# MARKET-LED AGRARIAN REFORM

This book offers a comprehensive, evidence-based critique of neo-liberal market-led agrarian reform and the challenges it poses for the rural poor and rural social movements.

Three-fourths of the world's poor are rural and most depend on the land for their livelihood. Access to land remains critical for their incomes and reproduction despite significant livelihood diversification in recent years. Land remains critical to any development discourse today. Market-led agrarian reform (MLAR) has gained prominence since the early 1990s as an alternative to state-led land reforms. This neo-liberal policy is based on the inversion of what its proponents see as the features of earlier approaches, and calls for redistribution via privatized, decentralized transactions between 'willing sellers' and 'willing buyers'. Its proponents, especially those associated with the World Bank, have claimed success where the policy has been implemented, but such claims have been contested by independent scholars as well as by peasant movements who are struggling to gain access to land.

This book presents three thematic papers and six country studies that explore recent experience with market-led agrarian reform in Africa, Asia and Latin America. The thematic papers address issues of formalisation of property rights, gendered land rights, and neo-liberal enclosure. These studies demonstrate the pervasive influence of neo-liberal ideas on property rights and rural development debates, well beyond the 'core' question of land redistribution. The limitations of the market-led approach, and the implications of the studies presented here for the future of agrarian reform, are considered in the editors' introduction.

This collection was previously published as a special issue of *Third World Quarterly*

**Saturnino M Borras Jr** is Canada Research Chair in International Development Studies at Saint Mary's University, Halifax, Nova Scotia.

**Cristóbal Kay** is Professor of Rural Development and Development Studies at the Institute of Social Studies, The Hague.

**Edward Lahiff** was formerly Senior Lecturer, Programme in Land and Agrarian Studies (PLAAS), School of Government, University of the Western Cape, South Africa.

# MARKET-LED AGRARIAN REFORM

## Critical Perspectives on Neoliberal Land Policies and the Rural Poor

*Edited by* Saturnino M Borras Jr, Cristóbal Kay and Edward Lahiff

Routledge
Taylor & Francis Group

LONDON AND NEW YORK

First published 2008 by Routledge
2 Park Square, Milton Park, Abingdon, Oxon, OX14 4RN

Simultaneously published in the USA and Canada
by Routledge
270 Madison Ave, New York NY 10016

*Routledge is an imprint of the Taylor & Francis Group, an Informa business*

© 2008 Edited by Saturnino M Borras Jr, Cristóbal Kay and Edward Lahiff

Reprinted 2009

First issued in paperback 2011

Typeset in Times by KnowledgeWorks Global Limited, Chennai, India

*British Library Cataloguing in Publication Data*
A catalogue record for this book is available from the British Library

ISBN 10: 0-415-46473-0 (hbk)
ISBN 10: 0-415-59088-4 (pbk)

ISBN 13: 978-0-415-46473-4 (hbk)
ISBN 13: 978-0-415-59088-4 (pbk)

# Contents

# Notes on Contributors

**Saturnino M Borras Jr** is Canada Research Chair in International Development Studies, Saint Mary's University, Canada. His recent publications are *Pro-Poor Land Reform: A Critique* (University of Ottawa Press, 2007); *Competing Views and Strategies on Agrarian Reform*, Vol 1, *International Perspective* and Vol 2, *Philippine Perspective* (Ateneo de Manila University Press, 2008). His co-edited books are *Land, Poverty and Livelihoods: Perspectives from Developing and Transition Countries* (2007) and *On Just Grounds: Struggling for Agrarian Justice and Citizenship Rights in the Rural Philippines* (2005). His latest co-publication with Marc Edelman and Cristóbal Kay is *Transnational Agrarian Movements Confronting Globalization* (2008).

**Cristóbal Kay** is Professor of Development Studies and Rural Development at the Institute of Social Studies, The Netherlands. His recent co-edited publications are *Disappearing Peasantries? Rural Labour in Africa, Asia and Latin America* (2000); *Latin America Transformed: Globalization and Modernity* (2004); *Land, Poverty and Livelihoods in an Era of Globalization* (2007) and *Political Economy, Rural Transformation and the Agrarian Question: Peasants and Globalization* (2008). He was for many years the editor of the *European Journal of Development Research* and is the co-editor of the *European Review of Latin American and Caribbean Studies* and the *Journal of Agrarian Change*.

**Edward Lahiff** was formerly Senior Lecturer at the Programme for Land and Agrarian Studies (PLAAS) University of the Western Cape, South Africa, where his research interests include agrarian reform, sustainable agriculture and rural social movements. His publications include 'State, market or the worst of both? Experimenting with market-based land reform in South Africa', PLAAS Occasional Paper 30, 2007; 'Land reform in the Eastern Cape: the ongoing struggle for resources and secure rights', *Social Dynamics*, 31 (1), 2005; and *An Apartheid Oasis: Agriculture and rural livelihoods in Venda* (Frank Cass, 2000). He now lives in Ireland.

**A Haroon Akram-Lodhi** is Professor of International Development Studies at Trent University. His principal research interest is in the political economy of agrarian change, and he has been working for several years on issues around land and landlessness, including its gender dimensions, in Vietnam, Pakistan and Fiji. His latest co-publication with Cristobal Kay is *Political Economy,*

*Rural Transformation and the Agrarian Question: Peasants and Globalization* (2008).

**Celestine Nyamu Musembi** is a Kenyan lawyer with interdisciplinary training in legal anthropology. She is currently a Fellow at the Institute of Development Studies, University of Sussex. She teaches and researches in the areas of human rights and development, gender and politics, local governance reform and property relations. Her recent publications include: 'Ruling out gender equality? The post-cold war rule of law agenda in sub-Saharan Africa', *Third World Quarterly*, 27 (7), 2006; 'From protest to proactive action: building institutional accountability through struggles for the right to housing', in Newell and Wheeler (eds), *Rights, Resources and the Politics of Accountability* (Zed, 2006); 'Toward an actor-oriented perspective on human rights', in N Kabeer (ed), *Meanings and Expressions of Citizenship: Perspectives from the North and South* (Zed, 2005); and 'Are local norms and practices fences or pathways? The example of women's property rights', in A An-Na'im (ed), *Cultural Transformation and Human Rights in Africa* (Zed, 2002).

**Shahra Razavi** is Research Co-ordinator at United Nations Research Institute for Social Development (UNRISD), Geneva. Her recent books include *Gender and Social Policy in a Global Context: Uncovering the Gendered Structure of 'the Social'* (Palgrave, 2006); *Agrarian Change, Gender and Land Rights*, special issue of *Journal of Agrarian Change* (2003); *Gender Justice, Development and Rights* (Oxford University Press, 2002); and *Gendered Poverty and Well-being*, special issue of *Development and Change* (1999). She coordinated the preparation of the UNRISD report, *Gender Equality: Striving for Justice in an Unequal World* (2005). Her current research areas include gender and social policy, and the rise of Islamic-based politics and gender equality.

**Leonilde Servolo de Medeiros** is a Professor in the Postgraduate Programme of Social Sciences on Development, Agriculture and Society of the Federal Rural University of Rio de Janeiro, Brazil. She has written numerous books and articles about Brazilian rural social movements, agrarian reform and land settlements. Her research is supported by CNPq and Faperj. Her recent publications include *Movimentos sociais, lutas políticas e reforma agrária de mercado no Brasil*, (UNRISD, 2002); *História e atualidade da luta pela terra* (2003); *Impactos dos assentamentos, um estudo sobre o meio rural brasileiro* (Editora da Unesp/Nead, 2004); and 'Agrarian reform and poverty reduction: lessons from Brazil', in A Akram-Lodhi, S Borras & C Kay (eds), *Land, Poverty and Livelihoods in an Era of Globalization* (Routledge, 2007).

**Susana Gauster** is a sociologist from the University of Vienna, and is currently a researcher at the Institute of Agrarian and Rural Studies (CONGOOP), Guatemala. Her recent co-authored works include: 'Perspectivas para la agricultura familiar campesina de Guatemala, en un contexto DR-CAFTA', (CONGOOP, 2006); 'Soberanía alimentaria y economía campesina: los desafios para Guatemala en las negociaciones agrícolas en la OMC' (CONGOOP, 2005); 'Balance de la aplicación de la política agraria del Banco Mundial en Guatemala 1996–2005' (CONGOOP, 2005); and 'FONTIERRAS, el modelo de mercado y el acceso a la tierra en Guatemala: balance y perspectivas' (CONGOOP, 2002).

**Ryan Isakson** is Assistant Professor of International Development Studies at Saint Mary's University, Canada. His research interests lie at the intersection of rural livelihood strategies, poverty alleviation, and the ownership and sustainable management of environmental assets. He recently completed his PhD in economics at the University of Massachusetts at Amherst, where his dissertation research explored the impact of market integration upon peasant livelihood strategies and the on-farm conservation of crop genetic diversity in the Guatemalan highlands.

**Ariane de Bremond** is Research Associate at the H John Heinz III Center for Science, Economics and the Environment, Washington, DC. She received her PhD from the Environmental Studies Department at the University of California, Santa Cruz in 2006 and recently completed a Switzer Environmental Leadership Post-doctoral Fellowship. Her latest publications include 'Harvesting peace from landscapes of conflict: land, livelihoods, and nature in post-war El Salvador', in *Contentious Geographies: Environment, Meaning, and Scale* (Ashgate, 2007) and 'Regenerating conflicted landscapes: war, identity and environmental governance in Cinquera, El Salvador', in *Ecologies of Hope* (SAR Press, forthcoming 2008).

**Danilo Carranza** is a veteran community-based rural activist working with autonomous peasant movements and NGOs in the Philippines. His recent publications include 'Hacienda Luisita massacre: a tragedy waiting to happen', *Agrarian Notes*, 2005, at www.peace.net.ph; and 'Land, poverty, and state–society interaction in the Philippines', in Akram Lodhi, Borras Jr & Kay (eds), *Land, Poverty and Livelihoods: Perspectives from Developing and Transition Countries* (Routledge, 2007).

**Jennifer C Franco** is Research Co-ordinator of the Rural New Politics Sub-programme at the Transnational Institute (TNI), Amsterdam. She is author of *Elections and Democratization in the Philippines* (Routledge, 2001) and co-edited *On Just Grounds: Struggling for Agrarian Justice and Citizenship Rights in the Rural Philippines* (TNI, 2005). She is currently completing a book, '*Balimbing (In)Justice': Plural–Legal Continuity and Social–Political Change in the Philippine Countryside* (for Ateneo de Manila University Press, forthcoming).

**Ray Bush** is Professor of African Studies and Development Politics in the School of Politics and International Studies, University of Leeds. He is also co-chair of *The Review of African Political Economy*. He is the author of

*Economic Crisis and the Politics of Reform in Egypt* (Westview, 1999) and editor of *Counter Revolution in Egypt's Countryside: Land and Farmers in the era of Economic Reform* (Zed, 2002); and *Poverty and Neoliberalism: Persistence and Reproduction in the Global South* (Pluto, 2007).

# Market-led Agrarian Reform: policies, performance and prospects

EDWARD LAHIFF, SATURNINO M BORRAS, JR &
CRISTÓBAL KAY

There was no evidence...that effective land reforms could result from 'market-friendly' policies alone. Registering land titles and facilitating real estate transactions between willing sellers and willing buyers do not by themselves change power relationships in favour of the rural poor. In many situations, such policies are likely to reinforce agrarian structures by providing large landholders and speculators with additional legal protection, while leaving the bargaining power of the poor unchanged or diminished. (Solon Barraclough)[1]

Market-led agrarian reform (MLAR) has gained prominence worldwide since the early 1990s as an alternative to the state-led approaches widely implemented over the course of the 20th century. This neoliberal policy framework, most actively promoted by the World Bank, is based on the inversion of what its proponents see as the key features of earlier approaches, and calls for redistribution via privatised, decentralised land transactions between 'willing sellers' and 'willing buyers'.[2] MLAR embraces the textbook 'willing seller-willing buyer' model but also a range of variations that include a liberalised share tenancy – land rental market approach, the doing away with existing land-size ceiling laws, formalisation – privatisation of 'non-private' lands and various combinations of these policies, sequentially or simultaneously.[3] MLAR programmes have been implemented in various forms in countries of Asia, Africa and Latin America, with varying outcomes. Successful results are claimed in countries such as Colombia, Brazil, Guatemala, El Salvador, South Africa and the Philippines, but this is challenged by a growing body of literature from academics and other researchers.[4] Resistance to MLAR has come from various movements of peasant and the landless, based on several factors, including the high degree of discretion it grants to existing landowners, the targeting of a narrow range of better-off, more commercially oriented beneficiaries, and a generally slow pace of land transfer. Vociferous demands are being made by groups across the developing world for a more interventionist approach by national governments that will challenge the power of landowning classes and provide both land and developmental support to resource-poor farmers. Whether this implies a return to a more traditional, state-led approach, based on expropriation of larger holdings, or some hybrid of state- and market-based policies, remains an open question and one more likely to be resolved through political struggle than via technical debates among academics or policy advisors.

This book brings together both thematic and country case studies. A total of six country studies on MLAR experiences since the 1990s in Latin America, Asia and Africa are examined by scholars who have followed closely the MLAR processes in these countries (Brazil by Leonilde Servolo de Medeiros, Guatemala by Susana Gauster and Ryan Isakson, El Salvador by Ariane de Bremond, the Philippines by Saturnino Borras Jr, Danilo Carranza and Jennifer Franco, Egypt by Ray Bush and South Africa by Edward Lahiff). MLAR in these countries has taken variegated forms: from those closest to the textbook version (Brazil, Guatemala, Philippines) to a hybrid type (El Salvador, South Africa), and to a more generic neoliberal land policy type (Egypt). Common themes that emerge across the studies include the success of landowners in minimising the impact of reform, and a lack of post-transfer support for new farmers that translates into generally low levels of productivity and limited impact on poverty. These common features, and their implications for market-led programmes and for the future of agrarian reform more generally, are considered in more detail below.

The three thematic studies, focusing on formalisation of property rights, gender and land rights and neoliberal enclosures, demonstrate the pervasive influence of neoliberal ideas on multiple aspects of property rights and rural development debates.

Nyamu Musembi interrogates the claim that the procedural act of formalisation of property rights has a causal link with the empowerment of poor people. This is done primarily through an examination of the work of Hernando de Soto,[5] in light of similar arguments made in earlier policy prescriptions on formalisation of land title in rural sub-Saharan Africa, with a particular focus on Kenya. The positions advanced by de Soto and like-minded theorists linking formal land title to productivity, it is argued, tend to ignore the lessons of earlier waves of tenurial reform in sub-Saharan Africa, and therefore reproduce their shortcomings, particularly with regard to what Nyamu Musembi refers to as a gendered pattern of exclusion. An explicit link is made between debates around formalisation of property rights and the rise of market-led agrarian reform policies. MLAR, it is argued, presumes the existence of a property system that gives rigid legal protection to existing property interests and leaves little room to facilitate the acquisition of property interests by a wider cross-section of society. Both MLAR and de Soto's prescriptions of formalisation of title as a tool for empowerment of the poor gloss over the unequal power relations that are behind demands for property rights reform, thus side-stepping the question of substantive redistribution.

In a comprehensive review of the debate around liberalisation and women's access to land, Razavi argues that the shift from a household model of land rights to an individual model in recent years has tended to obscure the highly unequal power of women and men within households, and wider societies, and their divergence even within the same household. While the principle of gender equality in access to resources, including land, has been endorsed by a diverse range of policy actors, various tensions and ambiguities have emerged, including questions about the market as a vehicle for women's inclusion. There are also, Razavi argues, troubling implications from a gender perspective in the current endorsement of 'customary' systems of land tenure and decentralisation of land management by a wide range of international development agencies, which can play into the hands of powerful interest groups hostile to women's rights.

A further critique of MLAR is provided by Akram-Lodhi, who focuses on the socially embedded character of both land and markets. Using an agrarian political economy approach, Akram-Lodhi argues that MLAR is premised on two faulty assumptions: that land is solely an economic resource and that markets are institutions in which participants are equal. It is suggested that agrarian political economy offers an understanding of the processes surrounding land transfers that is predicated on the socially embedded character of such transfers, especially through the concept of enclosure. Neoliberal re-enclosure, Akram-Lodhi argues, is facilitating the emergence of a 'bifurcated' agrarian structure in contemporary developing and transition countries, in which emergent capitalist farming governed by the dictates of the market sits side-by-side with a 'classic' peasant subsistence-oriented agriculture sub-sector. This, in turn, is giving rise to an ongoing process of expanded commodification of both rural products and rural labour, contributing to an ongoing and significant process of de-peasantisation.

Together, these country studies and thematic papers provide a far-reaching critique of market-oriented land policies and highlight the need for alternative approaches.

### Origins of MLAR and overview of recent debates

As has been widely observed, the 1990s saw the re-emergence of land and agrarian reform as a critical policy issue across much of the developing world. Various factors contributed to this, including the general failure of the World Bank/IMF-inspired structural adjustment programmes in the 1980s and 1990s to deliver economic growth and expanded employment, and renewed pressure from rural social movements. The deregulation of agricultural markets and dramatic reductions in state support to farmers have had differential effects across commodity groups and types of producers, but have, in the main, been highly detrimental for peasant producers and agricultural labourers, contributing to a growing crisis of rural poverty, unemployment and landlessness.[6] At the same time the rise of neoliberal ideology on a global scale has promoted the expansion of market relations into areas, such as land, which had hitherto remained outside the market to a greater or lesser extent, and to areas of policy, such as agrarian reform, that had long been predicated on direct state intervention.

The deteriorating social and economic conditions across much of Africa, Asia and Latin America have not gone uncontested, and the past decade has seen the emergence of new (and the revitalisation of some old) peasant movements, many of them now linked to national and international networks of anti-globalisation organisations.[7] Growing popular opposition to neoliberalism in many countries posed the threat of a reversion to old-style agrarian reform, either on the back of popular land invasions, as in Brazil and Zimbabwe, or in the coming to power of more radical populist governments, as in Venezuela and Bolivia.

In this context of widespread and persistent rural poverty and inequality, MLAR has emerged as the latest in a long series of policy initiatives aimed at stimulating growth and employment in the agricultural sector. Combining elements of neoliberalism and what Byres calls 'agrarian neo-populism',[8] MLAR advocates the redistribution of land from large to smaller owners via market transactions in order to achieve objectives of both social equity and economic efficiency—the latter through the assumption of an inverse relationship between farm size and productivity.[9] New 'family farmers' are to be drawn into increasingly liberalised markets for land, commodities and agricultural services.

Various strategies, including provision of grants and loans, are recommended to enable the poor to enter the land market and to encourage landowners to sell off unwanted or under-used land (eg compensation in cash, at full market value). Further measures are promoted to reduce 'distortions' in land markets, including the removal of restrictions on land rentals and subdivision, removal of direct and indirect subsidies to landowners and the introduction of land taxes that would encourage sales of under-utilised land and discourage land speculation or hoarding.[10]

Early versions of MLAR were attempted in Zimbabwe throughout the 1980s, as well as in some Latin American countries in the 1970s and 1980s.[11] Since then MLAR has, to varying extents, been implemented in Colombia from 1995 to 2003 through the Agrarian Law 160 of 1994,[12] in South Africa since 1995,[13] in Brazil from 1998 to 2001,[14] before being renewed and expanded during the Lula administration,[15] in Namibia since the 1990s,[16] and in Guatemala since the 1990s in the context of the peace agreement and what Holt-Gimenez calls 'neoliberal territorial restructuring',[17] among others. A small pilot project was also carried out in the Philippines, although a much larger MLAR -like voluntary land transfer (VLT) scheme has also been implemented there.[18] Negotiations on a MLAR-like programme were also attempted in Nepal.[19]

The leading proponents of MLAR have been associated with the World Bank, which has been responsible for the design and/or funding of the flagship market-led ('community-based' or 'negotiated') land reforms in Brazil, Colombia, the Philippines and (to a lesser extent) South Africa.[20] While MLAR has been enthusiastically endorsed by many national governments and multilateral organisations, it has been vigorously contested 'from below' by a range of peasant movements and others and has provoked a lively academic debate. Civil society organisations opposed to MLAR policies have launched co-ordinated local, national and international campaigns to expose their shortcomings and demand more aggressive action against landowners and a greater role for the state. One of the most important initiatives is that being currently co-ordinated internationally by *La Via Campesina*, the FoodFirst Information and Action Network (FIAN), and the Land Research and Action Network (LRAN).[21] While much of this opposition is undoubtedly ideological—based on scepticism about the limited role for the state and the generous terms being offered to landowners—it has been fuelled by the slow pace of reform in most countries where MLAR policies have been pursued and by questions around the sustainability of the new forms of agricultural production that have resulted.

There are numerous grounds on which the neoliberal critique of conventional state-led agrarian reform has been put forward.[22] But for the purposes of this current issue, the pro-market critique of conventional state-led agrarian reform will be summarised under what we see as the three most important headings, namely distortions of the land market, poor programme design and implementation, and excessive cost.

State-led programmes are criticised for introducing a range of distortions to land and agricultural markets through restrictive measures such as land-size ceilings and restrictions on land rentals and land sales, which, it is argued, have generally failed to achieve the desired results of a more equitable distribution of land.[23] Simultaneously, according to the neoliberal critique, the failure to address the system of taxation and other areas of public policy that encourage concentration and under-utilisation of land has remained unaddressed and thus has undermined attempts at redistribution.

Second, according to the neoliberal critique, the manner in which state-led agrarian reform programmes have been planned and implemented is deemed to have been both inefficient and, ultimately, ineffective, with all responsibility for funding and implementation being assumed by the state. For Deininger:[24]

> This complete reliance on government spawned complex regulations and cumbersome bureaucratic requirements to implement land reform, stretched available administrative capacity . . . and resulted in highly centralized processes of implementation. Government bureaucracies at the central level—justified by the need to provide technical assistance and other support services to beneficiaries—proved expensive and, unable to utilize information from the local level, often also quite ineffective.

The combination of political motivation and a 'supply-driven' approach, it is argued, has resulted in two undesirable outcomes, namely, the acquisition of lands that are not suitable for resettlement and the inclusion of households that are not 'qualified' to become land reform beneficiaries. Conventional land reforms start either by identifying lands for expropriation, and then looking for possible beneficiaries, or by identifying potential beneficiaries and then looking for lands to be expropriated. This, it is argued, leads to efficiency losses in agriculture as large productive farms are expropriated and subdivided into smaller, less productive units, or when environmentally fragile (usually public) lands are distributed by the state. Because beneficiaries are identified by state officials, opportunities are created for patronage and corruption. Political affiliation and other non-economic factors may also lead to the inclusion of beneficiaries who already have land or who have little interest in farming, while those in the greatest need, or with the greatest ability to farm, may be overlooked.[25]

Because state-led agrarian reforms have tended to be expropriatory and coercive, with limited compensation for landowners, they may provoke resistance, evasion and protracted legal battles over property rights, leading to a situation of greater uncertainty for investments. Binswanger and Deininger explain that, 'although landowners receive the nominal value of their bonds, time erodes the real market value of the bonds received, and the government offers no compensation for this loss. Most landowners naturally oppose such thinly disguised confiscation.'[26] Legal and political battles launched by landlords have frequently slowed down, if not prevented, reform implementation.[27]

Furthermore, a failure to carry out farm-level planning before land transfer is further seen as contributing to poor productivity on resettled land

and a failure by the state to deliver post-settlement support services in a co-ordinated and timely manner.[28]

Third, state-led programmes are accused of being excessively expensive and breeding large and unaccountable bureaucracies, which consume inordinate quantities of the available land-reform budget. Operational costs are compounded by the need for ongoing support and subsidies to resettled farmers. A widespread failure to extract loan repayments or other contributions from resettled farmers has added to the operational costs and further undermined the sustainability of such programmes.[29]

In place of such state-led approaches, MLAR proposes a package of reforms that rely heavily on voluntary land transactions via the market, embedded within the wider neoliberal agenda for the restructuring and reorientation of the agricultural sector. A vibrant land market is assumed to allow the most efficient use of land resources by the most efficient users. It requires that sources of distortions in agricultural land prices, such as subsidised input and output markets, must be abolished completely, in order to bring the market value of land closer to its productive value.[30] Thus the MLAR model strongly advocates the abolition of prohibitions on land sales and rentals, in order to allow for a more fluid land market.[31]

Reforming agrarian structures has been central to historical processes of development and democratisation which have, until recently, been almost entirely of the conventional state-led (or revolutionary) variety.[32] Like other versions of agrarian reform, MLAR should, therefore, be seen not just as a means of redistributing land or alleviating rural poverty, but as part of the wider (market-oriented) structural adjustment of national economies being implemented as part of neoliberal globalisation. Indeed, this critical point is underscored by the thematic contributions in this special issue, where Akram Lodhi locates MLAR in the broad historical political–economic context of neoliberal globalisation, Nyamu Musembi interrogates the MLAR variant being applied to non-private lands ('formalisation–privatisation' drives), the neoliberal claims on gender land rights and development are critically examined by Razavi and the particular case of Egypt is explained by Bush.[33]

## Critical perspectives

In this section the main claims of the MLAR approach are identified and interrogated on the basis of emerging evidence from around the world. Three broad policy areas are highlighted, namely, gaining access to land, post-land-purchase farm and beneficiary development, and programme financing.[34]

### Gaining access to land

MLAR is predicated on voluntary transactions between sellers (landowners) and buyers (tenants, small farmers, landless people and farm workers). Only landlords who are willing to sell land, and only the quantity of lands they are selling, will be included in the land reform process. In exchange landlords will be fully compensated, with cash payment at commercial value of the land. It is this fundamental conflict-free framework that pro-market scholars hope will secure the cooperation of landlords.

Meanwhile, MLAR programmes are 'demand-driven': only those people who have actually demanded land will be considered for the land reform process. Potential beneficiaries will carry out a 'self-selection' process to decide who will eventually be included in the land reform process. It is believed that this is a way to make sure that only those who are actually, or who have the potential to become, economically efficient and commercially viable farmers can become programme beneficiaries. In order to find these 'fittest' beneficiaries, a 'self-selection' process among the prospective buyers is undertaken in order to put the beneficiaries in the 'driver's seat'.[35] This would, in theory, exclude less promising applicants because peers would not allow them to join the organisation that would negotiate for the land purchase and credit access.

The creation of efficient and competitive individual family farms is the main objective of the MLAR project.[36] However, in order to strengthen the bargaining power of the buyers during the land purchase negotiation, beneficiaries have to form an organisation. The formation of a beneficiary organisation is also necessary to achieve economies of scale in the input and output markets. These organisations will also carry out a 'peer monitoring' process partly in order to bring down the programme's transaction costs.[37]

The MLAR policy model is designed to be a private transaction between a willing seller and a willing buyer, and thus adopts a decentralised method of implementation aimed at achieving speedy transaction as well as transparency and accountability.[38] The role of the state, and especially of national government, is thus greatly reduced compared with state-led programmes, and does not extend to direct involvement in every land transaction.[39] It is in this context that MLAR needs local governments for land purchase mediation and tax collection, although the land taxation advocated as part of MLAR has not always materialised. Local governments are thought to be nearer to the people and so should be more responsive to the actual needs of the local communities. Furthermore, the MLAR model has emphasized the roles of local NGOs in its implementation, particularly in the area of community facilitation, and of the private sector, particularly in the provision of post-settlement support services.

With its decentralised transaction, and the incentive of full market prices paid in cash, the MLAR model is assumed to be faster in acquiring land than other approaches, avoiding long delays associated with disputes about compensation levels.[40] The speed with which beneficiaries get access to land would then depend on the level of annual appropriations, rather than on long drawn out expropriation proceedings for specific farms, and the scale of such appropriations would itself be set in response to popular demand.[41] Finally, land prices are expected to be lower, mainly because of the cash payment to landlords who are expected to factor away transaction cost incurred under previous systems that offered a mix of cash and bonds over a longer period. Because it is a voluntary process between willing sellers and willing buyers, political and legal complexities and problems that slowed down processes of conventional land reform are expected to be absent. Therefore, the pace of the programme implemented is expected to be relatively swift and conflict-free.[42]

In practice, MLAR has failed to live up to the many claims made for it in the area of beneficiary selection and land acquisition. First, the volume of land transferred has been extremely low relative to programme targets and alternative approaches. In the Philippines, for example, less than 1000 hectares was transferred in four years via the textbook MLAR experiment,[43] as compared with seven million hectares under the previous state-led approach.[44] In South Africa less than 4% of agricultural land was transferred in the first 10 years of reform, against a government target of 30% over five years (later extended to 20 years).[45] A similar figure is reported for Guatemala, over eight years.[46] In Brazil over 10 times the number of people have benefited from 'traditional' (ie expropriatory) reform than from the various market-led approaches currently being implemented.[47] Much more was achieved in El Salvador, where some 10% of agricultural land was transferred over a six-year period, but it is important to note that this was part of a major peace settlement with heavy involvement by the state—what de Bremond refers to as a 'state-market hybrid'.[48] The case of Egypt is different: here the generic neoliberal agrarian and land policy imposed by international financial institutions resulted in the passage of Mubarak's Law 96 of 1992. By revoking the Agrarian Reform Law of 1952 Law 96 became the main pillar to ensure that control of land was returned to its owners and Nasser's legal guarantees for smallholders and the landless were ended.[49] Overall, MLAR's impact on land redistribution to date remains extremely low when compared with the conventional approach, as shown in Tables 1 and 2.

Furthermore, the lure of market-related cash payments does not appear to have brought more land onto the market. Studies from Brazil, Guatemala and South Africa suggest that little 'new' land is coming on to the market, and what is available is generally of inferior quality. Moreover, prices paid for land have often exceeded market prices—by as much as 100% in some cases—contributing to programme costs that far exceed those of more traditional approaches. In the Philippines the very limited transfers under the market-led CMARPRP cost, on average, six times the cost of the state-led CARP per hectare of land transferred.[50] The entirely voluntary nature of MLAR clearly offers opportunities to landowners to engage with the programme when it is in their interest, and to hold back when it is not, but does not necessarily offer the same advantages to the state or to the intended beneficiaries.

Contrary to earlier predictions, the implementation pace of MLAR has been mixed. In some cases it has been long drawn out and dominated by bureaucratic processes, in terms of applications for grants, processing of applications, negotiations with landowners, processing of payments and the preparation of often complex farm plans by state officials or private

TABLE 1. Land redistribution outcomes of *all* major market-led agrarian reform programmes in several countries

| Country | Period | Redistributed land as % of total agricultural land | Number of beneficiaries as % of total agricultural households |
|---|---|---|---|
| Brazil | 1997–2005 | 0.4 | 1.32 |
| Colombia | 1994–2001 | 0.22 | 0.33 |
| El Salvador | 1990s | 10 | 1.4 |
| Guatemala | 1997–2005 | 4.0 | 1.30 |
| Philippines | 2000–05 | 0.01 | 0.03 |
| South Africa | 1994–2006 | 4.1 | n/a |
| Zimbabwe | 1980–96 | 16.6 | 5.83 |
| Namibia | 1990–2005 | 6.0 | 0.16 |

*Notes*: The entry for South Africa has been slightly revised from that of the source and is based on Lahiff, in this issue.
The entry for El Salvador comes from de Bremond, this issue and is calculated from www.faostat.org.
*Source*: S Borras & T McKinley, *The Unresolved Land Reform Debate: Beyond State-led or Market-led Models*, United Nations Development Programme, International Poverty Centre, Policy Research Brief no 2, November 2006.

TABLE 2. Land redistribution outcomes of state-led land reform programmes in a *few* selected countries

| Country | Period | Redistributed land as % of total agricultural land | Number of beneficiaries as % of total agricultural households |
|---|---|---|---|
| Bolivia | 1952–77 | 74.5 | 83.4 |
| Rep of Korea | since 1945 | 65 | 77 |
| Chile | 1964–73 | nearly 50 | 20 |
| Taiwan* | 1949–53 | 48 | 48 |
| Peru | 1963–76 | 42.4 | 32 |
| Mexico | 1970 data | 42.9 | 43.4 |
| Philippines | 1972–2005 | nearly 50 | 40 |
| Japan | 1945 on | 33.3 | 70 |
| Ecuador | 1964–85 | 34.2 | no data |
| El Salvador | 1980–90s | 20 | 12 |
| Venezuela | Up to 1979 | 19.3 | 24.4 |
| Egypt | 1952–61 | 10 | 9 |
| Brazil | 1964–2005 | 7.6 | 18.5 |
| Costa Rica | 1961–79 | 7.1 | 13.5 |

*Note*: *Taiwan Province.
*Source*: S Borras & T McKinley, *The Unresolved Land Reform Debate: Beyond State-led or Market-led Models*, United Nations Development Programme, International Poverty Centre, Policy Research Brief no 2, November 2006.

contractors. In Guatemala project implementation can take upwards of two years;[51] similar times are reported for other countries. In South Africa landowners are reported to be avoiding land reform transactions because of the complex and uncertain bureaucratic processes involved, and lengthy delays in receiving payment after deals have been confirmed.[52] In other cases the process has indeed been quick—but with anti-poor outcomes, as in the cases if Egypt and in some MLAR experimental cases in the Philippines.

In terms of beneficiary selection, too, implementation outcomes are significantly different from the theoretical predictions. This is most evident in the socioeconomic profile of programme participants, who have tended to be drawn disproportionately from the better-off peasants, artisans and professionals, rather than from the relatively poor and landless. Particular difficulties have been experienced by women-headed households in the case of Guatemala, where Guaster and Isakson report that fewer than 1% of beneficiary households are headed by women.[53] Marginalisation of the poor and less-educated can, in part, be attributed to the complexity of the application process, which involves approaching landowners, preparation of application forms and dealing with state bureaucracy, but also to deliberate policy orientation, as in the case of Brazil.[54] In South Africa early experiences with a pro-poor approach were quickly replaced by the LRAD programme that promotes 'emerging farmers' and favours those with their own resources; in Guatemala the law admits applicants earning up to four times the statutory minimum wage. In an earlier experiment in Colombia the MLAR project was completely taken over by the non-poor and elite individuals. Embarrassed by the failure of this experiment, the World Bank closed this programme in 2003.[55]

*Farm and beneficiary development*

MLAR emphasises the importance of farm project plans being put in place before any land purchase can be made. The World Bank argues that: 'Farm enterprise planning and identification of marketing channels etc are undertaken *before* land is being transferred, thus enabling beneficiaries to start production from day one after they receive the land'.[56] Similarly Deininger emphasises that the creation of productive projects 'are a core element of market-assisted land reform that is designed to establish economically viable and productive projects at a socially-justifiable cost rather than to transfer assets'.[57]

Given the importance accorded to post-land transfer development in the MLAR policy model, extension and other agricultural support services are a critical issue. Unlike in state-led agrarian reforms, where extension services are bureaucratic, centralised and 'supply-driven', under MLAR, these are privatised, decentralised and strictly demand-driven. Deininger and Binswanger explain that: 'by drawing on the private sector, nongovernmental organizations, and the community to develop, finance, and administer projects, the approach promises to overcome some of the informational imperfections that have plagued the implementation of land reform by government bureaucracies'. Furthermore, such an approach 'would help to develop a menu of project options more attuned to the specific needs of different groups within the target population'.[58]

11

Traditional obstacles to credit and investments are supposedly addressed under MLAR through the removal of prohibitions on land sales and rentals. In addition, proponents of MLAR advocate the abolition of such restrictions on lands already awarded to peasants under previous (state-led) programmes, so that it can be used as collateral for bank loans and to attract external investors.[59] Moreover, credit and investments are expected to materialise without delay because land is acquired via outright purchase, with immediate transfer of titles that may be used in negotiations with financial institutions.

In practice, the model of farm planning and post-transfer support proposed under MLAR has not, in the main, led to highly productive projects or major increases in income for participants, for which the lack of post-transfer support is a primary cause. Close to half of all resettlement projects in Guatemala, and over 70% in South Africa's Limpopo province, are described as dysfunctional, producing little or nothing relative to their potential. Farm planning is carried out by a range of state and private-sector consultants, often with minimal consultation with the intended beneficiaries, resulting in unworkable plans that fail to attract the financial or technical support they require. In Guatemala three different systems of technical support from the private sector have been attempted and abandoned; in South Africa a majority of redistribution projects have received no support whatsoever from either state or private sector; in Brazil estimates of projects that receive no post-transfer technical assistance range from 23% to 61%, and what there is is described as sporadic.[60] Support has been mixed in the Philippines: in instances where the government delivered some support services to the redistributed lands, it was the non-poor who benefited most because they were the ones who got lands under the MLAR experiment. The landlords who recovered their lands in the 1990s were also rewarded with government services in Egypt.

Lack of support to beneficiaries under MLAR has occurred in the context of massive disinvestment in state agricultural services as part of structural adjustment. Shortages of working capital have also made it difficult or impossible for beneficiaries to access private-sector agricultural services, which remain largely oriented towards serving the needs of established commercial farms. The requirement for applicants to pool their grants in order to buy large farms has also given rise to unwieldy, and often unworkable, agricultural collectives, often imposed as a condition of the grant, with high rates of desertion from projects reported from countries such as Brazil, Guatemala, the Philippines and South Africa.

Unwieldy group structures, inappropriate planning and a general lack of post-transfer support have resulted, not surprisingly, in minimal impacts on incomes and employment. In Guatemala households under the Fontierras programme are reported to have an income equivalent to one-third of the legal minimum wage. In Brazil research carried out by the World Bank, among others, reports some increase in welfare for participants under the various market-led programmes, but not generally sufficient to raise households above the poverty line.[61] In South Africa after 10 years of implementation, a World Bank discussion paper talks of '*the promise* of increasing efficiency, equity and generating jobs', but is unable to present any evidence that this was happening in practice.[62]

While, on the one hand, it is difficult to determine the extent to which national government delivered support services to farmers who got lands through MLAR and the various formalisation–privatisation drives, it is relatively easier for us to conclude there has been no empirical evidence to show that households used their land titles to secure commercial loans. Instead, in varying degrees, all the country case studies and thematic contributions in this special issue tend to suggest otherwise: that, in general, poor people did not use their land titles or land certificates to secure commercial loans.

*Financing*

According to its proponents, the financial costs to the state of MLAR implementation will be lower than the previous state-led agrarian reforms, and the financing scheme will be more efficient, making the policy model more desirable and workable. There are two basic features of the financing scheme under MLAR. On the one hand, MLAR proponents acknowledge that peasants cannot afford to purchase land on the open market, especially on a cash basis, and they cannot afford to purchase all the necessary farm inputs and needed infrastructure. Thus there is a need to facilitate a subsidy in the form of a loan and/or a grant. On the other hand, the beneficiaries of MLAR should shoulder at least some of the land cost, including the interests incurred on the loans secured to finance the land purchase. This expense is thus passed from the state (under the state-led land reform) on to the peasant beneficiary (under the MLAR policy model) resulting, it is argued, in radically reduced spending for the state, which is now focused on land development rather than on land acquisition.[63]

More specifically, the textbook MLAR model adopts a flexible loan-grant financing scheme. This means that each beneficiary is given a fixed sum of money, which s/he is free to use in whatever way is deemed cost efficient, but in accordance with this rule: whatever portion is used to buy land, that portion is considered a loan and has to be repaid by the beneficiary—100% of the amount at market rates on loan interest rates. Whatever is left after the land purchase is given to the beneficiary as a grant to be used for post-transfer development projects and is not to be repaid by the beneficiary. This flexible approach is believed to be a safeguard against possible fund manipulation, and instils the value of 'co-sharing' of risks to avoid a 'dole-out' mentality among beneficiaries. The expectation is that the peasant beneficiaries will look for the best bargain in their land purchase in order to spend less on land and have more money left to finance farm development.[64] Deininger explains that: 'without effective beneficiary contribution and assured access to financial markets as a part of the land reform package either beneficiary self-selection or the sustainability of project operations will be compromised'.[65]

13

The MLAR policy model also avoids the practice of 'universal subsidies', as it is argued that, '[grants] are superior to subsidies because they are immediate, transparent, can be targeted and their distortionary effects are small'.[66] This mechanism is also thought to be a factor in reducing the cost of land because peasants will go for the best bargain for their money, and will not be inclined to overspend.[67]

Finally, it is predicted that the overall cost of land being sold under the programme will be lower than for deals transacted under the conventional state-led land reform. The main reason, it is argued, is that the land is being sold for cash at full market value. Thus landowners need not resort to factoring in the cost of delayed payment as in the state-led land reforms.

In practice, the textbook rule on flexible financing has only been adopted in a few countries, including Brazil, Colombia and the Philippines. But in these countries the predicted positive effect of such a scheme has not materialised, with the worst case reported in Colombia, while land value manipulation has been significantly present in Brazil and the Philippines. The textbook rule on financing was not adopted in South Africa, where a one-off land purchase grant (usually equivalent to 100% of the purchase price) was instead provided.

Moreover, contrary to expectations, expenditure by the state under MLAR has been considerable, especially as prices paid are generally equal to or above prevailing market prices. Unlike other (state-led) programmes, a large volume of this expenditure has gone directly to (former) landowners, rather than to the provision of support services and infrastructure for the rural poor and landless.

The average cost to the state per beneficiary in the Philippines under CMARPRP has been over US$3000; in Guatemala, over $9000. In Brazil the combined value of credit and grants may be up to $18 000 per beneficiary; in South Africa grants alone may reach $20 000, with up to $80 000 available to some better-off beneficiaries in the form of loans from the state-owned Land Bank. MLAR programmes are also more directly constrained by fiscal allocations. In South Africa, for example, planned projects were deferred in successive years because the budgetary allocation for land purchase had been exhausted.[68]

Direct costs to beneficiaries have also been high, with much of this sunk in land purchase, leaving little over for working capital or longer-term investment. The relatively high costs of participating in a MLAR programme have been widely cited as a disincentive to participation by the poor.[69] High rates of default on loans are reported from all countries where these are provided under MLAR, a direct result of the low productivity on newly resettled lands discussed above, which not only puts individual projects in jeopardy but also undermines the sustainability of reform programmes that depend on loan financing. Gauster and Isakson report that 80% of farms transferred in Guatemala were behind with their payments, and consider it 'impossible' that such loans could ever be paid off in full.[70] For Brazil Medeiros reports that the majority of participants under the CF-CPR were unaware of the interest rates to be paid on their land purchase loans,[71] while under the Cédula da Terra programme, another study found that only 10% of farmers knew that their land was at risk should they default on their loans.

### Conclusion: what future for agrarian reform?

The most notable features of MLAR worldwide to date are two-fold: its very limited impact on patterns of landholding where reforms have actually been carried out, and its pro-elite/anti-poor character. It appears highly unlikely that MLAR is capable of bringing about a radical restructuring of landholding or of providing sufficient land to meet the demand from the rural poor and landless. Some general conclusions emerging from our review of MLAR internationally are elaborated below, together with some thoughts on the future of agrarian reform.

First, as shown in all the thematic and country case studies in this special issue the fundamental problem in MLAR lies in its basic assumption that land is treated solely as an economic factor of production. By doing this, it misses numerous social, political, cultural, religious and environmental dimensions, as well as class-, gender- and ethnic-based relations.

Second, neoliberal reforms of the systems of property registration and of the land market have benefited existing landowners and other elites through formal registration of property, increased marketability (and thus increased value) of land, and, in some cases, through the effective privatisation of former communal resources—what de Bremond calls 'asset streamlining'.[72]

Third, while local elites have often been the main beneficiaries of MLAR and other market-oriented land policies, relatively few poor people (landless peasants and rural workers) have benefited from land transfers or subsequent support services. Worse, in some cases, MLAR and its variants have resulted in the net transfer of wealth and power from poor people to the landed elite, as in the case of Egypt and in some cases in the Philippines. In many cases poor people have obtained little benefit from the support services provided as part of MLAR programmes, which were directed mainly to commercial (ie better-off) producers. Moreover, its claims of promoting gender equality are also questionable.

Fourth, while MLAR proponents continue to declare that such polices are complementary to existing state-led approaches, MLAR is more often a deliberate effort to counter such alternatives that continue to enjoy widespread popular and legislative support. In Brazil, for example, MLAR constitutes a direct challenge to the constitutional provisions on land reform that grant fundamental rights to land seekers and limit compensation to landowners. In the Philippines MLAR has contributed to the undermining of progress made under the state-driven CARP. In El Salvador, despite the fact that agrarian reform was an integral part of the peace settlement between the revolutionary FMLN and the Salvadoran government, it was subordinated to voluntary agreements with landowners, making it 'instantly more difficult to implement—land became harder to acquire and to finance'.[73] Similarly in South Africa a constitutional commitment to land reform that includes provision for expropriation at below market prices 'in the public interest' has been subordinated to market processes under 'willing buyer, willing seller'—what Lahiff terms 'the landowner veto'—without any clear legal basis.[74]

Fifth, MLAR tends to downplay or obscure the importance of land as a source of power, and the resulting highly political nature of agrarian reform. Granting an effective veto over the process to existing landowners ensures that they will engage with MLAR only in so far as it advances their interests. The evidence from this collection suggests that the advantages to landowners can be considerable, and can lead to the disposal of limited portions of land, but this alone cannot translate into a large-scale redistribution to the rural poor and landless. Even if it were somehow in the economic interest of individual landowners to sell off substantial portions of their land, it stretches credulity (and the body of evidence presented here) to suggest that large landowners *as a class*—a very distinct and politically well organised class in the highly unequal agrarian societies discussed here—would accept the erosion of the material basis of their power and wealth through a large-scale redistribution of land to peasants and workers.

Sixth, another impact of MLAR is the postponement of the resolution of difficult political questions in countries with often fragile democratic institutions. For El Salvador, de Bremond describes the state–market hybrid approach as 'saturated' with the politics and power relations characterising Salvadoran society at the close of the war.[75] In South Africa, and to an extent in neighbouring Namibia, the system of 'willing buyer, willing seller' has not only fallen far short of its targets but has effectively postponed the resolution of the land question inherited from colonialism and apartheid, a question that should have been squarely addressed at the moment of political transition, but which is now likely to be addressed under very different circumstances at an unknown date in the future. As the example of another neighbour, Zimbabwe, shows only too clearly, postponing such fundamental and politically sensitive issues can see them being resolved eventually under radically different, and much less favourable, political and economic circumstances, with grievous consequences.

What, then, is the future for agrarian reform? The fundamental arguments and pressures for agrarian reform, as part of a pro-poor development process, have not gone away, and are growing in many parts of the world. Among such pressures are the preponderance of rural poverty;[76] the persistence of what Fox calls (land-based) 'local authoritarian enclaves',[77] despite transitions away from dictatorships; continuing land-based violence;[78] increasing inequality within and between countries; and the growing assertiveness of local and (trans)national rural social movements for 'an alternative (rural) world'. In this highly polarised environment, MLAR policies that emphasise free markets and protection for private property, as part of the wider neoliberal agenda, are clearly on a collision course with the growing mass of peasants, agricultural workers and the unemployed who seek access to land primarily for survival purposes. Expecting the rural poor and landless to buy in—literally and metaphorically—to a market-oriented agricultural sector, within a resurgent system of private property rights, can surely only benefit a lucky few, and postpone the date of a more fundamental restructuring of landholding and agricultural markets—or can accelerate the transfer of rural poverty to urban slums. National governments, increasingly locked into neoliberal economic and political models on a global scale, are, with few exceptions, unable and unwilling to take on the leading role in agrarian reform as required by past models of the developmental state. Clearly, a new path is required, one that squarely confronts the scale of the agrarian problem across the developing world, which builds on the energy of popular movements and is willing to confront the narrow interests of wealthy landowning minorities.

The agrarian question today requires a broader understanding than in the past; it cannot be reduced to a solely economic issue, but has to be framed in an interdisciplinary and multidimensional context. The resolution of the agrarian question, understood in terms of achieving a dignified and sustainable living standard for the rural poor, cannot be achieved within the rural sector itself and within the global South alone; it requires a development strategy that builds on more equitable rural–urban and North–South linkages. Redistributive land reform is a necessary but not sufficient condition to eradicate poverty and inequality in the rural areas of the global South. Three broadly distinct but interrelated factors are also critical: 1) the ability of the rural poor to build their own independent movements and bring sustained political pressure 'from below'; 2) the creation of pro-reform national political coalitions that can use state power to implement development politics that includes land reform and 'growth with equity'; and 3) large-scale public investment in infrastructure and support services to ensure that the land reform is 'productivity-enhancing'. Only through a more equitable distribution of assets can the highly inequitable and anti-poor effects of today's global market forces be effectively contested—locally, nationally and internationally.

## Notes

The origin of this collective project is traced to the workshop on the same theme during the International Conference on Land, Poverty, Social Justice and Development at the Institute of Social Studies (ISS) in January 2006, where most of the contributors to this special issue presented preliminary versions of their papers. We would like to acknowledge the financial support extended by the Rural Development, Environment and Population Studies Group at ISS through its 'land project' (and by implication the project's funders, namely, ICCO, Cordaid, Novib and the Belgian Coalition of the North–South Movements or 11.11.11) and the Ford Foundation, which enabled the guest editors to meet in The Hague in late 2006 where steps towards the framing of this project were taken. We would like to thank Saint Mary's University for its logistical support, which enabled us, among others things, to recruit Michael Grime as editorial assistant, to whom we also extend our thanks. Several scholars assisted us in various ways in ensuring high quality papers in this collection, and we would like to acknowledge and thank them without, of course, implicating them in the final analysis in this special issue: Henry Bernstein, James Boyce, Robin Broad, Ben Cousins, Jonathan Fox, Jim Handy, Eric Holt-Gimenez, Philip McMichael, Trevor Parfitt, Reem Saad and Wendy Wolford.

1 Cited in C Kay, 'Solon L Barraclough: leading agrarian reform researcher and advocate', *Development and Change*, 37 (6), 2006, p 1400.
2 K Deininger & H Binswanger, 'The evolution of the World Bank's land policy: principles, experiences and future challenges', *World Bank Research Observer*, 14 (2), 1999. But see also S Borras, 'Questioning market-led agrarian reform: experiences from Brazil, Colombia and South Africa', *Journal of Agrarian Change*, 3 (3), 2003, pp 367–394.

3 MLAR is also the general land policy framework in most transition economies. However, it takes a significantly different context, and so we purposely do not include transition countries in this collection. For an overview of the mainstream position in this context, see K Deininger, 'Agrarian reforms in Eastern European countries: lessons from international experience', *Journal of International Development*, 14 (7), 2002, pp 987–1003. For a critical overview, see P Ho & M Spoor (guest eds), 'Whose land? The political economy of land titling in transition economies', *Land Use Policy*, 23 (4), 2006, pp 580–587; and M Spoor (ed), *Contested Land in the 'East': Land and Rural Markets in Transition Economies*, London: Routledge, forthcoming.

4 JM Riedinger, WY Yang & K Brook, 'Market-based land reform: an imperfect solution', in HR Morales & J Putzel (eds), *Power in the Village: Agrarian Reform, Rural Politics, Institutional Change and Globalisation*, Quezon City: Project Development Institute and University of the Philippines Press, 2001, pp 363–378; MR El-Ghonemy, 'The political economy of market-based land reform', in KB Ghimire (ed), *Land Reform and Peasant Livelihoods: The Social Dynamics of Rural Poverty and Agrarian Reforms in Developing Countries*, London: ITDG Publishing, 2001, pp 105–133; K Griffin, A Rahman Khan & A Ickowitz, 'Poverty and the distribution of land', *Journal of Agrarian Change*, 2 (3), 2003, pp 279–330; P Rosset, R Patel & M Courville (eds), *Promised Land: Competing Visions of Agrarian Reform*, Oakland, CA: Food First/Institute for Food and Development Policy, 2006; F Barros, S Sauer & S Schwartzman (eds), *The Negative Impacts of World Bank Market-Based Land Reform*, Brazil: Comissao Pastoral da Terra, Movimento dos Trabalhadores Rurais Sem Terra (MST) and Foodfirst Information and Action Network (FIAN), 2003; Borras 'Questioning market-led agrarian reform'; S Borras, 'Questioning the pro-market critique of state-led agrarian reform', *European Journal of Development Research*, 15 (2), 2003, pp 105–128; E Lahiff, *State, Market or The Worst of Both? Experimenting with Market-based Land Reform in South Africa*, Occasional Paper 30, Programme for Land and Agrarian Studies, University of the Western Cape, 2007; H Akram-Lodhi, S Borras & C Kay (eds), *Land, Poverty and Livelihoods in the Era of Globalization: Perspectives from Developing and Transition Countries*, London: Routledge, 2007; H Bernstein, 'Land reform: taking a long(er) view', *Journal of Agrarian Change*, 2 (4), 2002, pp 433–463; and R Herring, 'The political impossibility theorem of agrarian reform: path dependence and terms of inclusion', in M Moore & P Houtzager (eds), *Changing Paths: The New Politics of Inclusion*, Ann Arbor, MI: University of Michigan Press, 2003, pp 58–87.

5 H De Soto, *The Mystery of Capital: Why Capitalism Triumphs in the West and Fails Everywhere Else*, New York: Basic Books, 2000.

6 H Bernstein, 'Once were/still are peasants? Farming in a globalising "South"', *New Political Economy*, 11 (3), 2006, pp 399–406; P McMichael, 'Peasant prospects in the neoliberal age', *New Political Economy*, 11 (3), 2006, pp 407–418; J Boyce, P Rosset & E Stanton, 'Land reform and sustainable development', *PERI Working Paper* 98, University of Massachusetts, Amherst, 2005; and E Lahiff & I Scoones, 'Sustainable livelihoods in southern Africa: institutions, governance and policy processes', *Sustainable Livelihood Southern Africa, (SLSA) Research Paper* 2, Brighton: Institute of Development Studies, 2000.

7 See the recent collection edited by Ghimire, *Land Reform and Peasant Livelihoods*; S Moyo & P Yeros, 'The resurgence of rural movements under neoliberalism', in Moyo & Yeros (eds), *Reclaiming the Land: The Resurgence of Rural Movements in Africa, Asia and Latin America*, London: Zed Books, 2005; and Rosset *et al*, *Promised Land*. See also S Borras Jr, 'La Via Campesina: an evolving transnational social movement', TNI *Briefing Paper Series 2004/6*, Amsterdam: Transnational Institute, 2004, available at www.tni.org.

8 TJ Byres, 'Neo-classical neo-populism 25 years on: déjà vu and déjà passé'—towards a critique', *Journal of Agrarian Change*, 4 (1–2), 2004, p 20.

9 K Deininger, *Making Negotiated Land Reform Work: Initial Experience from Brazil, Colombia and South Africa*, Policy Research Working Paper 2040, World Bank, 1999; Deininger & Binswanger, 'The evolution of the World Bank's land policy'; and World Bank, *Land Policies for Growth and Poverty Reduction*, Washington, DC: World Bank, 2003.

10 World Bank, *Land Policies for Growth and Poverty Reduction*.

11 See P Dorner, *Latin American Land Reforms in Theory and Practice*, Madison, WI: University of Wisconsin Press, 1992.

12 H Mondragon, 'Colombia: either land markets or agrarian reform', in Barros *et al*, *The Negative Impacts of World Bank Market-based Land Reform*, pp 103–169.

13 P Jacobs, E Lahiff & R Hall, *Evaluating Land and Agrarian Reform in South Africa: Land Redistribution*, Cape Town: Programme for Land and Agrarian Studies, University of the Western Cape, 2003; L Ntsebeza & R Hall (eds), *The Land Question in South Africa: The Challenge of Transformation and Redistribution*, Cape Town: HSRC Press, 2006; and Lahiff, this issue.

14 Z Navarro, 'The "Cédula da Terra" guiding project—comments on the social and political–institutional conditions of its recent development', 1998, at www.dataetrra.org.br; S Sauer, 'A ticket to land: the World Bank's market-based land reform in Brazil', in Barros *et al*, *The Negative Impacts of World Bank Market-based Land Reform*, pp 45–102.

18

15 CD Deere & L de Medeiros, 'Agrarian reform and poverty reduction: lessons from Brazil', in Akram-Lodhi *et al*, *Land, Poverty and Livelihoods in an Era of Neoliberal Globalization*; W Wolford, 'Land reform in the time of neoliberalism: a many-splendored thing', *Antipode*, 39 (3), 2007, pp 550–570; JMM Pereira, 'The World Bank's "market-assisted" land reform as a political issue: evidence from Brazil (1997–2006)', *European Review of Latin American and Caribbean Studies*, 82, 2007, pp 21–49; and Medeiros, this issue.

16 JK van Donge, G Eiseb & A Mosimane, 'Land reform in Namibia: issues of equity and poverty,' in Akram-Lodhi *et al*, *Land, Poverty and Livelihoods in an Era of Neoliberal Globalization*.

17 E Holt-Gimenez, 'Territorial restructuring and the grounding of agrarian reform: indigenous communities, gold mining and the World Bank', paper presented at the Canadian Association for the Study of International Development (CASID) Congress, University of Saskatchewan, 31 May–2 June 2007.

18 S Borras, 'Can redistributive reform be achieved via market-based land transfer schemes? Lessons and evidence from the Philippines', *Journal of Development Studies*, 41 (1), 2005, pp 90–134.

19 R Bhandari, 'Searching for a weapon of mass production in Nepal: can market-assisted land reforms live up to their promise?', *Journal of Developing Societies*, 22 (2), 2006, pp 111–143.

20 Deininger & Binswanger, 'The evolution of the World Bank's land policy'; and Deininger, *Making Negotiated Land Reform Work*.

21 See S Borras, '*La Via Campesina*: an evolving transnational social movement', TNI *Briefing Paper Series*, 6, Amsterdam: Transnational Institute, 2004, available at www.tni.org.

22 For a comprehensive summary, refer to Borras, 'Questioning the pro-market critique of state-led agrarian reform'.

23 Deininger & Binswanger, 'The evolution of the World Bank's land policy', p 263.

24 Deininger, *Making Negotiated Land Reform Work*, p 653.

25 See World Bank, *Land Policies for Growth and Poverty Reduction*. See also Borras, 'Questioning the pro-market critique of state-led agrarian reform'.

26 H Binswanger & K Deininger, 'South African land policy: the legacy of history and current options', in J van Zyl, J Kirsten & HP Binswanger (eds), *Agricultural Land Reform in South Africa: Policies, Markets and Mechanisms*, Oxford: Oxford University Press, 1996, p 71.

27 See also A de Janvry & E Sadoulet, 'A study in resistance to institutional change: the lost game of Latin American land reform', *World Development*, 17 (9), 1989, pp 1397–1407.

28 Deininger, *Making Negotiated Land Reform Work*.

29 Deininger & Binswanger, 'The evolution of the World Bank's land policy', p 267. See also Borras 'Questioning market-led agrarian reform', p 368.

30 K Deininger & H Binswanger, 'The evolution of the World Bank's land policy: principles, experiences and future challenges', in A de Janvry, G Gordillo, JP Platteau & E Sadoulet (eds), *Access to Land, Rural Poverty, and Public Action*, Oxford: Oxford University Press, 2001, p 426.

31 Deininger & Binswanger, 'The evolution of the World Bank's land policy', 1999, p 269; Deininger & Binswanger, 'The evolution of the World Bank's land policy', 2001, pp 426–427; A Banerjee, 'Land reforms: prospects and strategies', paper presented at the Annual World Bank Conference on Development Economics, Washington, DC, April 1999; and de Janvry *et al*, *Access to Land, Rural Poverty, and Public Action*.

32 See, for example, B Moore, *Social Origins of Dictatorship and Democracy: Lord and Peasant in the Modern World*, London: Penguin, 1967; E Tuma, *Twenty-Six Centuries of Agrarian Reform: A Comparative Analysis*, Berkeley, CA: University of California Press, 1965; J Putzel, 'Land reforms in Asia: lessons from the past for the 21st century', *LSE Working Paper Series*, 00-04, London: London School of Economics, 2000; and C Kay, 'Why East Asia overtook Latin America: agrarian reform, industrialisation and development', *Third World Quarterly*, 23 (6), 2002, pp 1073–1102.

33 This volume. See also B Cousins, 'More than socially embedded: the distinctive character of "communal tenure" regimes in South Africa and its implications for land policy', *Journal of Agrarian Change*, 7 (3), 2007, pp 281–315.

34 This section draws from Borras, 'Questioning market-led agrarian reform'; and Borras, 'Questioning the pro-market critique of state-led agrarian reform'.

35 World Bank, *Land Policies for Growth and Poverty Reduction*, p 69.

36 World Bank, 'The theory behind market-assisted land reform', at http:///www.worldbank.org/landpolicy/, nd, p 3.

37 Deininger & Binswanger, 'The evolution of the World Bank's land policy', 1999; and MA Buainain, JM da Silveira, HM Souza & M Magalhães, 'Community-based land reform implementation in Brazil: a new way of reaching out to the marginalized?' Paper presented at the GDN conference in Bonn, Germany, December 1999, available at www.gdnet.org/bonn99/confpapers.f1ml.

38 H Binswanger, 'Rural development and poverty reduction', in van Zyl *et al*, *Agricultural Land Reform in South Africa*, p 155.
39 J van Zyl, J Kirsten & H Binswanger, 'Introduction', in Zyl *et al*, *Agricultural Land Reform in South Africa*, p 9.
40 Binswanger, 'Rural development and poverty reduction', p 155.
41 H Binswanger, 'The political implications of alternative models of land reform and compensation', in van Zyl *et al*, *Agricultural Land Reform in South Africa*, p 143.
42 Deininger, *Making Negotiated Land Reform Work*.
43 The Philippine case also shows a variant of MLAR that has been carried out since 1988 and to a larger scale. This is analysed in Borras, 'Can redistributive reform be achieved via market-based land transfer schemes?'.
44 Borras *et al*, this issue.
45 Lahiff, this issue.
46 Gauster, this issue.
47 Medeiros, this issue.
48 de Bremond, this issue.
49 Bush, this issue.
50 Borras *et al*, this issue
51 Gauster & Isakson, this issue.
52 Lahiff, this issue.
53 Guaster & Isakson, this issue.
54 Navarro, 'The "Cédula da Terra" guiding project'; and Sauer, 'A ticket to land'.
55 Deininger, *Making Negotiated Land Reform Work*. But see also Mondragon, 'Colombia'; and Borras, 'Questioning market-led agrarian reform'.
56 World Bank, *Land Policies for Growth and Poverty Reduction*, p 69, emphasis in the original.
57 Deininger, *Making Negotiated Land Reform Work*, pp 666–667.
58 Deininger & Binswanger, 'The evolution of the World Bank's land policy', 1999, pp 267–268.
59 *Ibid*, p 265.
60 Medeiros, this issue.
61 *Ibid*.
62 R Van den Brink, G Thomas, H Binswanger, J Bruce & F Byamugisha, *Consensus, Confusion, and Controversy: Selected Land Reforms Issues in Sub-Saharan Africa*, World Bank Working Paper 71, Washington, DC: World Bank, 2006, emphasis added.
63 World Bank, 'The theory behind market-assisted land reform', p 1.
64 Buainain *et al*, 1999.
65 Deininger, *Making Negotiated Land Reform Work*, p 667.
66 J van Zyl & H Binswanger, 'Market-assisted land reform: how will it work?', in van Zyl *et al*, *Agricultural Land Reform in South Africa*, p 419.
67 See Deininger, *Making Negotiated Land Reform Work*.
68 R Hall, *Land and Agrarian Reform in South Africa: A Status Report 2004*, Cape Town: Programme for Land and Agrarian Studies, University of the Western Cape, 2004.
69 F Zimmerman, 'Barriers to participation of the poor in South Africa's land redistribution', *World Development*, 28 (8), 2000, pp 1439–1460; Guaster & Isakson, this issue; and Medeiros, this issue.
70 Gauster & Isakson, this issue.
71 Medeiros, this issue.
72 de Bremond, this issue.
73 *Ibid*.
74 Lahiff, this issue.
75 de Bremond, this issue.
76 Akram-Lodhi *et al*, *Land, Poverty and Livelihoods in the Era of Globalization*.
77 J Fox, 'The difficult transition from clientelism to citizenship: lessons from Mexico', *World Politics*, 46 (2), 1994, pp 151–184.
78 C Kay, 'Reflections on rural violence in Latin America', *Third World Quarterly*, 22 (5), 2004, pp 741–775; C Cramer, 'Does inequality cause conflict?', *Journal of International Development*, 15 (4), 2003, pp 397–412; N Pons-Vignon & HB Solignac Lecomte, 'Land, violent conflict and development', *OECD Development Centre Working Paper* No 233, Paris: OECD, 2004; and S Baranyi & V Weitzer, 'Transforming land-related conflict: policy practice and possibilities', Policy Brief, North–South Institute, Ottawa, 2006.

# Land, Markets and Neoliberal Enclosure: an agrarian political economy perspective

A HAROON AKRAM-LODHI

Market-led agrarian reform (MLAR) is premised on two assumptions: that land is principally an economic resource; and that markets are institutions in which participants are equal. These assumptions are argued, in the next part of this article, to be faulty because of the socially embedded character of land and markets. In this light it is suggested that agrarian political economy offers an understanding of the processes surrounding and subsuming land transfers that are predicated on the socially embedded character of such transfers, especially through the concept of enclosure, which is reviewed in the third section. This leads into a discussion about the characteristics of enclosure under processes of neoliberal globalisation in the fourth part of the article. Neoliberal enclosure uses market-based imperatives, as a consequence of which capitalist social property relations in the South are deepened. It is argued in the fifth section that neoliberal enclosure is facilitating the reconfiguration of a 'bifurcated' agrarian structure in the South in which emergent export-oriented capitalist farming governed by the market imperative sits side-by-side with a 'classic' peasant subsistence-oriented agricultural sub-sector that is not as strictly governed by the market. In part, this is because of ongoing processes of expanded commodification of both rural products and rural labour, which is resulting in widespread semi-proletarianisation.

The treatment that is offered here is theoretical and analytical. As befits such an approach, space precludes presentation of the ample evidence that can be used to substantiate the arguments that are advanced. However, country-based case study evidence that backs up many of the propositions made can be found in recent collections by Akram-Lodhi *et al*, Rosset *et al*, and the earlier work of de Janvry *et al*, as well as in other articles found in this special issue of *Third World Quarterly*, among others.[1]

## Land and markets: faulty assumptions

Early versions of MLAR commenced in the 1970s and 1980s. Later, in the 1990s, it was implemented, under the guidance of the World Bank, in countries as diverse as Brazil, Colombia, South Africa and the Philippines.[2] Following the clear assignment of property rights, 'textbook' MLAR sees landlords being paid the full market value for land that they are voluntarily willing to sell privately to smaller farmers and the landless. Buyers usually bear the full costs of the land transfer that they demand, in the form of a debt that is acquired from a rural financial institution or the state, a debt that must be repaid over time. However, in some 'non-textbook' versions of MLAR, such as South Africa, the costs of land acquisition may take the form of a one-off non-repayable grant. Nonetheless, in both cases MLAR seeks to replace previous state-led land and agrarian reform efforts with a 'willing buyer, willing seller' model in which market-facilitated and price-mediated transactions are undertaken to generate improvements in economic efficiency and social welfare.[3]

MLAR is part of a broader set of policies that seeks to liberalise international trade in food and agricultural products, deregulate the operation of domestic agricultural markets, privatise rural parastatals, and formalise the ownership and control of property that had been held in public, in common or, in some cases, privately but monopolistically. Thus MLAR is one element in a broader project that facilities neoliberal agrarian restructuring. This project was first introduced under structural adjustment programmes and has continued under their successor, Poverty Reduction Strategy Papers. Within neoliberal agrarian restructuring what makes MLAR distinct is that orthodox structural adjustment made no claim to distribute land more equitably. MLAR was, then, introduced on top of broader neoliberal agricultural reforms in countries where there was a strong political imperative for a redistribution of land downward towards smallholders and the landless. This imperative may be driven from below, by rural social movements, or from above, by dominant elites seeking to build markets. This political imperative remains far from universal in the South. Thus MLAR is a highly constrained attempt within neoliberalism to engineer a redistribution of assets within the context of market-oriented reforms. Understanding MLAR therefore requires a broader understanding of the processes underpinning and facilitating neoliberal agrarian restructuring. That is the perspective that I will emphasise.

Neoliberal agrarian restructuring is predicated on two assumptions that I would contest. The first assumption is that land is, strictly speaking, an economic resource that should be allocated in order to maximise the benefits that accrue from its ownership and control. The global resurgence of peasant and indigenous people's movements for land is not solely based upon the role of land in constructing a livelihood. For many people an understanding of land is located within a determinate set of social, political, economic, ecological and cultural relations. As a consequence land is woven into the construction of identity. This is not to say that the place of land within rural identities is uniform across individuals even within communities, let alone across communities, or that such a role is unchanging over time and as the character of the political economy alters. It is merely to say that an exclusive emphasis on the character of land as an economic resource, as is practised by neoliberals, who do not deny its non-economic dimensions but argue that it is not possible to build policy around them, remains faulty in the extreme. Indeed, I would go so far as to say that this helps to explain part of the widespread policy failures that have been witnessed under neoliberalism.

An alternative understanding of land, which is more consistent with that of rural social movements, would be rooted in what social anthropologists term 'landscape'. Landscape consists of four distinct elements: the physical elements that comprise the actual landform; the living elements, including flora, fauna and other aspects of 'nature'; the abstract elements, such as lighting and weather; and the human elements of the landscape, which are the outcome of conscious transformative activity. These elements interact in spatially and temporally specific ways, generating sets of material outcomes that are contingent upon the prevailing set of social relations within which cultural forms are constructed. Thus landscapes are embedded within sets of social relations, and a key aspect of capitalist development in agriculture is to transform the socially embedded character of land into that of a more abstract, and hence alienated, commodity.[4]

However, it can be argued that, before the maturation of agrarian capitalism, land is inexorably relational in character. Social relations are reflected in the structure of property rights and the security attached to such rights. Social relations are also exposed by the resulting distribution of land between individuals within communities. Social relations surrounding the terms and conditions by which land is accessed affect how farmers decide to organise production. In so doing, social relations affect the terms and conditions by which labour and other non-land resources are used. As a consequence social relations embedded within the terms and conditions governing access to land affect and reflect the development of rural capitalism. Land thus shapes and is shaped by its place within a determinate set of social relationships, of which only one aspect is its economic characteristics.

The second assumption underpinning neoliberal agrarian restructuring that can be contested is the proposition that in well functioning markets people meet as equals to mutually and voluntarily agree a price upon which to exchange a commodity, an exchange that is equally beneficial to both if it is based upon comparative advantage and specialisation. Neoclassical economics argues that 'agents' operating in markets face constraints that are outside their control when seeking to optimise their production and consumption decisions. If markets are unencumbered by state or monopoly, neoclassical economics can easily demonstrate that equilibrium prices must result in the marginal cost of production being equal to the marginal revenue gained from that production by the producer, as well as the marginal benefit received by the purchaser of the product. In other words, unencumbered 'free' markets produce the best possible outcome for both the producer and the consumer. Admittedly this is a simplified view of Adam Smith's 'invisible hand'. However, neoclassical economists have a strong view of how the world should work, and seek through policy reforms to make the world more closely mirror that view. In this sense, then, this simple description of neoclassical economics remains accurate.

In any system of commodity-based production, in which production for sale dominates production for use, such a framework is problematic, for four reasons.[5] First, the extent to which exchange in markets is voluntary is debatable. In many markets the identity of those conducting an exchange is essential to its terms and conditions, including the price.[6] As a consequence exchange is often not anonymous. A lack of anonymity may, however, limit the degree to which market transactions are voluntary.[7] Second, it is common for commodities and wider market conditions not to be as well understood by the buyer as they are by the seller. Within neoclassical economics the price contains all the information required by the seller and the buyer. Yet prices may fail to give adequate information to the buyer because of an asymmetrical distribution of information regarding the qualities of the product and its place within specific market conditions.[8] Third, in light of asymmetrical information it follows that, in order for markets to operate, there is a need for supplementary non-market institutions to co-ordinate and control aspects of resource allocation so as to deal with the uncertainty and bounded rationality arising out of asymmetrical information. Non-market institutions of resource co-ordination such as the household, the community, the farm, the firm and the state thus become a necessary precondition of exchange.[9] Finally, buying and selling must be logically and temporally preceded by the production of the commodity, which makes it available for exchange.[10] This also implies a role for non-market institutions that co-ordinate resource allocation in production before any sale. In short, the neoclassical conceptualisation of markets lacks sufficient recognition that market transactions are built upon non-market institutions which structure resource control and allocation. Thus markets, like land, are embedded within wider social processes and relations.[11]

These four propositions have major implications for MLAR and its place within neoliberal agrarian restructuring. In many circumstances the identity of those proposing to undertake a land transfer is essential to the terms and conditions, including the price, governing the sale. This is well understood within the literature on sharecropping,[12] but also applies to MLAR. Moreover, the proposed price may fail to give adequate information about the land that is to be transferred to the buyer because of the asymmetrical distribution of information regarding the qualities of and meanings attached to the land. This is precisely the reason why land transfers require non-market institutions such as enforceable property rights: they deal with problems arising out of asymmetrical information. Hence MLAR requires a broader set of interventions associated with the governance reforms that are part of neoliberal agrarian restructuring. Thus MLAR is built upon non-market institutions that structure resource control and allocation.

That markets, including those that are constructed as a consequence of MLAR, are embedded within social relations is an important aspect of political economy. One of Marx's theoretical insights, when discussing the buying and selling of labour-power, was that the presumed equivalence of members of different classes involved in labour markets under the capitalist mode of production, an equivalence that is so central to neoclassical economic theory, is an illusion.[13] Mackintosh, from the perspective of institutionalism, deconstructed this insight when arguing that 'real' markets—as opposed to the 'abstract' markets of neoclassical economics—operate on the basis of four factors.[14] The first factor is the terms of entry into markets. In particular, differences in wealth among those who take part in markets mean that not all are equal. As Bernstein has similarly argued, members of dominant classes, controlling disproportionately large shares of the means of production, will be able to enter markets from a position where they can 'regulate' the operation of the market to their advantage.[15] When markets are regulated by members of dominant classes, members of subordinate classes that enter markets with disproportionately limited shares of the means of production will be regulated by a market organised to the material advantage of the dominant classes. Second, then, it is necessary to examine the ways in which those with disproportionate shares of the means of production seek to influence the conditions under which markets operate. In particular, members of dominant classes may use principal–agent relations to shape the available information, bounded rationality and uncertainty that are witnessed in markets. Third, it is necessary to understand the central role played by merchant capital in markets, as it plays a critical intermediary role linking a structure of production relations with a structure of consumption relations. Finally, it is necessary to analyse the circumstances under which regulated market-based co-ordination is supplemented or replaced by the direct actions of non-market institutions such as firms or the state that seek to structure resource allocation.

This political economy analysis suggests that MLAR has reified the market. Granted, neoclassical theorists accept that land markets may be 'imperfect', in that vested interests may seek monopolistic outcomes. The solution, proponents of MLAR suggest, is attention to the reform of wider economic policy, including the taxation of land and hidden subsidies to landlords and large-scale producers, as well as clearly defined property rights and the well established juridical and legal procedures that underpin good governance.

What proponents of MLAR would not accept is that, under a reasonable set of 'ideal-type' economic and governance conditions, it might still be possible for the powerful to regulate the market, or indeed bypass it altogether. In other words, even with good economic policy, clear legal rights and responsibilities, and apparent transparency, transactions in land may reflect a pre-existing distribution of wealth. This possibility would suggest, in turn, that there would be a need to consider the ways in which land transfers between individuals and social classes may be the result of the prevailing structure of social relations. Thus it can be argued that there is a need to consider how agrarian political economy examines land transfers between individuals and social classes.

## Agrarian political economy and the enclosure of land

Agrarian political economy is interested in understanding the underlying laws of motion of contemporary capitalism and its relationship to the countryside. As Kautsky described it,[16] agrarian political economy is concerned with whether 'capital, and in what ways is capital, taking hold of agriculture, revolutionising it, smashing the old forms of production and of poverty and establishing the new forms which must succeed'.[17] Whether capital is or is not revolutionising agriculture in general or at different paces in different times and places is, of course, both shaped by and shapes the conditions governing access to land, in that land is the principle agrarian means of production, and thus a key determinant of social, political, economic, ecological and cultural relationships. In other words, the way in which land is held will affect the capacity of capital to transform agriculture. For agrarian political economy, then, MLAR is, in a sense, about 'agrarian questions of land': who controls it, how it is controlled, and the purpose for which it is controlled will determine and reflect the distribution of power, property and privilege in the countryside and the capability of capital to overcome these limits. In seeking to understand the answers to these questions the key terrain of analysis is not the conditions under which property rights are transferred *between* individuals and social classes; rather, it is the conditions under which property rights are vested *in* individuals and social classes.

In this context agrarian political economy is predicated on the proposition that there is a near-global history of country-specific transformations in property rights over land that has resulted in restrictions in access to it. Termed 'enclosure', these restrictions have been, historically and in the political economy literature analytically, an important condition of the development of capitalism.[18] The importance of enclosure to the structure of social relations in the countryside was highlighted by Marx when he wrote:

> in the history of primitive accumulation, all revolutions are epoch-making that act as levers for the capitalist class in course of formation; but this is true above all for those moments when great masses of men are suddenly and forcibly torn from their means of subsistence, and hurled onto the labour-market as free,

unprotected and rightless proletarians. The expropriation of the agricultural producer, of the peasant, from the soil is the basis of the whole process. The history of this expropriation assumes different aspects in different countries, and runs through its various phases in different orders of succession, and at different historical epochs. Only in England, which we therefore take as our example, has it the classic form.[19]

Marx thus recognised the possibility that there could be different types of enclosure through which a set of capitalist social relations would be established or consolidated. In Marx's 'classic' example independent yeoman farmers began to be dispossessed from the land as the enclosure of the commons that were an important part of their social and material reproduction deepened the crisis of the peasant economy and, in so doing, facilitated a process of socioeconomic differentiation in the late 15th century. Within two centuries a rural labouring class and a class of capitalist tenant-farmers faced each other, beneath the dominant landlord class.[20]

Although the concept of enclosure resembles the idea of privatisation in David Harvey's thesis of 'accumulation by dispossession', its use here is different.[21] Enclosure is about more than the privatisation of space-specific assets, in either their physical or geographical aspects, although these dimensions will be critical for people who live through the process. Neither should enclosure be considered to be the result of changes in the technical and commercial characteristics of farming. Finally, enclosure is not a consequence of the emergence of capitalist manufacturing. Rather, as Wood has emphasised, in understanding enclosure it is necessary to focus upon how the emergence of capital is rooted in changes in the content and meaning of social property relations.[22] Capital is, in this materialist sense, a social relation, and not a thing, and the emergence of capital through processes of enclosure reflects deeper processes than simply the transfer of the private ownership of material assets at a given point in history. Enclosure is about more than just land, and needs to be more widely situated.

This proposition has been emphasised by Massimo De Angelis.[23] However, while De Angelis argues that 'the separation of producers and means of production is... the central category... of Marx's critique of political economy',[24] separation is not just 'the historical process of divorcing the producer from the means of production', what Marx refers to as the 'so-called primitive accumulation' that was a consequence of enclosure.[25] Rather, 'once capital exists, the capitalist mode of production itself evolves in such a way that it maintains and reproduces this separation on a constantly increasing scale'.[26] Bonefeld puts it thus: 'primitive accumulation... is the presupposition and condition of capital's existence'.[27] In other words, it can be suggested that 'enclosures are a continuous characteristic' of capital and not just a historical phenomenon: if capital is a social relation, capital accumulation is an 'accumulation of social relations'[28] in which 'the silent compulsion of economic relations [that] sets the seal on the domination of the capitalist over the worker' continuously sits side-by-side with the imposition of 'direct extra-economic force'.[29]

This understanding of Marx's political economy allows De Angelis to present an analytical framework to understand enclosures. Enclosure takes place in the capitalist mode of production whenever 'producers set themselves up as an obstacle to the reproduction of their separation from the means of production', in that capital develops 'social processes or sets of strategies aimed at dismantling those institutions that protect society from the market'.[30] The 'space of enclosure' is predicated upon capital identifying 'a limit in order to transcend it'. Two types of limit are identified: the frontier, defined as 'a space of social life that is still relatively uncolonised by capitalist relations of production'; and political re-composition, defined as 'the need and strategic problem of dismantling' a social barrier to commodification that is predicated upon people having 'access to public wealth without a corresponding expenditure of work'.[31] Such access constitutes a form of social provisioning that may or may not be monetised but is not mediated by money and is the outcome of social and political struggle against capital to construct public goods.[32] Commodification is thus intimately entwined with enclosure: capital 'makes the world through commodification and enclosures'.[33]

What then is common in the multiple taxonomies in which enclosure may be seen is that under the capitalist mode of production there is witnessed 'the forcible separation of people from whatever access to social wealth they have which is not mediated by competitive markets and money as capital'. Two modes of this 'forcible separation' can be observed: those that occur as a result of the deliberate recourse to extra-economic power; and those that occur as a by-product of the process of accumulation.[34] De Angelis notes that these latter processes may be seen as 'negative externalities, that is costs that are not included in the market price of a good, because the costs are incurred by social agents who are external to the producing firm', although this does not exhaust the possibilities of enclosure as a by-product of accumulation, for example through taxation, debt or some other by-product that fosters commodification.[35]

Neoliberal agrarian restructuring, of which MLAR is an aspect, demonstrates both modes of forcible separation. Thus, regulated markets can generate, as a by-product of accumulation, the market-led appropriation of land by dominant classes, and hence enclosure. At the same time such appropriation can be replaced or supplemented by the direct action of the state and dominant classes seeking to structure resource allocation through the economic and governance reforms that underpin the commodification of land. In these senses, then, MLAR facilitates enclosure.

De Angelis thus offers a distinction between enclosure that shapes the historical emergence of social property relations and enclosure that theoretically and politically recognises the contemporary character of it as a means of sustaining, by both reproducing and extending, capitalist social property relations. Enclosure is therefore an intrinsic part of the logic of capital and hence of the law of value, in which 'territorial restructuring' is demonstrated: a reconfiguration of the 'control over the places and spaces where surplus is produced by shaping and controlling the institutions and social relations that govern production, extraction and accumulation'.[36] Moreover, forcible separation through enclosure is fundamental to the 'transformation of subject into object' and thus 'echoes Marx's analysis of alienated labour' and hence the understanding of commodity fetishism. Finally, and critically, reconfiguration does not go uncontested: 'the fact that capital encloses...[generates] real social struggles against the many forms of capitalist enclosure'.[37] Indeed, De Angelis' argument is centrally concerned with trying to understand how 'alternatives to capital pose a limit to accumulation by setting up rigidities and liberating...counter-enclosures, of spaces of commons'.[38] Certainly recent literature on rural social movements, while not articulating the language of counter-enclosures, demonstrates the ways in which the power of peasants can pose limits to the accumulation of capital.[39]

## Neoliberal enclosure

The continuous character of enclosures, either by deliberate recourse to extra-economic power or as a by-product of the process of accumulation, as part of the immanent if not immutable drive of capital, must be situated within the specific characteristics of neoliberal globalisation. Neoliberal globalisation dates from the 1980s, and has witnessed a sustained reassertion of enclosure in shaping rural livelihoods in the South. Indeed, Araghi memorably calls it 'the great global enclosure of our times'.[40] Dominant classes in the South, working in conjunction with neoconservative dominant classes in the North, have used the policy conditionalities imposed with their agreement upon the countries in the South, in the form of structural adjustment programmes, to compress the state, to enhance the role of markets in social and cultural life, and in so doing to broaden and deepen the role of capital and the capitalist mode of production in the countries of the South.[41] Neoliberal globalisation has thus sought to promote the deeper capitalist transformation of societies in the South, in the form of a marked sharpening of capitalist social property relations.

Neoliberal globalisation has, as a consequence, promulgated changes in the character of the rural economy in many countries, most vividly around access to land. These alterations commenced with a series of legislative changes in several countries that sought to terminate or roll-back a wide variety of state-led agrarian reforms produced during the first three-quarters of the 20th century. These had constituted a form of counter-enclosure, in that 'access to public wealth without a corresponding expenditure of work'[42] had resulted in the creation of commons, that is to say 'non-commodified means to fulfil social needs, eg to obtain social wealth and to organise production...created and sustained by communities...that are not reduced to the market form'.[43] Of course, the most famous examples of this termination of counter-enclosure were witnessed with Chinese and Vietnamese decollectivisation, as well as with the collapse of collective agriculture in the former Soviet Union; the former created opportunities for relatively egalitarian capitalist farming, while the latter created opportunities for large-scale capitalist farming. However, neoliberalism was equally hostile to state-led agrarian reforms that distributed land non-collectively to individual peasant households, such as in Bolivia, Brazil, Chile, Egypt, India and Zimbabwe, among others. Thus a less well known but equally dramatic roll-back of state-led agrarian counter-enclosure occurred; Egypt and Chile offer stark examples. Often predicated on the subdivision and privatisation of the collectives or co-operatives that had emerged out of a state-led agrarian reform process, such as the *ejidos* in Mexico, and with the common objective of seeking to attract foreign capital into landscapes that were not fully colonised by capital, these transformations of counter-enclosure were a result of direct action by the state designed to facilitate a market-led appropriation of land under conditions regulated by dominant classes. Thus neoliberal globalisation has produced changes that have, as a general if not universal rule, reshaped the rural production process, in that there has been, to differing degrees, a reassertion of forms of enclosure carried out in sub-sectors of the rural economy that have served, in some cases, to reinforce, and, in other cases, to resurrect, inequalities in access to land and, as a result, to sustain a bias in the pattern of rural accumulation so that it works to the benefit of a minority.

This common process I will term 'neoliberal enclosure'. Neoliberal enclosure can be differentiated from previous enclosures in that its objective is not to establish capitalist social property relations but rather to deepen the already prevailing set of capitalist social property relations by diminishing the relative power of peasants and workers in favour of dominant classes. This is achieved principally through the use of market-based processes supplemented by the direct action of the state. In this sense neoliberal enclosure is often a by-product of the accumulation process, using capitalist economic rationality as a mechanism to achieve its ends. However, neoliberal enclosure required, in the first instance, fundamental alterations by the state in the structure of rights to property in the juridical and legal sphere that it monopolised, and which thus reflected the power of dominant class forces to regulate the underlying social relations that govern the extraction of surplus labour. Indeed, I would argue that this is the context within which MLAR arises: state alterations of the juridical sphere have facilitated the capacity of dominant classes to regulate neoliberal enclosure, establishing market imperatives that promote the use of capitalist economic rationality, and thus have resulted in a deepening of capitalist social property relations in the South as it underwent neoliberal agrarian restructuring.

Notwithstanding common aspects in processes of neoliberal enclosure, the impact of such transformations demonstrates significant taxonomies of variation in changing access to land, which must be contextually evaluated. Thus neoliberal enclosure can be geographically specific, as in the Bolivian region of Santa Cruz, in Punjab and Haryana in India, in the southern coastal region of Mozambique, or in the Central Highlands region of Vietnam, among others. It can also be commodity-specific, as in the case of fruit production in Ecuador and Tunisia, coffee production in Nicaragua and Vietnam, or game farming in Namibia. Neoliberal enclosure can be market-specific, as in the case of export-oriented agricultural production in Chile, Iran, Kenya, the Philippines and Uzbekistan. Finally, it can be ownership-specific, as in the case of state-owned enterprises in Vietnam, newly privatised agro-enterprises in Uzbekistan and the political elite's private takeover of what had been European settler farms in, for example, Mozambique and Zimbabwe, a process that led to fractions of the elite being effectively transformed through enclosure into a class of proto-capitalist farmers. Moreover, there are, in some instances, cases in which multiple and overlapping neoliberal enclosure processes are found. These taxonomic complexities, within what I suggest is a common set of underlying processes of neoliberal agrarian restructuring that is largely derived from the accumulation strategies of capital, helps explain why neoliberal enclosure has resulted in substantive trajectories of variation in changing access to land. This is uneven rural development on a world scale.

### Neoliberal enclosure and agrarian structure: analytical distinctions

The process of neoliberal enclosure has reshaped the character of the agrarian political economy in the South. In particular, changes in access to land restructured the rural production process. The result, in a diverse set of countries, has been the reconfiguration of an agrarian structure that I will term 'bifurcated'. A bifurcated agrarian structure can be distinguished from a 'bi-modal' rural system in the sense that the latter is epitomised by Latin American *latifundio* and *minifundio* existing 'side-by-side' in such a way as to ensure that both are, in neoclassical economic terms, inefficient. In a bifurcated structure, however, while two quite different productive sub-sectors remain located side-by-side, figuratively and sometimes empirically, and indeed can be quite closely connected with each other, such need not be the case. Indeed, it is precisely this possibility—that linkages between the two productive sub-sectors can be varied—that opens up the possibility of substantive variation in the differential ways that rural economies are incorporated into global capitalism.

It is important to note that my key analytical distinctions here between the productive sub-sectors is not the size of the producing unit. Neither is it scale of production. Rather, I have two key analytical distinctions, both of which are important to an agrarian political economy perspective. The first distinction is that of commodification. In particular, the two productive sub-sectors can be distinguished by the extent to which they produce for use or they produce for sale. Production for use and production for sale between the two sub-sectors can be strongly linked, but need not be. My second distinction is related to the extent of commodification, in that one productive sub-sector strives under the imperatives of the market to improve its competitive profitability within an increasingly globalised circuit of capital. By way of contrast, the market imperative for the other productive sub-sector is often but not exclusively that of the market for labour-power rather than commodities. It is these two distinctions, of commodification and the type and strength of market imperatives, that produces differential incorporations into global capitalism, an uneven development that results, not surprisingly, in substantive diversity.

Bifurcation clearly describes much of African, Asian and Latin American agriculture over the past century. Under neoliberal agrarian restructuring, however, bifurcated agrarian structures have been reconfigured, in the sense that the market imperative to improve competitive profitability by enhancing the production of surplus-value within an increasingly globalised circuit of capital has become far, far sharper than was previously the case. This has resulted in the emergence of an export-oriented capitalist sub-sector that is both more closely integrated into the global agro-food system than ever before and more important to the internationalised circuit of capital. This is because it acts as a provider of agro-food commodities that lower the value of labour-power in the North and hence raise the rate of relative surplus-value, while at the same time having the potential to act as a source of the agri-fuels that could power capitalist production. By way of contrast, for the peasantry the market imperative that has become more binding than was previously the case is that of the market for labour-power that is productive, often for the first time, of surplus-value.

## The emerging export-oriented capitalist sub-sector

The emerging export-oriented sub-sector is or may be about to emerge as being capitalist. It is more capital-intensive and less labour-absorbing in its technical coefficients of production, seeking to utilise those economies of scale and scope that can be unlocked in the production of crops principally but not singularly destined for export markets that are primarily but not exclusively located in the North.[44] As such, understanding the characteristics of this productive sub-sector relies not so much on understanding just access to land as locating the productive sub-sector within the circuit of capital. As it produces almost exclusively for the market, this productive sub-sector is subject to the logic of the market imperative, in that it must continually strive to improve competitiveness by reducing per unit costs and improving per unit quality in order to generate the surplus-value that sustains enhanced profitability. However, the markets in which the productive sub-sector participates are heavily regulated by dominant class forces. Thus the productive sub-sector is closely linked to agro-food transnational capital operating in the spheres of production, processing, distribution, retailing and finance in what is now a buyer-driven global agro-food system.

The linkages between agro-food capital and emerging export-oriented capitalist farms may be direct, through the physical ownership of capitalist farms or the control of production through contract farming. However, they may also be indirect, operating through public or private intermediaries that arbitrate between on-farm production, global processing, and global wholesale and retail distribution. In this sense, then, agro-food capital plays a key role in shaping the configuration of this productive sub-sector, imposing, as it were, 'capitalism from above'.[45]

This productive sub-sector often has limited backward linkages, but such need not be always the case. Thus in contemporary Vietnam intensified commodification was predicated on growth in which agro-food capital played a key intermediary role for an export-oriented emerging capitalist sub-sector that nonetheless has extensive backward linkages, particularly in employment. Forward linkages in this productive sub-sector into domestic markets may also be limited, in that crops are not necessarily produced for local consumption, although again this need not be the case, as the dynamic commodification of domestic food markets that is witnessed, for example, in China, Vietnam, and in parts of sub-Saharan Africa demonstrates.

Linkages into export markets are, however, exceedingly important and much more diverse, albeit in a manner that is restricted by the regulatory activities of transnational capital. These include, very importantly, the global supermarket chains that have an increasing influence over what should be produced, how it should be produced, and by whom it should be produced, and which are seeking providers of agro-food commodities that lower the value of labour-power in the North and in so doing enhance the rate of relative surplus-value. They also include the seed and chemical companies that are in the midst of turning themselves into energy companies, producing agri-fuels to replace the hydrocarbons that fuel capitalist production within internationalised circuits of capital.

In general, then, the emerging export-oriented capitalist sub-sector witnesses the generation of surplus-value under a market imperative regulated by dominant classes that has sharpened global value relations[46] in a world food system governed by highly internationalised circuits of capital seeking to raise the rate of relative surplus-value. The key point, then, is that enclosures, broadly defined so as to include the array of interventions that come under neoliberal agrarian restructuring, including MLAR, enhance the rate of relative surplus-value and, in so doing, of capital accumulation.

*The peasant sub-sector*

While the second productive sub-sector resembles a 'classic' peasant-producing farm sector it is important to be nuanced in recognising its characteristics. First, in this sub-sector the social, political and ecological characteristics of landscapes may shape behaviour and identity, and in this sense economic relations are refracted through a broader set of social relations. Nonetheless, in terms of its economic characteristics this productive sub-sector is far more labour-intensive in its technical coefficients of production, with correspondingly lower levels of capitalisation and greater challenges involved in reaping economies of scale and scope. This productive sub-sector is not homogeneous; even marginal differences in the technical coefficients of production and the ability to capture incremental economies of scale and scope can lead to the emergence of stratification among farms as the capacity to produce output surplus to consumption requirements generates processes of differentiation. The peasant sub-sector produces a greater diversity of crops, principally but far from exclusively for direct consumption by the producing household, or for sales in the home market, whether it is local or regional. The peasant sub-sector thus has, through its impact on product as well as on labour markets, significant forward and backward linkages into the domestic economy.

However, as farmers within this productive sub-sector produce for the market, for use, or both, farms within the peasant sub-sector may be differentially incorporated into the logic of the market imperative which nonetheless remains regulated by dominant classes. There are thus those peasants who are relatively more strongly incorporated into dynamic markets for farm commodities that are regulated by dominant classes and who must seek to improve competitiveness as rural capitalism slowly emerges 'from below'. For these farmers the ownership of land and other means of production must be set beside the fact that the capacity of dominant classes to regulate markets has resulted in the effective loss of control of much of the labour-process, and hence an emerging loss of access to non-market-based subsistence, as surpluses are transferred from the direct producer to dominant classes and production is therefore carried out 'by the peasan-try...but not for the peasantry' under the logic of capital.[47]

For those peasants who are less incorporated into the market the issue of control of land is critical for their very survival. The ability to construct a counter-enclosure brings with it the possibility of production for direct use, a subsistence guarantee that gives peasants a degree of autonomy from capital that may secure a livelihood—although it will not open up the possibility of accumulation. Conversely, reliance on landowners for access to land means that surpluses will be, as in the case of those peasants who are more strongly integrated into market processes, transferred from the direct producer to dominant classes. Production for those that rely on landowners is thus once again by peasants but not for peasants.

The characteristics of the peasant sub-sector thus demonstrate how the issue of access to land, by shaping the rural labour-process, extends far beyond the immediate terrain of social struggles over land and into the more general terrain of rural social relations, including social property relations and the processes by which surpluses generated within the political economy can be accumulated by the direct producer, as rural capitalism emerges from below, or be transferred from the direct producer to the landowner in ways that may or may not facilitate the emergence of rural capitalism.

*Semi-proletarianisation*

Standing beside those in this bifurcated agrarian structure is a significant and increasing proportion of the global peasantry that is seeking refuge in their small plot of land, producing agricultural products for food security reasons while increasingly engaging in selling their labour-power to capitalist farmers, to richer peasants or to non-farm capitalists.[48] Their 'de-agrarianisation'[49] is an outcome of the shift towards more capital-intensive production, usually for the purpose of export, and is mediated by capital, a 'dispossession through displacement'[50] that can be seen in Vietnam, India, China, Brazil and Bolivia. It has led to the concentration of land in fewer hands as a result of appropriation through the operation of land markets regulated by dominant classes, or as a consequence of some other by-product of neoliberal accumulation such as debt and taxation.

This stratum was described by Lenin as being semi-proletarian. He defined it as:

> peasants who till tiny plots of land, ie those who obtain their livelihood partly as wage-labourers... and partly by working their own rented plots of land, which provide their families only with part of their means of subsistence... the lot of these semi-proletarians is a very hard one.[51]

Semi-proletarians retreat from the market imperative in terms of their food production, as they can no longer compete with cheap food imports or with local capitalist farmers. Nonetheless, for semi-proletarians the market imperative holds, in that, in order to survive, they must be able to sell their labour as a commodity—labour-power—which is productive of surplus-value. Indeed, an inability to sell labour-power results in pauperisation. If, then, as in many cases, the amount of available employment is far less than the demand for employment, the result is an expansion of the global reserve army of labour, with attendant implications for both the rate of exploitation and intra- and international migration.

This is why semi-proletarians are not included within the productive sub-sectors: with insufficient means of production, they do not produce but rather sell their ability to work and, indeed, their potential to generate surplus-value. While neither peasant nor proletarian, this part of the rural population is nonetheless the result of the drive of capital to enclose, and thus to separate, producers to a greater or lesser extent from the means of production. Indeed, it can be suggested that context-specific factors contributing to or constraining semi-proletarianisation can help explain a significant fraction of the variation in processes of agrarian change in the South, or indeed the lack thereof. For example, in countries where a MLAR has been implemented, rural labour that is settled on inadequate amounts of land must work the land highly intensively, increasing the relative surplus-value that they generate when working off-farm, but with an inability to accumulate that could lead, over time, to a process of differentiation that will eventually force them to sell part or all of their holding to richer peasants or rural capitalists. In this way MLAR can facilitate enclosure by capital when labour is fragmenting into a semi-proletarian class.[52]

### Contrasts and outliers

Of course, it is important not to over-generalise, and to emphasise, in addition to the areas of comparability, the areas of contrast that may be witnessed in the contemporary bifurcated agrarian structure. Thus the specific form of the capital-intensive export-oriented emerging capitalist sub-sector can differ. In some instances farms in this productive sub-sector are classic capitalist farms, such as in Bolivia. In other instances they may be more traditional plantations, such as in Vietnam. Clearly, moreover, these two forms of production can exist alongside each other, as in Kenya. In addition, the export-oriented emerging capitalist sub-sector may utilise the surplus redistributive characteristics of landlord – peasant relationships, with the result that the peasant sub-sector, even when internally differentiated, may seek to produce for export, as in the Philippines.

There are, moreover, outliers to these general processes: for example, countries in the Caucasus such as Armenia, and Ethiopia. Each case is similar, in that the agricultural sector is not bifurcated; a petty peasant sector dominates the rural economy of each, with high degrees of labour absorption in labour-intensive technical coefficients of production, limited links to local and global capital, and pervasive linkages across the rural economy. Indeed, in parts of the Caucasus a process of 're-agrarianisation' can be observed. Even these outliers, however, are not homogeneous. Once again, marginal differences in the technical coefficients of production and the ability to capture even incremental economies of scale and scope can lead to the emergence of stratification among farms as the capacity to produce output surplus to consumption requirements generates processes of differentiation. In this context, then, even outliers may, in particular instances and contexts, generate processes promoting the eventual capitalisation of some agrarian producers as neoliberal agrarian restructuring deepens and enclosures begin to occur.

*Expanded commodification*

Relentlessly expanding commodification is part of the immanent if not immutable drive of capital which results in enclosures being a continuous characteristic of accumulation. Under neoliberal globalisation expanded commodification has occurred in terms of products, in terms of labour, and in terms of space. Thus, in terms of products, in a multiplicity of countries state development policies, as 'a particular historical form of capital's inherent drive',[53] have focused on promoting the expanded commodification of the rural economy. The relentless privatisation of state-held rural productive and distributive assets, particularly in activities necessary to sustain farm production, such as marketing, storage and processing facilities as well the provision of credit and technical assistance, bears witness to expanded commodification. Moreover, in many countries the private sector has been allowed to commence activities in operations that were once the exclusive preserve of public sector enterprises, thus commodifying economic 'space' and transferring it to capital, a clear sign of an enclosure of space that had been held in common. Indeed, it can be argued that MLAR is itself intimately intertwined with expanded commodification, in that within the context of neoliberal agrarian restructuring MLAR seeks to deepen land markets, and hence the status of land as a commodity.

Capital has expanded commodification for two interrelated reasons. The first reason has been to facilitate an expansion of an increasingly diversified set of higher-value agricultural exports destined for wealthier markets, especially in the North. Policies are thus constructed around what could be termed a 'neoliberal agricultural export bias' designed to raise the rate of relative surplus-value and thus to offset the tendency for the organic composition of capital to rise in the North. In some instances there can be little doubt that the promotion of agricultural exports has made a significant contribution to the rate of accumulation in the South, although the actual percentage change in poverty reduction with respect to the percentage change in growth commonly remains far less impressive, as evidenced by the contrast between, say, Brazil and Vietnam.

Second, expanded commodification has boosted agricultural productivity and profits within the international circuit of capital. In part this has been carried forward by stimulating increased investment in particular and specific branches of agriculture. This has led to the further and more deeply imposed market imperatives of continual specialisation, per unit cost reductions, technological innovations, improved competitiveness, and hence the enhanced production of surplus-value upon which accumulation is predicated.

Expanded commodification is thus a by-product of strategies to facilitate accumulation. It leads to a socially regressive redistribution of surplus labour within the circuit of capital away from the direct producers and towards the dominant classes as surplus-value. However, the transfer of assets and space to capital has not, in many instances, been reflected in a marked increase in the rate of accumulation. Granted, there are some cases, such as Vietnam, where there can be little doubt that the effective privatisation of land sparked dramatic increases in poverty-reducing economic growth during the 1990s. However, there are many counter-examples, such as Armenia, where the privatisation of land has not been reflected in accumulation, while in cases such as Bolivia the privatisation of state enterprises in marketing and distribution has had, if anything, a negative impact on accumulation. Thus for rural labour there is little doubt that relentlessly expanding commodification is a socially regressive aspect of neoliberal agrarian restructuring.

## Conclusion

Neoliberal agrarian restructuring is taking place in the South. However, the premise of neoliberal agrarian restructuring—that land is an economic resource—is highly simplistic. Moreover, in viewing market participation as a voluntary exchange between equals, neoliberal agrarian restructuring reifies the market. Agrarian political economy offers an alternative that emphasises, in the first instance, the way in which the control of land and the landscape shapes and is shaped by the political economy of rural change.

In the history of capitalism the control of land has been obtained through processes of enclosure. However, enclosure is not just a characteristic of history. Enclosure is a central aspect of capital's drive to accumulate, as enclosure reproduces the separation of the direct producer from the means of production and in so doing facilitates the reproduction of capital. Enclosure can be witnessed in the attempts of capital to colonise spaces not under its sway, and in the attempts of capital to reassert through commodification control of spaces that have been, as a consequence of struggle, disconnected from the logic of the market. Enclosure can be imposed directly by dominant classes or the capitalist state, or can be an indirect by-product of the accumulation process.

In this light, in this article neoliberal enclosure has been examined in detail. Neoliberal enclosure seeks to deepen prevailing capitalist social property relations through the use of market imperatives and capitalist economic rationality. Neoliberal enclosure has resulted in transformations in access to land and a restructuring of rural production, fostering, as a general if not exclusive rule, the reconfiguration of a bifurcated agrarian structure in which an emerging export-oriented capitalist agricultural sub-sector sits beside a subsistence-oriented peasant producer sub-sector. This bifurcated agrarian structure is an outcome of a set of processes in which dominant global class forces promote, as a by-product of accumulation, a market-led appropriation of land in order to foster the competitive improvements required by the market imperative. Neoliberal enclosure is thus about increasing the rate of relative surplus-value generated within the circuit of capital; MLAR is one aspect of this. Central to the reconfiguration of this bifurcated agrarian structure have been relentless processes of expanded commodification of products, labour, nature and space, which, through their impact on the landscape, affect the relationship between the emerging export-oriented capitalist and peasant production sub-sectors. As a consequence beside the two productive sub-sectors just noted lie those within the peasantry that are becoming dislocated from the capacity to achieve livelihood security on the land, and are being transformed into semi-proletarians. Indeed, factors contributing to or constraining semi-proletarianisation help explain a significant fraction of the variance in processes of agrarian change in the South.

It must be emphasised that some outliers to these overarching processes can be identified; I do not claim to capture all facets of the complexity fostered by the differential incorporation of rural economies into the capitalist mode of production. Rather, agrarian political economy is concerned with teasing out the underlying laws of motion of contemporary capitalism and its relationship to the countryside and its landscapes. In this regard this article has argued that agrarian political economy offers clear explanatory power in facilitating an understanding of neoliberal agrarian restructuring and, within this, of MLAR.

# Notes

I would like to offer my thanks to Henry Bernstein, Saturnino M Borras, Jr, James K Boyce, Cristóbal Kay, Edward Lahiff and an anonymous referee for their comments on earlier versions. The undoubted errors that remain are mine.

1 AH Akram-Lodhi, S Borras & C Kay (eds), *Land, Poverty and Livelihoods in an Era of Globalization: Perspectives from Developing and Transition Countries*, London: Routledge, 2007; P Rosset, R Patel & M Courville (eds), *Promised Land: Competing Visions of Agrarian Reform*, Oakland, CA: Food First Books, 2006; and A de Janvry, G Gordillo, JP Platteau & E Sadoulet (eds), *Access to Land, Rural Poverty and Public Action*, Oxford: Oxford University Press, 2001.

2 S Borras, 'The Philippine land reform experience in comparative perspective: some theoretical and methodological implications', *Journal of Agrarian Change*, 6 (1), 2006, pp 69–101.

3 K Deininger & H Binswanger, 'The evolution of the World Bank's land policy: principles, experience and future challenges', *World Bank Research Observer*, 14 (2), 1999, pp 247–276; World Bank, *Land Policies for Growth and Poverty Reduction*, Washington, DC: World Bank/Oxford University Press, 2003; World Bank, *World Development Report 2006: Equity and Development*, Oxford: Oxford University Press, 2005, pp 156–175; and World Bank, *World Development Report 2008: Agriculture for Development in a Changing World*, Oxford: Oxford University Press, forthcoming.

4 Albeit one that is fictitious, according to Polanyi. K Polanyi, *The Great Transformation: The Political and Economic Origins of Our Time*, Boston, MA: Beacon Press, 2001.

5 AH Akram-Lodhi, 'A bitter pill? Peasants and sugarcane markets in northern Pakistan', *European Journal of Development Research*, 12 (1), 2000, pp 206–228.

6 A Evans, 'Gender issues in rural household economics', *IDS Bulletin*, 22, 1991, pp 51–59.

7 A Bhaduri, 'Forced commerce and agrarian growth', *World Development*, 14 (2), 1986, pp 267–272.

8 W Gerrard, *Theory of the Capitalist Economy: Towards a Post-Classical Synthesis*, Oxford: Basil Blackwell, 1989.

9 FCvN Fourie, 'The nature of firms and markets: do transactions approaches help?', *South African Journal of Economics*, 57 (3), 1989, pp 142–160.

10 M Sawyer, 'The nature and role of the market', in C Pitelis (ed), *Transactions Costs, Markets and Hierarchies*, Oxford: Basil Blackwell, 1993.

11 Polanyi, *The Great Transformation*.

12 TJ Byres (ed), 'Sharecroppers and sharecropping', special issue of *Journal of Peasant Studies*, 10 (2–3), 1983.

13 K Marx, *Capital*, Vol I, London: Penguin Books, 1976, pp 279–280.

14 M Mackintosh, 'Abstract markets and real needs', in H Bernstein, B Crow, M Mackintosh & C Martin (eds), *The Food Question: Profits versus People?*, London: Earthscan Publications, 1990.

15 H Bernstein, 'The political economy of the maize *filière*', in Bernstein (ed), *The Agrarian Question in South Africa*, London: Frank Cass, 1996.

16 K Kautsky, *The Agrarian Question*, two vols, London: Zwan Publications, 1988.

17 J Banaji, 'Summary of selected parts of Kautsky's *The Agrarian Question*', in H Wolpe (ed), *The Articulation of Modes of Production: Essays from Economy and Society*, London: Routledge, 1980, p 46.

18 Marx, *Capital*.

19 *Ibid*, p 876.

20 Key contributions on the transition from feudalism to capitalism include M Dobb, *Studies in the Development of Capitalism*, New York: International Publishers, 1964; P Sweezy, 'A critique', in Paul Sweezy *et al*, *The Transition from Feudalism to Capitalism*, London: Verso, 1976; Sweezy *et al*, *The Transition from Feudalism to Capitalism*, London: Verso, 1976; RH Hilton, 'Introduction', in Sweezy *et al*, *The Transition from Feudalism to Capitalism*; R Brenner, 'The origins of capitalist development: a critique of neo-Smithian Marxism', *New Left Review* (first series), 104, 1977, pp 25–92; and TH Aston & CHE Philpin (eds), *The Brenner Debate: Agrarian Class Structure and Economic Development in Pre-Industrial Europe*, Cambridge: Cambridge University Press, 1985. More recent texts include TJ Byres, 'The agrarian question and differing forms of capitalist transition: an essay with reference to Asia', in J Breman & S Mundle (eds), *Rural Transformation in Asia*, Delhi: Oxford University Press, 1991; and Byres, *Capitalism from Above and Capitalism from Below: An Essay in Comparative Political Economy*, London: Macmillan, 1996.

21 D Harvey, *The New Imperialism*, Oxford: Oxford University Press, 2005.

22 E Wood, *The Origin of Capitalism: A Longer View*, London: Verso, 2002.

23 M De Angelis, 'Marx and primitive accumulation: the continuous character of capital's "enclosures"', *The Commoner*, 2, 2001; and De Angelis, 'Separating the doing and the deed: capital and the continuous character of enclosures', *Historical Materialism*, 12 (2), 2004, pp 57–87.

24 De Angelis, 'Separating the doing and the deed', p 63.

25 Marx, *Capital*, pp 874–875.

26 K Marx, *Theories of Surplus-value*, Vol 3, Moscow: Progress Publishers, 1971, p 271.

27 W Bonefeld, 'The permanence of primitive accumulation: commodity fetishism and social constitution', *The Commoner*, 2, 2001.

28 De Angelis 'Separating the doing and the deed', pp 60, 65.

29 Marx, *Capital*, pp 899–900.

30 De Angelis 'Separating the doing and the deed', p 69.

31 *Ibid*, pp 72, 73, 80.

32 M Wuyts, 'Deprivation and public need', in M Wuyts, M Mackintosh & T Hewitt (eds), *Development Policy and Public Action*, Oxford: Oxford University Press, 1992.

33 De Angelis, 'Separating the doing and the deed', p 61.
34 *Ibid*, pp 75, 77.
35 *Ibid*, p 78.
36 E Holt-Giménez, 'Territorial restructuring and the grounding of agrarian reform: indigenous communities, gold mining and the World Bank', paper presented to the Canadian Association for the Study of International Development Annual Congress, University of Saskatchewan, 1 June 2007, p 2; and W Assies, 'Land tenure legislation in a pluri-cultural and multi-ethnic society: the case of Bolivia', *Journal of Peasant Studies*, 33 (4), 2007, pp 569–611.
37 De Angelis, 'Separating the doing and the deed', pp 65, 57.
38 *Ibid*, p 73.
39 S Borras, '*La Via Campesina*: an evolving transnational social movement', Transnational Institute *Briefing Series* no 2004/6, 2004; T Brass (ed), *New Farmers' Movements in India*, London: Frank Cass, 1995; Brass (ed), *Latin American Peasants*, London: Frank Cass, 2003; A Desmarais, *La Via Campesina: Globalization and the Power of Peasants*, London: Pluto, 2007; and J Petras & H Veltmeyer, 'Are Latin American peasant movements still a force for change?', *Journal of Peasant Studies*, 28 (2), 2001, pp 83–118.
40 F Araghi, 'The great global enclosure of our times: peasants and the agrarian question at the end of the twentieth century', in F Magdoff, JB Foster & F Buttel (eds), *Hungry for Profit: The Agribusiness Threat to Farmers, Food and the Environment*, New York: Monthly Review Press, 2000.
41 AH Akram-Lodhi, 'Neoconservative economic policy, governance and alternative budgets', in AH Akram-Lodhi, R Chernomas & A Sepehri (eds), *Globalization, Neoconservative Policies and Democratic Alternatives*, Winnipeg: Arbeiter Ring Publishing, 2005; Akram-Lodhi, 'What's in a name? Neo-conservative ideology, neoliberalism and globalisation', in R Robison (ed), *The Neoliberal Revolution: Forging the Market State*, London: Palgrave 2006.
42 De Angelis, 'Separating the doing and the deed', p 80.
43 M De Angelis, 'Reflections on alternatives, commons and communities, or building a new world from the bottom up', *The Commoner*, 6, 2003, p 1.
44 China is a key actor in world food markets, both in terms of its domestic production and its international trade, but it is important not to underestimate the role of agro-food transnational capital in the internationalisation of Chinese agricultural production and markets.
45 TJ Byres, 'Paths of capitalist agrarian transition in the past and in the contemporary world', in VK Ramachandran & M Swaminathan (eds), *Agrarian Studies: Essays on Agrarian Relations in Less-Developed Countries*, London: Zed Press, 2003.
46 F Araghi, 'Food regimes and the production of value: some methodological issues', *Journal of Peasant Studies*, 30 (2), 2003, pp 41–70.
47 Araghi, 'The great global enclosure of our times', p 151.
48 This process is described, in the Latin American context in C Kay, 'Latin America's agrarian transformation: peasantization and proletarianization', in DF Bryceson, C Kay & J Mooij (eds), *Disappearing Peasantries? Rural Labour in Africa, Asia and Latin America*, London: ITDG Publishing, 2000.
49 DF Bryceson, 'Peasant theories and smallholder policies: past and present', in Bryceson *et al*, *Disappearing Peasantries?*.
50 Araghi, 'The great global enclosure of our times', p 146.
51 VI Lenin, 'Preliminary draft theses on the agrarian question', in *Collected Works*, Vol XXXI, Moscow: Progress Publishers, p 153.
52 H Bernstein, 'Is there an agrarian question in the 21st century?', *Canadian Journal of Development Studies*, 27 (4), 2006, pp 449–460.
53 De Angelis, 'Separating the doing and the deed', p 76.

# De Soto and Land Relations in Rural Africa: breathing life into dead theories about property rights

CELESTINE NYAMU MUSEMBI

In international development circles there is currently an interest in making a causal link between between formalisation of property rights and poverty reduction, or the empowerment of poor people.[1] This current interest echoes an earlier belief in a direct causal relationship between formalised property rights and economic productivity, which belief was abandoned in the early 1990s, following four decades of land tenure reform experiments that failed to produce the anticipated efficiency results.[2] Central to this revival is the work of Hernando de Soto.[3] In a book regarded as widely influential de Soto argues that formal property rights hold the key to poverty reduction by unlocking the capital potential of assets held informally by poor people.

The premise of de Soto's argument is that the poor inhabitants of the non-Western world have failed to benefit from capitalism because of their inability to produce capital, despite holding vast assets.[4] The key to transforming assets into capital lies in instituting a system of property rights and information on property that is applied nationally and is 'legible' to outsiders. Instead of a national formal system of law and information, property relations in developing countries and former socialist states are governed through webs of informal norms based on trust, which do not extend beyond narrow local circles. As a result most assets are not adequately documented, and therefore 'cannot readily be turned into capital, cannot be traded outside of narrow local circles where people know and trust each other, cannot be used as collateral for a loan and cannot be used as a share against an investment'.[5] Formal title would enable all these, facilitate enforcement of property transactions and establish an accountable address for collection of taxes and debts, and thus enable delivery of public utilities.[6]

By contrast, the West benefits from capitalism because, over time, disparate micro-rules on property were assembled into one co-ordinated system of formal property rights.[7] Unless the Third World can do what the West did, a large majority of its people will continue to be 'trapped in the grubby basement of the pre-capitalist world', holding dead assets that cannot be translated into capital.[8] Formal title breaths life into dead assets and transforms them into capital.

De Soto's argument has found favour with development agencies across the political spectrum, as evidenced in his appointment as co-chair of the UN High Level Commission on Legal Empowerment of the Poor.[9] For the left the notion of 'property rights for poor people' or 'pro-poor property rights' wraps a social justice mantle around an issue that is otherwise more closely associated with a conservative agenda. It keeps the intractable (and now seemingly unfashionable) question of substantive redistribution off the agenda.[10] For the right the idea of unlocking poor people's own assets to alleviate poverty is consistent with the notion of a lean but capable state that merely facilitates voluntary market transactions by putting in place the necessary legal and institutional framework.[11]

This notion of the state also dictates the mindset behind the promotion of a market-led approach to agrarian reform (MLAR), sometimes described by its proponents as the 'negotiated' approach to land reform.[12] This approach eschews a substantive role for the state in implementing redistribution of land and related resources, restricting the state's role simply to that of a facilitator of transactions between willing sellers and willing buyers.[13] The debate around MLAR presumes or takes for granted the existence of a particular form of legal protection of property rights. This presumption backgrounds the debate and without it the debate would not happen in the first place: it is presumed that, since the entitlements of current owners (of land and related resources) are legally justified, the owners' full power to use and dispose of the resources and to exclude non-owners should not be restricted without the owners' consent, except for limited and reasonable government regulation. Taking the existing distribution of resources as a given, the consent of existing owners is the paramount value to be protected. The MLAR debate presumes the existence of a property system that gives rigid legal protection to existing property interests and leaves little room for the legal system to facilitate the acquisition of property interests by a wider cross-section of society. In short, the debate presumes the existence of what has been described as a 'classical' system of property rights.[14] As a consequence, any debate on any measures that implicate redistribution is constrained right from the start: the starting point becomes 'how much intereference in private property rights is allowable?', rather than 'how shall we structure the legal framework and public policy so that everyone has the right (in a substantive sense) to get property?'

Both the MLAR and de Soto's prescription of formalisation of title as the tool for empowerment of the poor succeed in glossing over the unequal power relations that are behind demands for property rights reform, thus side-stepping the question of substantive redistribution. Critical analysis of MLAR and its assumptions has been addressed comprehensively in other contributions to this volume and elsewhere.[15] This article focuses on interrogating the ambitious claim linking the procedural act of formalisation of property rights with empowerment of poor people. The article explores this claim primarily through examining the work of Hernando de Soto in light of similar arguments made in earlier policy prescriptions on formalisation of land title in rural sub-Saharan Africa, with a special focus on Kenya, which has had the longest history (over 50 years) of experimentation with formal titling in the region.[16]

De Soto's work has breathed life into these previously discredited theories on land rights, land tenure reform and productivity, and enabled the current debate to proceed as though the negative lessons learned from African experiments of the past four decades never happened.

It is necessary to foreground the lessons learnt from the failure of earlier programmes when scrutinising the arguments being advanced in the current debate, not least because current arguments espouse the idea of formalisation of property rights as the route to economic empowerment of poor people, without taking too much trouble to specify the context(s) in which this is possible.[17] This article identifies and discusses five shortcomings in the contemporary arguments, which mirror shortcomings in past arguments. The five shortcomings are as follows.[18]

1. A narrow construction of legality to mean only formal legality. Legal pluralism is equated with extra-legality. This narrow construction of legality, combined with a social evolutionist bias results in a normative assumption that formal legal title must replace informal social norms in order for property systems to function efficiently.
2. There is an underlying social evolutionist bias that presumes inevitability of the transition to private (conflated with individual) ownership as the destiny of all societies.
3. The presumed link between formal title and access to credit facilities has not been borne out by empirical evidence.

4.  Markets in land are understood narrowly to refer only to 'formal markets'.
5.  The argument ignores the fact that title spells both security and insecurity.

Discussion of these five shortcomings will be substantiated with empirical findings from research by the author in Eastern Kenya, and using secondary literature based on experiences elsewhere in sub-Saharan Africa. The empirical research was conducted in Makueni district between June 1998 and January 1999. The data comprise a village level survey with 111 respondents (49 women and 62 men) by means of in-depth semi-structured interviews, interviews with local administrators and district-level land officials, clan leaders and women's groups' leaders, as well as observation of dispute proceedings and review of land records. The research is discussed in more detail elsewhere.[19]

### Narrow construction of legality

> The only real choice for the governments of these nations is whether they are going to integrate those resources into an orderly and coherent legal framework or continue to live in anarchy.[20]

According to this view, the absence of formal legality means anarchy. The existence of plural informal legal orders (legal pluralism) is equated with extra-legality, meaning being outside the law. De Soto therefore uses 'legality' when he really means formal legality. By posing the choice as one between a formal property system and anarchy, de Soto reveals an apparent internal contradiction in his own argument: while his work shows how central the informally regulated sector is to the economies of non-Western countries, he at the same time discounts the ordering force of informal legality.

Local informal norms and formal law are presented as mutually opposed: the former as politicised and anarchic and the latter as impersonal and orderly. Yet informal legality is an enduring feature of property relations everywhere including the USA and other Western contexts which, according to de Soto, have successfully replaced these multiple informal orders with one orderly and coherent legal framework where neighbourhood relationships or local arrangements no longer play a role in property relations.[21] The messiness of informality continues to intrude, for instance in the USA to render land titles much more ambiguous than de Soto admits, making costly title insurance a mandatory feature of land sales.[22]

Kenya's Registered Land Act also embodies the legal-centric myth when it states that: 'Except as otherwise provided in this Act, no other written law and no practice or procedure relating to land shall apply to land registered under this Act so far as it is inconsistent with this Act' (section 4). The social reality, however, is different. Although the official idea of ownership anchored on formal title does exist in some form, it is not the defining feature of property relations. It coexists, and is constantly in tension, with broader and dynamic social processes and institutions that shape property relations by constantly balancing between various competing claims and values, rights and obligations.

Justifications of private title over-valorise the role of formal state institutions as the anchor for property rights. Much as the legal-centric view would like to present property rights as simply 'juridical constructs enforced by the centralized state',[23] the legitimacy of property rights ultimately rests on social recognition and acceptance. Social institutions such as family networks and locally based dispute resolution processes play a much more central and immediate role in day-to-day interaction. When formal title is introduced it does not drop into a regulatory vacuum; it finds itself in a dynamic social setting where local practices are continually adapting to accommodate competing and changing relations around property. In these day-to-day local practices, the meaning of formal title gets transformed through the informal rules that people develop in their land relations. These informal rules and the concomitant expectations they produce become the immediate points of reference in people's land relations, more often than not relegating the formal laws and institutions to a marginal role, or modifying them to suit the reality of their lives.

Experience in Eastern Kenya illustrates this. The area in which I conducted research has sections that were titled in 1969/70, and sections that were titled in the mid-1980s. Formal title has therefore been in this area for periods ranging from 10 to 30 years. One statement that kept recurring both among land officials and local administrators, as well as among people I interviewed, was that one advantage that formal title had brought about was a reduction in boundary disputes, as these had become easier to solve. On further inquiry it emerged that a set procedure had emerged for dealing with boundary disputes: on an agreed date each of the disputing parties would bring two witnesses (often other neighbours), and the chief or assistant chief would attend.[24] Each of the disputing parties would then be required to identify the spot he/she claimed to be the boundary. A centre-point between the two disputed spots would then be identified. From this centre-point a distance of three paces in the direction of each party's piece of land would be measured and marked out, resulting in a strip six paces wide. This strip is marked off as a buffer zone between the two pieces of land. Each party agrees to fence off his/her land, leaving this buffer in between to avoid further disputes. They sign an agreement to this effect, which is witnessed by their respective selected witnesses, and stamped by the chief or assistant chief.[25]

The procedure stipulated in section 21 of the Registered Land Act is far from this local arrangement. The Registered Land Act requires that, in the event of a boundary dispute, the parties shall make a request to the Registrar of Lands to make a site visit, bringing along the official map showing the boundaries demarcated at registration. Among the people I interviewed not a single person had used this statutory procedure, or knew of anyone who had. Leaving aside the obvious reasons of cost and avoidance of lengthy bureaucratic or court procedures,[26] the reality of unregistered sub-divisions and transfers that have taken place since the initial official demarcation of boundaries in 1969/70 or the mid-1980s have rendered the registrar's official information obsolete. Similarly, in dealing with succession or inheritance, it is family and clan procedures that apply, backed up when necessary by local administrators.[27]

Therefore, even though people reflexively associated orderly resolution of property disputes with formal title, the formal property system cannot take credit for this. The only official 'rubber stamp' present is that of the chiefs or assistant chiefs who apply a mixture of the community norms in which they are embedded and their own understanding of what would be viewed as officially acceptable by their superiors. A property system is a social system and it takes shape according to the cultural context in which it is rooted. The content and shape of formal title varies with local context, and can be very different from what the officials and proponents of formalisation have in mind. Thus, given the reality of legal pluralism, to argue that formalisation of title yields an efficiently functioning property system is to make a hollow claim.

## The social evolutionist bias

De Soto's work brings a 19th century idea back into popular discourse: that formal private ownership of property carries with it the mark of civilised progress ('efficiency' in present-day terminology). He digs into the history of property relations in pre-industrial revolution England and the pre-19th century USA and suggests that this historical reality is a snapshot of present-day property relations in the Third World.[28] In order for the Third World to make the progress that the West has made, it has much to learn from the West's experience of consolidation of a formal property system.[29] Although de Soto is careful to mention that he is not calling for slavish imitation of the US transition, he leaves no doubt as to a shared destination. De Soto presumes the inevitability of transition to formal private ownership as the universal route to efficiently functioning property systems.

Whether wittingly or unwittingly, the simple dichotomisation between capitalist and *pre*-capitalist (not *non*-capitalist) property relations, and de Soto's juxtaposition of *contemporary* Third World realities with *historical* realities in the West allies him with 19th and early 20th century social evolution theories. These theories placed all societies on an evolutionary ladder on the basis of criteria such as mode of political organisation, the degree of rationality in their legal systems, and degree of complexity in division of labour.[30] These theories were imported wholesale into analysis of land tenure systems in Africa and have been deeply implicated in justifications for expropriation of land in colonial times, as well as land tenure reform experiments in the decades that followed. The evolutionist justification for formalising and privatising ownership of land was taken for granted and spoken of explicitly, as this quote from Sir Frederick Lugard, one of the chief architects of British colonial rule illustrates:

Speaking generally, it may, I think, be said that conceptions as to the tenure of land are subject to a steady evolution, side by side with the evolution of social progress, from the most primitive stages to the organization of the modern state... These *processes of natural evolution, leading up to individual ownership*, may, I believe, be traced in every civilisation known to history.[31]

This evolutionary view eventually provided the impetus for the introduction of formalisation programs in British colonies in East and Central Africa in the late 1950s.[32]

One key difference between these colonial-era views and de Soto's is that de Soto affirms that informally held property rights are quite well defined and upheld within each narrow setting, and only need to be represented in a form that outsiders (such as the state and financial institutions) recognise. The colonial-era views, in contrast, view customary property relations as unable to give rise to defined rights. Chanock and Klug have hypothesised that this portrayal of African customary tenure was necessary to give the impression that no defined rights were implicated in the expropriation of African lands for European settlement.[33]

Such arguments are influenced by abstract contrasting images between communal and individual tenure, which gloss over the immense variety of relations over property that can exist within any given system. Property relations in any society are dynamic and adaptable and allow several types of property-holding arrangements to coexist depending on the type of property in question, the types of uses, and even the types of social relationship between the people using and managing the property.

As the following example from Akamba[34] customary land tenure illustrates, different senses of 'ownership'(control and use) exist for different types of land.[35] Broadly people speak of five types of land: *Weu, Kisesi, Kitheka, Muunda* and *Ng'undu. Weu* refers to unsettled land, often used as common grazing and hunting areas accessible for use by anyone within a given locality. These hardly exist anymore.[36] *Kisesi* also refers to grazing areas, but it differs from *weu* in the sense that individual families, or groups of families that are not necessarily biologically related could fence off an area and claim it for themselves. *Isesi* (plural) were seasonal pasture usually relatively far away from homes, which served mostly as temporary grazing areas in drought emergencies. They would usually be abandoned when conditions improved in grazing areas closer to home.[37] Interests in *isesi* are regarded as temporary. They are not heritable, and cannot be reclaimed once they are abandoned. When a particular family's use of a *kisesi* ceased, the land reverted to *weu* and could be used by anyone else.

*Kitheka* refers to uncultivated land usually close to the home, which could be used for grazing, gathering firewood, bee-keeping and growing of timber. The boundaries between various people's *itheka* (plural) are usually clearly marked or known to the families involved, even though the state presumes that until demarcation has been carried out there are no clear or 'official' boundaries. *Muunda* refers to cultivated land. This belongs to a distinct family, and within the family, particularly if it is polygamous, to a distinct household identified by reference to the particular wife. Finally, *Ng'undu* also refers to cultivated land, but land that has been farmed by the same family for several years, spanning at least three or four generations. Thus, a piece of land that may have started off as an unsettled *Kisesi* could end up as *ng'undu* as a result of subsequent settlement and cultivation.

The strength of the claims of individuals and distinct households increases as we move towards *ng'undu*, the importance of individual or family claims being determined by the type of use. Where the land is being used (or was at some point in the past used) to produce food for the basic survival of the family, the claims are given stronger recognition. Unlike *kisesi, ng'undu* is regarded as heritable (can be passed down patrilineally). In the event that there are no heirs, the land does not revert to *weu*. Instead, it passes to the clan (*mbai*), which has the power to allocate it to a member of the clan and to exclude non-clan members.

The point of referring to this is to show that contrary to evolutionist assumptions of a linear progression from communal to individual control, the reality is one of 'multi-tenure systems with different land uses calling for different tenures'.[38] Variety in property holding arrangements is a reality in Western societies as well, as writings on property and social relations in the USA illustrate.[39]

It is important to expose evolutionist biases in contemporary arguments for formalisation of property rights for two reasons: first, because the simplistic dichotomisation into capitalist and *pre*-capitalist brushes aside the vast differences among and within Third World countries and charts only one direction in which change ought to proceed for all. Second, formalisation of property rights has long been conflated with individualisation of property rights and there is significant slippage between the two, both at the level of discourse,[40] and at the level of policy implementation. It is fair to say that the evolutionist impulse operates in the background to dictate a weeding out of any vestiges of communalism and its parochial norms on property relations, in favour of according legal validity only to those interests that most closely resemble individual or absolute ownership. Even when contemporary arguments for formalisation acknowledge the need to give legal recognition to 'communal' interests in land, they still perceive such recognition as a transitional step toward individualisation. For instance, some of them urge a government role in facilitating 'a gradual evolution of communal systems to meet emerging needs, possibly for greater individualization of property rights over time'.[41] At the level of policy implementation, the tacit assumption that formalisation equals individualisation is illustrated by two examples taken from Kenya's experience of formal titling. First, during my field work I observed that, although the Land Adjudication Act mandates the registration of all existing interests,[42] not merely interests amounting to ownership,[43] the exercise proceeds as though only interests amounting to 'ownership' in the absolute exclusionary sense matter. Neither in the land adjudication cases that I examined nor in the finalised registers that I perused did I find registered any other types of interests, other than interests amounting to ownership. The training manuals used by the Land Adjudication Officials do not guide them in the direction of registering broader interests either.[44] The second example relates to a special law—the Land (Group Representatives Act)—that was enacted in 1968 to facilitate the formalisation of group title in the pastoralist areas where individual title was seen as unsuited to land-use practices such as migratory grazing. There too the registration of 'group ranches' as landholding entities is, in official circles, viewed as a step towards eventual individualisation of landholding.[45]

It must be noted, however, that, although this narrow understanding of formalisation (to mean individual and exclusive ownership) has been the dominant trend in experiences of land titling, there is a handful of sub-Saharan African governments who, since the late 1990s, have been experimenting with more inclusive land registration policies. Examples include Ethiopia, Ghana, Mozambique and Tanzania.[46] Land policies in these countries have experimented with what has been described in the literature as an 'adaptation' model. This entails giving legal recognition to the whole range of existing interests recognised under local tenure arrangements, which interests are then gradually and on an on-demand basis formalised further through mapping and written documentation. To varying degrees of success in the countries in question, the adaptation model seeks to base certainty of legal title more firmly on local legitimacy.[47]

## Where is the credit?

> In the United States, for example, up to 70 per cent of the credit new businesses receive comes from using formal titles as collateral for mortgages. Extralegality also means that incentives for investment provided by legal security are missing.[48]

That formal title enables access to credit and therefore increases economic productivity is one of the principal arguments for formalisation. The security that formal title brings with it, so the argument goes, gives landowners an incentive to invest, using their land as collateral. The ability to use land as collateral is also expected to increase the supply of credit from formal sources.[49] A World Bank report on sub-Saharan Africa in the 1980s placed much emphasis on the centrality of land tenure security in improvement and transformation of agriculture: 'Accordingly, farmers must be given incentives to change their ways . . . Secure land rights also help rural credit markets to develop, because land is good collateral'.[50]

De Soto reiterates the argument linking formalisation of land ownership to access to credit and productivity, despite the fact that such arguments have long since been discredited by empirical evidence, including in de Soto's native Peru.[51] It is also worth noting that earlier wholesale celebration of de Soto's ideas in some influential quarters has had to be reconsidered, given the glaring absence of evidence for the claim linking formal title to access to credit. The August 2006 issue of *The Economist*, after reviewing recent studies in Argentina and Peru, concedes that there are factors other than lack of title that make the poor risk-averse, and that biases in the commercial lending sector still persist. Therefore poor people with title are no more likely to obtain loans from commercial banks than those without.[52]

Empirical studies in sub-Saharan Africa have failed to establish the link between formal title and access to credit for smallholder farmers. A study of a sub-location of South Nyanza district in Western Kenya found that only 3% of the 896 titles had been used to secure loans, seven years after completion of the formalisation exercise in the sub-location. A similar study in a sub-location of Embu district in Eastern Kenya found that only 15% of the titles had been mortgaged to secure loans, 25 years after the formalisation exercise.[53] A study of a pilot registration scheme in Uganda's Rukungiri district found that, out of 228 households surveyed, only 15 had acquired loans in the previous five years, over 80% of those from sources other than commercial banks.[54] A comparative study of two coffee-growing areas, one in a formally titled area in Kenya, the other in a non-titled area in Tanzania, found that only two out of the 115 households in the Kenyan site had land-secured loans, not that different from the Tanzanian site.[55] A recent study in Ethiopia's Amhara region suggests that farmers do not necessarily relate land titling with facilitation of access to credit: only 2% had such an expectation.[56] In addition, several studies have established that access to non-farm income (largely through wage employment), rather than credit, is the key factor in agricultural investment in the rural smallholder sector.[57]

My own fieldwork findings in Makueni district, Eastern Kenya are consistent with these studies. Out of the 111 people interviewed, only two had ever taken out commercial loans. Several of the interviewees spoke of two families that had taken out loans, and then defaulted, leading to foreclosure and loss of land in one, and near loss in the other.[58]

The reasons why smallholders' access to credit has not improved significantly with formal titling may be summed up as follows. First, based on a cost–benefit analysis commercial banks tend to shun small-scale (particularly rural or agriculture-dependent) landholders. Title does little to change these institutionalised practices and biases.[59] In 2003, for example, Tanzania passed an amendment to its 1999 Land Act, ostensibly to make it easier for smallholders to use their land as collateral (in addition to permitting outright sale of land for the first time). In spite of this law, the reality is that commercial banks will not give loans against the security of holdings of under 20 acres, ruling out a majority of small-scale farmers.[60] The second reason is the existence of a vibrant informal micro-lending network.[61] The credit obtained from informal networks is not secured on land and is therefore more attractive in a context where people fear losing their family land. There is a strong attitude against risking family land for credit. My field research established this, as have studies in other parts of the country.[62] Third, I found that many registered landowners had not gone to pick up their official documents of title from the land registries several years after the formalisation exercise. Most people only have the parcel number and sketch map issued to them following demarcation, the first step in the formalisation process. Without the certificate of title they cannot transact with formal financial institutions, and, since they do not get to transact with these institutions anyway, they have not bothered to pick up the documents and pay the requisite collection fee. Out of the 111 people interviewed in my study, 33 had picked up documents of title (about 30%). Studies in other parts of the country also show a low incidence of collection of title documents. A study carried out at the Kisumu District land registry showed that in Lower Nyakach, out of 109 545 titles that had been processed, only 24 893 (23%) had been picked up. In upper Nyakach only 28% had been picked up since completion of the registration exercise in the 1960s.[63] In Mbeere, Eastern Kenya only 22% of the households had picked up their title documents since the registration exercise in 1970.[64]

Finally, the overall link between formal ownership and productivity has similarly been discredited by empirical data that show that holders of unregistered land have made equally productive investments. The comparative study of two coffee-growing regions in Kenya and Tanzania discussed above concluded that land titling had little or no impact on agricultural investments or credit markets, contrary to conventional and official justifications—an observation that brought the authors of the study to the conclusion that titling is simply unimportant.[65] Another study conducted in the Njoro area in Kenya concluded that it is difficult to identify and measure the impact of tenure reform on productivity. The results were inconclusive because the richer ('more productive') farmers, who are most likely to benefit from the titling programmes, are also the ones more likely to seek title and loans. The poorer ('less productive') farmers are less able to acquire title and leverage loans. Thus, making a simple comparison of productivity and access to credit in such a context tends to overstate the supposed benefits of title.[66]

## Which market, which land?

> Any asset whose economic and social aspects are not fixed in a formal property system is extremely hard to move in the market.[67]

Proponents of formalisation make two assumptions that are refuted by empirical evidence: that 'market' refers only to 'formal market' and that 'commodity' or 'asset' captures all the dimensions of meaning that people attach to their possessions. These views could not be further from the reality when it comes to rural land in sub-Saharan Africa. The presumption that markets in land can only operate when there is formal private ownership is strong in arguments for formalisation. On this point, however, de Soto makes a less ambitious claim. He at least acknowledges that there are vibrant markets in the informal economy, and that the contribution that formal title could make is to scale up people's ability to transact beyond narrow informal circles.[68] In its conventional form the argument linking formal title to markets in land is expressed in economic terms as follows: a formalised private property regime is the only means by which individuals are enabled to take advantage of increases in land values brought about by factors such as market integration, land scarcity or technological innovation. Informal communally based systems do not enable this capturing of economic rents because there is no institutional mechanism allowing assignment of valuable economic rents to any specific person or group. Individuals therefore capture these rents by demanding a shift toward private property rights that will enable them to take advantage of the new benefits. Formalisation and individualisation of ownership is therefore the state's appropriate response to this demand. A market in land is thus encouraged to develop since formalisation lowers transaction costs in land transfers because of reduced ambiguities in property rights, a view that has been much criticised.[69]

Contrary to this view, a market in land does exist *in the absence of formal title*, and informal transactions in land do take place *in spite of formal title*. This market in land is regulated primarily by informal social structures and only marginally, if at all, by formal official structures. There has always been evidence of a thriving market in land, mostly in the form of sales of portions of a family's holding, land exchanges and leasing of farm land and grazing land.[70] In the Eastern Kenya study I found that, in a sale transaction, it is common practice for the intending buyer and seller to simply call witnesses and draw up and sign an agreement of sale of land. Often a local administrator such as the chief, assistant chief or village headman is called in to witness the agreement, to give the transaction an appearance of official backing. One of the assistant chiefs in my area of study showed me a standard form agreement that he had developed for people transacting before him.[71] Thus, formal title and its institutional apparatus are only marginally relevant or useful in the rural land market.

A further presumption often made is that people everywhere regard land as a commodity and view the freedom to dispose of it as central to their right to land. The 1996 *World Development Report* carried the following definition of property rights: 'Property rights include the right to use an asset, to permit or exclude its use by others, to collect the income generated by the asset, and to sell or otherwise dispose of the asset'.[72]

Formal legal definitions similarly underline the owner's absolute ownership, emphasising the freedom to dispose of the property.[73] Land tenure reforms have often focused disproportionately on the commodity aspect or marketability of land, ignoring the multidimensional nature of land.[74] In a rural smallholding setting, land is much more than simply one more input in an agricultural enterprise.[75] It is impossible, for most people, to abstract land from the social and cultural meanings associated with it. Besides being the main source of livelihood for the majority of families, land also supports a wide network of kin relationships, and functions as a status symbol. To sell land—particularly ancestral land—is a monumental decision. Thus the sale of land takes place mostly in emergency situations, such as meeting unexpected medical expenses, or to pay for children's education when there is no other source of income. Usually it will involve sale of only a portion of the land, sometimes in an agreement expressed as a redeemable sale, and almost always on an informal basis, with no official transfer registered.

Arguments that link formalisation to creation of land markets portray holders of property rights as abstract autonomous individuals able to transact freely on the basis of their formally recognised rights of ownership.

The reality is different. Social institutions such as the clan or other kinship groups play a major role in instilling a level of restraint in transacting in land. In the location where I conducted research, 17 clans are represented, of which 10 have written rules. All 10 had a clause concerning land transactions. Even the clans without written rules had widely cited oral rules concerning land transactions. An example from the *Atwii* clan captures the spirit of clan rules on land transactions:

> It is not permitted for a member of our clan to sell land without the knowledge and consent of the clan committee. Land belonging to a *Muutwii* [member of the *Atwii* clan] must first be offered for sale to the family, and then to other clan members, before it can be offered to outsiders.[76]

A clan member who intends to sell land must satisfy the clan committee that he is in agreement with his family members and that he has valid reasons for selling the land, and, most importantly, that he will still have sufficient land left for his family's needs. Even in other communities where this rule may not be formally spelled out, there is a general expectation of consultation of family members before any sale of land. This is an illustration of the fact that the commodity view of land promoted by officials and proponents of formalisation competes with a different social vision of property as primarily a means through which social responsibilities are met; even though individual rights and entitlements do matter, these are conceived of broadly in order to enable the fulfilment of those social responsibilities. Individual entitlements are conceived of broadly so as to include rather than exclude. An argument that links formal title to the emergence of land markets on the expectation that individuals are always motivated by the desire to capture economic rents ignores the fact that the social context of which they are a part plays a role in shaping their preferences.[77]

### Security for whom? The distributional consequences of title

> When we ask ourselves whether a social or legal practice works, we must ask ourselves 'works *for whom?*' Who benefits and who loses from existing political, economic and legal structures?[78]

If we take the relational and inherently distributional nature of property rights seriously,[79] the argument that formal title ensures security of tenure must necessarily be met with the question 'security for whom?'. De Soto celebrates the promise of 'lifting the bell jar' to enable inclusion of poor people into formal property systems so much that he fails to acknowledge that there are negative distributional consequences involved. Specifically, as some critics have pointed out, his emphasis on alienability and fungibility as the primary desired outcome of formalisation has potentially adverse consequences for 'poorer holders of land rights more prone to distress sales'.[80] Any redefinition of property rights produces winners and losers.[81] People who acquire title can both gain and lose, as in the case of formalisation in urban slum contexts, where the land does gain value, but this has often meant that poor beneficiaries of land titling programmes come under pressure to sell off their holdings to developers and slum-lords, forcing them into further marginality and widening inequality.[82]

In the context of sub-Saharan Africa the negative distributional consequences of formalising rights to land, with an emphasis on absolute individual ownership in rural areas governed by customary tenure, have been well documented.[83] Title formalisation programmes in many African countries have been driven—explicitly or implicitly—by an impulse to replace customary land tenure with individual title, reflecting in large part the thinking of international financial institutions.[84] Thus, entitlements based on customary rights to land have been rendered vulnerable, for instance, when title holders assert their absolute rights of ownership against family members whose claims are unregistered. Courts in Kenya have overwhelmingly ruled in favour of holders of formal title, ignoring the reality that the vast majority of people regulate their property relations based on custom, even after land has been formally registered.

Prevailing judicial attitudes against unregistered interests translate into systemic gender bias in interpreting property rights within the family, given the low incidence of registration by women, whether as individual or joint owners.[85] The remainder of this section focuses on the displacement of women's claims to family land to illustrate the distributional nature of formal titling as it has been practised in Kenya, and to refute the simplistic equation of formal title with security.

### Displacing women's claims to family property

A low incidence of joint registration, coupled with the established practice of registering land in the name of the 'head of household' has meant that formalisation weakens women's claims to family property. This insecurity has been spoken of in some writings as if it were unique to women.[86] However, it needs to be understood within the general context of the systemic narrowing of existing social criteria for recognising entitlement. Framed this way, we are able to see that the problem is with the previously discussed narrow and limited understanding of registrable interests employed in the titling programmes, which inevitably results in exclusion.

This exclusion does have gender-differentiated consequences that translate into particular expressions of insecurity for women. For the vast majority of married women interests in family land are held on account of the marriage relationship, which for most women is based on customary law. The precariousness of customary land rights in the eyes of a legal system that pretends to be blind to the reality of plural and overlapping rights to land is obvious. Unmarried daughters living on land registered in their fathers' or brothers' names are in a similarly precarious position. In the absence of legal recognition of customary interests in registered land, the entitlements of women in these situations have no independent legal existence. They derive from the title-holder's interests, and their security depends primarily on the stability of their relationship with the title holder. The Kenyan Court of Appeal ruled in 1988 that a wife's interests under customary law cease to exist once her husband becomes the formally registered owner. Therefore she could not rely on her customary law entitlements as a widow in the face of third parties with competing registered claims, in this case, a financial institution to which the land had been mortgaged.[87]

But it is not just exclusion from formal title that renders women's interests in family land insecure. The formalisation process reinforces the existing relative insecurity of women's customary land rights. By relative insecurity I mean relatively weaker capacity to mobilise social support for one's claim to property. It refers specifically to a person's position in the property-holding entity—a family or kinship network. Relative insecurity does not have to be based on comparison between men and women only. It could be between people born into a family versus those who have married in; or between women at different stages of the life cycle; or between those with children and those without; those with a regular source of income and those without. A husband or eldest brother occupies a position of authority within the family. He enjoys economic power that derives from exercising control over valued resources, as well as social power to allocate resources, which implicates others' loyalty, dependency and obligations.

Against this background, formalisation of title has become synonymous with transformation and increased visibility of men's control rights over land, and the simultaneous disappearance or invisibility of women's established usage rights under customary law by legal fiat. The formalisation programme relies on one understanding of ownership, namely ownership as absolute authority. Empirical work conducted by Achola Pala in the Luo community in Western Kenya illustrates the gendered effects of such a narrow approach to formalisation.[88] She shows that in the Luo language, the term for 'owner of land' (*wuon lowo*) is understood at two levels. First, it refers to the person (often male, generally in the position of a grandfather) who has the power or right to allocate land to others. At the second level it refers to a person (female or male) who has a recognised right to use a particular piece of land over a long period of time. This right exists by virtue of his or her relationship to the person who has authority to allocate the land. She argues that the process of formalisation of title has focused on the first level only (which is exclusively male), and ignored the second sense of land ownership (which would allow for more gender inclusiveness). Thus only men end up registered as owners of land.

By equating ownership of land to only the first sense of *wuon lowo*, the process transforms men's allocative authority into an absolute right of ownership, which includes the right to alienate the land, without any safeguards for the rights exercised by women and other family members as owners and users of land in the second sense. Parker Shipton, writing on the same community, concludes that registration has effected 'a hardening of men's land rights into absolute legal ownership to the exclusion of women and children'.[89]

Fiona Mackenzie, writing on central Kenya, makes a similar argument regarding the absence of protection for 'lesser rights', and the rendering of men's interests in land into rights of outright ownership.[90] She argues that the precarious position of these 'lesser rights' is made even less secure in light of the weakening of social institutions that would otherwise have played a supervisory role in the way men exercise these interests.

This discussion does not in any way suggest that the situation will be remedied by simply recognising customary claims. Customary tenure arrangements have the capacity to both facilitate and impede the security of women's property rights, and the need for a pragmatic but critical and balanced approach to their recognition has been discussed in detail elsewhere.[91] The countries that have recently undertaken land tenure reforms employing a more inclusive adaptation model have also put in place special measures to protect the property interests of wives and ex-wives. The enormity of this task, and the need for solutions beyond legal measures, is illustrated by the fact that, even in the brief history of these special measures, there has been evidence of practices that circumvent the law and result in dispossession.[92]

A final illustration of the way in which a narrow approach to formalisation results in the weakening of women's claims to family property is drawn from the manner in which courts have decided cases concerning marital property in Kenya.[93] Since there is no Act of Parliament specifying the rights of spouses to family property following marital breakdown, courts apply an English statute, the Married Women's Property Act of 1882. This statute follows the common law doctrine of separate property, which means that each spouse retains as his/her individual property whatever he or she owned before marriage, as well as what he or she acquired during marriage. The property holding unit is the individual, not the family unit. Marriage alone does not confer a proprietary interest on the other spouse. The starting point in any dispute therefore is to establish legal ownership. In the case of land this would be evidenced by title. The court then enquires into any claim of beneficial ownership made by the non-title-holding spouse. The most common claim made is that the non-title-holding spouse made a significant contribution in the form of money or labour. The law requires that such a claim must be proved strictly. Thus wives pursuing marital property claims with no formal title documents to show are forced into an uphill battle of proving significant contribution. Regardless of the duration of a marriage, such a wife must strictly prove her contribution to the assets acquired during the marriage.

In a context where formalisation of property rights in land has resulted predominantly in individual registration of men as heads of households, application of a strict separate property regime produces a gendered pattern of exclusion. Any discussion of formalisation of property systems that engages seriously with this gendered pattern of exclusion, with inequalities at the micro-level of family relations and beyond, cannot credibly make an unqualified claim that equates formalisation of title with the securing of property rights.

## Conclusion

By disregarding the lessons learnt from the failure of tenure reform experiments of the past four decades, de Soto's work re-popularises previously discredited theories of property rights and reproduces their shortcomings. This article has discussed five such shortcomings with reference to the context of rural land in Africa. First, a narrow construction of legality to refer only to formal law results in over-valorisation of formal title and a downplaying of the central role played by informal norms and practices. Second, dichotomisation of property systems into capitalist and *pre*-capitalist glosses over the dynamic and multi-tenure nature of land-holding arrangements and echoes 19th century notions of the inevitability of social evolution towards private individual ownership. This evolutionist impulse is at work in formalisation programmes that work with a narrow notion of interests that most closely resemble absolute individual ownership as the only registrable interests. Third, the assertion of a causal link between formal title and access to credit is repeated without any acknowledgement of the overwhelming evidence discrediting it. Fourth, in arguing that formal title scales up markets in land de Soto does acknowledge that markets in land, albeit on a small and informal scale, exist in the absence of formal title. However, he overlooks the fact that informal transactions do persist in spite of formal title, and fails to take account of the multiple dimensions of meanings that people attach to land and other valued possessions besides 'commodity' or 'asset'. The fifth shortcoming—failure to engage with the insecurity that a narrow approach to formalisation often brings with it or with the ways in which such formalisation might reinforce existing inequalities—casts doubt on the 'pro-poor' credentials of the property rights reform agenda.

We must not lose sight of the fact that debates around land reform and reform of property systems are taking place within a broader context of a search for ways to tackle deep inequality. Priority should therefore be given to policy recommendations that maintain rather than distract from a focus on substantive inequality. We must be wary of policy proposals that pin too many hopes on procedural reforms and formal abstractions in the face of empirical evidence to the contrary, thus glossing over the real challenges of overcoming substantive inequality. Arguments such as de Soto's fall into this category for the reasons discussed here and, not least, for the ambitious claim that 'the benefits of capitalism' will trickle down to the poor once 'the firm foundations of formal property are in place'.[94]

## Notes

The author thanks the following for comments on earlier versions of this article: Peter Houtzager, Ian Scoones, Ben Cousins, Elizabeth Daley, Birgit Englert and Robin Palmer.

1 K Deininger, D Ayalew & T Yamano, 'Legal knowledge and economic development: the case of land rights in Uganda', *World Bank Policy Research Working Paper* No 3868, Washington, DC: World Bank, 2006; World Bank, *Land Policies for Growth and Poverty Reduction*, Washington, DC: World Bank/New York: Oxford University Press, 2003; and High Commission on Legal Empowerment of

Poor People (HCLEP), 'Overview Paper', 2006, at http://legalempowerment.undp.org/pdf/HLCLE-P_Overview.pdf.

2 World Bank, *Land Policies for Growth and Poverty Reduction*; and J Bruce & S Migot-Adholla (eds), *Searching for Land Tenure Security in Africa*, Dubuque, IA: Kendall/Hunt Publishing Company, 1994.

3 H De Soto, *The Mystery of Capital: Why Capitalism Triumphs in the West and Fails Everywhere Else*, New York: Basic Books, 2000.

4 *Ibid*, p 5.

5 *Ibid*, p 6.

6 *Ibid*, pp 7, 59.

7 *Ibid*, p 52.

8 The notion that adoption of Western legal forms and legal cultures is inevitable for social and economic development in Africa is also present, albeit implicitly, in contemporary donor-funded 'good governance' reforms. The area of property systems has been a prime candidate for such reforms, particularly after the end of the Cold War—and not only in Africa. *Ibid*, p 55; P McAuslan, 'Making law work: restructuring land relations in Africa', *Development and Change*, 23(3), 1998, pp 525–552; and McAuslan, *Bringing the Law Back in: Essays in Land, Law and Development*, Aldershot: Ashgate, 2003.

9 The commission is co-chaired by Hernando de Soto and Madeleine Albright, the former US ambassador to the UN, and hosted by the United Nations Development Programme (UNDP). See http://legalempowerment.undp.org/; http://www.desotowatch.net/.

10 I Shivji, 'Lawyers in neoliberalism: authority's professional supplicants or society's amateurish conscience?', mimeo, University of Dar es Salaam, Tanzania, 2006, at http://www.oxfam.org.uk/what_we_do/issues/livelihoods/landrights/downloads/shivji_valedictory_lecture.pdf); and A Manji, *The Politics of Land Reform in Africa: From Communal Tenure to Free Markets*, London: Zed Books, 2006. Manji observes how the question of land reform in Africa has seen a revival since the late 1990s, but unlike in the period leading up to the 1970s, the preoccupation now is not with substantive redistribution of land to the landless. Rather, substantive redistribution has been displaced by a procedural agenda of reforming systems for the administration of land (pp 33–34. See also F Von Benda-Beckman, 'Mysteries of capital or mystification of legal property?', *Focaa—European Journal of Anthropology*, 41, 2003, pp 187–191.

11 World Bank, *World Development Report 1996: From Plan to Market*, Washington, DC: World Bank, 1996.

12 K Deininger & H Binswanger, 'The evolution of the World Bank's land policy: principles, experience, and future challenges', *World Bank Research Observer*, 14 (2), 1999, pp 247–276.

13 S Borras, 'Questioning market-led agrarian reform: experiences from Brazil, Colombia and South Africa', *Journal of Agrarian Change*, 3 (3), 2003, pp 367–394.

14 J Singer, 'Property and social relations: from title to entitlement', in C Geisler & G Daneker (eds), *Property and Values: Alternatives to Public and Private Ownership*, Washington, DC: Island Press, 2000, pp 3–19.

15 Borras, 'Questioning market-led agrarian reform'.

16 RJM Swynnerton, *A Plan to Intensify the Development of African Agriculture in Kenya*, Nairobi: Kenya Department of Agriculture, 1954.

17 While at times it is clear that de Soto is writing within the context of urban slums, at other times he writes as if making a general argument for a causal relationship between formalisation of title and economic empowerment. Those who have seized upon his work and popularised it in influential media are even less careful to make any contextual distinction. See, for example, 'No title', *The Economist*, 31 March–6 April 2001, pp 20–22; 'Breathing life into dead capital: why secure property rights matter', *The Economist*, 17 January 2004, pp 6–8; P Schaefer, 'Poor need resurrection of their dead capital', *Wall Street Journal*, 14 June 2005, A15; R Robb, 'Poor Africans need land rights', *Arizona Republic*, 15 July 2005; and K Dolan, 'A new kind of entitlement', *Forbes Magazine*, 23 December 2002.

18 Others have critiqued de Soto's work on different but related grounds. See, for example, J Manders, 'Sequencing property rights in the context of development: a critique of the writings of Hernando de Soto', *Cornell International Law Journal*, 37, 2004, pp 178–198; C Rakodi & RC Leduka, 'Informal land delivery processes and access to land for the poor in six African cities: towards a conceptual framework', *Working Paper No 1*, Birmingham. AB: School of Public Policy, International Development Department, 2003; D Hunt, 'Unintended consequences of land rights reform: the case of the 1998 Uganda Land Act', *Development Policy Review*, 22 (2), 2004, pp 173–191; M Rawson, 'Review of: The Mystery of Capital by Hernando de Soto', *Land and Liberty*, Summer 2001; S Kinsella, 'Book review: Hernando de Soto. The Mystery of Capital: Why Capitalism Triumphs in the West and Fails Everywhere Else', *Journal of Libertarian Studies*, 16 (1), 2002, pp 99–114; S Hendrix, 'Myths of property rights', *Arizona Journal of International and Comparative Law*, 12, 1995, pp 183–

223; and JK Winn, 'Book review: How to Make Poor Countries Rich and How to Enrich Our Poor', *Iowa Law Review*, 77, 1992, pp 899–939.

19 C Nyamu, 'Gender, culture and property relations in a pluralistic social setting', doctoral dissertation, Harvard Law School, 2000.

20 De Soto, *The Mystery of Capital*, p 27.

21 *Ibid*, p 53. On the coexistence of formal and informal legality in Western property relations, see R Ellickson, *Order Without Law: How Neighbours Settle Disputes*, Cambridge, MA: Harvard University Press, 1991; SE Merry, *Getting Justice and Getting Even: Legal Consciousness among Working Class Americans*, Chicago, IL: University of Chicago Press, 1990; and J Ruffini, 'Disputing over livestock in Sardinia', in L Nader & H Todd (eds), *The Disputing Process: Law in Ten Societies*, New York: Columbia University Press, 1978, pp 209–246.

22 Hendrix, 'Myths of property rights'.

23 K Firmin-Sellers & P Sellers, 'Expected failures and unexpected successes of land titling in Africa', *World Development*, 27, 1999, pp 1115–1128.

24 Chiefs and assistant chiefs are government-appointed local administrators who have a broad mandate to maintain law and order. Roughly half of their time is spent solving local disputes.

25 In terms of strict formal legality, a stamp by a chief or assistant chief bears no legal weight. The chiefs and assistant chiefs have no specific mandate to resolve disputes. However, a default mediation role has evolved out of their vague and all-embracing mandate to maintain law and order at the grassroots level, partly because in many places they are the only embodiment of officialdom around and partly because in their personal capacity some also have legitimacy as community leaders. Their involvement therefore confers both social legitimacy and the appearance of official sanction on the proceedings. For further discussion on the role of local administrators in resolution of property disputes, see C Nyamu-Musembi, 'Are local norms and practices fences or pathways? The example of women's property rights', in Abdullahi An-Na'im (ed), *Cultural Transformation and Human Rights in Africa*, London: Zed Books, 2002, pp 126–150. For references to similar involvement of officials in informal land transactions in other sub-Saharan African contexts, see A Chimhowu & P Woodhouse, 'Customary vs private property rights? Dynamics and trajectories of vernacular land markets in sub-Saharan Africa', *Journal of Agrarian Change*, 6 (3), 2006, pp 346–371.

26 Indeed, de Soto acknowledges the high cost of implementing rigid and outdated formal property laws inherited from colonial English and Roman jurisprudence, which are tilted more toward a rigid protection of ownership rather than facilitating and guaranteeing the security of transactions. As a result of this, de Soto argues, many assets have 'slipped out of the formal legal system in search of mobility' (*The Mystery of Capital*, p 62). However, by his singular focus on getting formality right, de Soto stops short of proposing that the solution lies in building on the very informal systems, such as customary land tenure, that have provided this alternative route to mobility, by providing the security needed for transactions such as settlement of boundary disputes, leases and exchanges of land, land sales and informal credit arrangements.

27 Nyamu, 'Gender, culture and property relations in a pluralistic social setting'; and C Nyamu-Musembi, 'Are local norms and practices fences or pathways?'.

28 The book contains several explicit references to the West's past as the Third World's present. See pp 10, 11, 13 and 16.

29 De Soto, *The Mystery of Capital*, pp 52, 55. The accuracy of de Soto's narrative claiming a causal link between capitalist development in the West and the consolidation of disparate informal systems into a formal property system has been questioned by accounts that highlight the greater significance of other factors, such as exploitative working conditions and cheap access to raw materials from the colonies, conditions that cannot be replicated for the present Third World. Von Benda-Beckman, 'Mysteries of capital or mystification of legal property?', p 190.

30 M Weber, *Law in Economy and Society*, ed Max Rheinstein, Cambridge, MA: Harvard University Press, 1954; and E Durkheim, *The Social Division of Labor in Society*, New York: Free Press, 1964; H Maine, *Ancient Law: Its Connection with the Early History of Society and its Relation to Modern Ideas*, Tucson, AZ: University of Arizona Press, 1986.

31 F Lugard, *The Dual Mandate in British Tropical Africa*, London: Cass, 1922 (author's emphasis).

32 Report of the Conference on African Land Tenure in East and Central Africa, Arusha, Tanzania, October, 1956 (Special Supplement to the *Journal of African Administration*), p 2.

33 M Chanock, 'A peculiar sharpness: an essay on property in the history of customary law in colonial Africa', *Journal of African History*, 32, 1991, pp 65–88; and H Klug, 'Defining the property rights of others: political power, indigenous tenure and the construction of customary law', *Working Paper No 23*, Johannesburg: Centre for Applied Legal Studies, University of Witwatersrand, 1995.

34 Akamba are the predominant ethnic group in four districts of Eastern Kenya, including Makueni district, the site of the empirical research referred to here.

35 This account is based on conversations I have had with various people before and during my field research. In particular, I draw from my interviews with clan elders and Land Adjudication Officers. I also rely on Penwill 1951. DJ Penwill, *Kamba Customary Law: Notes Taken in the Machakos District of Kenya Colony*, London: Macmillan, 1951.

36 Now references to '*weu*' exist almost exclusively in folk lore. See, for example, J Mbiti, *Akamba Stories*, Oxford: Clarendon Press, 1966.

37 Since there is hardly any land available for *isesi* now, a similar practice in the case of drought emergencies is the leasing of land in a different area, where herds are temporarily located for the duration of a drought.

38 JP Platteau, 'The evolutionary theory of land rights as applied to sub-Saharan Africa: a critical assessment', *Development and Change*, 27 (1), 1996, pp 29–86.

39 G Alexander, *Commodity and Propriety: Competing Visions of Property in American Legal Thought, 1776–1970*, Chicago, IL: University of Chicago Press, 1997; and J Singer, *Entitlement: The Paradoxes of Property*, New Haven, CT: Yale University Press, 2000; Singer, 'Property and social relations: from title to entitlement', in C Geisler & G Daneker (eds), *Property and Values: Alternatives to Public and Private Ownership*, Washington, DC: Island Press, 2000, pp 3–19.

40 The assumption of a liner progression from communal to individual ownership is more explicit in the earlier views referred to than in de Soto's. De Soto's case for formal property systems is framed broadly enough that most of the book permits a reading that accommodates multiple owners or users as long as their interests are clearly defined. However, in his articulation of one of the effects (benefits) of a formal property system, de Soto does appear to take it for granted that the end-result of formalisation will be individual ownership: 'By transforming people with property interests into accountable individuals, formal property created individuals from masses' (*The Mystery of Capital*, p 53). Other commentators have also observed that de Soto is not explicit about whether formalisation equates to individualisation, but it is suggested. See von Benda-Beckman, 'Mysteries of capital or mystification of legal property?' p 188. The authors unselfconsciously use the term 'secure property rights' interchangeably with 'secure individual property rights' and 'individual titling'. Deininger & Binswanger, 'The evolution of the World Bank's land policy', pp 248, 249.

41 Deininger & Binswanger, 'The evolution of the World Bank's land policy', p 248.

42 The statute that outlines the procedure to be followed in determining registrable interests in land before their formal registration.

43 Section 23 (2) (e) of the Land Adjudication Act lists such interests to include 'any lease, right of occupation, charge or other encumbrance, whether by virtue of recognized customary law or otherwise.' The statute requires the Recording Officer to determine the nature and extent of such interest in order to enable it to be registered in the name of the person or persons claiming it. In theory, a wife or other member of the family claiming a customary law right of occupation could invoke this section to have that interest officially registered. I have not come across any such use of this provision nor any legal argument on its possible use.

44 The officers in the Makueni land adjudication office rely on two handbooks, neither of which refers to the registration of claims other than ownership claims. Government of Kenya, *A Handbook for the Guidance of Officers of the Land Adjudication Department*, Nairobi: Ministry of Land and Settlement, 1970; Government of Kenya, *Handbook on Land Use Planning, Administration and Development Procedures*, Nairobi: Ministry of Lands and Housing, 1991.

45 HWO Okoth-Ogendo & W Oluoch-Kosura, *Final Report on Land Tenure and Agricultural Development in Kenya*, Nairobi: Ministry of Agriculture, Livestock Development and Marketing, 1995, p 44.

46 D Tsikata, 'Securing women's interests within land tenure reforms: recent debates in Tanzania', *Journal of Agrarian Change*, 3 (1), 2003, pp 149–183; N Kanji, L Cotula, T Hilhorst, C Toulmin & W Witten, *Research Report 1: Can Land Registration Serve Poor and Marginalized Groups?*, Summary Report, London: IIED, 2005; B Adenew & F Abdi, *Research Report 3: Land Registration in Amhara Region, Ethiopia*, London: IIED, 2005; A Teklu, *Research Report 4: Land Registration and Women's Land Rights in Amhara Region, Ethiopia*, London: IIED, 2005; M Haile, W Witten, K Abraha, S Fissha, A Kebede, G Kassa & G Reda, *Research Report 2: Land Registration in Tigray, Northern Ethiopia*, London: IIED, 2005; A Chilundo, B Cau, M Mubai, D Malauene & V Muchanga, *Research Report 6: Land Registration in Nampula and Zambezia Provinces, Mozambique*, London: IIED, 2005; and A Manji, *The Politics of Land Reform in Africa: From Communal Tenure to Free Markets*, London: Zed Books, 2006.

47 R, Crook, 'Law, Legal Institutions and the Protection of Land Rights in Ghana and Cote d'Ivoire: Developing a More Effective and Equitable System', *IDS Research Report No. 58*, Brighton: Institute of Development Studies, 2007, p 33.

48 De Soto, *The Mystery of Capital*, p 86.

49 Deininger & Binswanger, 'The evolution of the World Bank's land policy', p 250.

50 World Bank, *Sub-Saharan Africa: From Crisis to Sustainable Growth*, Washington, DC: World Bank, 1989.

51 Hendrix. 'Myths of property rights'; and Winn, 'Book review'.

52 'Of property and poverty', *The Economist*, 26 August 2006, pp 11–12.
53 P Shipton, *Land and the Limits of Individualism: Population Growth and Tenure reforms South of the Sahara*, Discussion Paper No 320, Harvard Institute for International Development, 1989, p 35.
54 M Roth, J Cochrane & W Kisamba-Mugerwa, 'Tenure security, credit use, and farm investment in the Rujumbura Pilot Land Registration Scheme, Rukungiri District, Uganda', *Land Tenure Center Research Paper No 112*, Madison: University of Wisconsin-Madison, 1993, pp 22, 23.
55 TC Pinckney & PK Kimuyu, 'Land tenure reform in East Africa: good, bad or unimportant?', *Journal of African Economies*, 3(1), 1994, p 9.
56 Adenew & Abdi, *Research Report 3*, p 22.
57 Chimhowu & Woodhouse, 'Customary vs private property rights?', p 354.
58 Interviews in Kathulumbi Location, Makueni District, October 1998.
59 Government of the United Republic of Tanzania, *Report of the Presidential Commission of Enquiry into Land Matters*, Vol 1, Dar-es-Salaam: Ministry of Lands, Housing and Urban Development, 1994.
60 Shivji, 'Lawyers in neoliberalism'.
61 One Kenyan study demonstrates the wide range of alternative institutions providing credit to low and middle income groups. The study shows that the informal credit sector registers substantially more flows than the formal sector, and that it services anywhere between 30% and 95% of rural and urban populations, an observation that is made in several other African countries. See S Johnson, '"Milking the elephant": financial markets as real markets in Kenya', *Development and Change*, 35 (2), 2004, p 249.
62 P Shipton, 'Debts and trespasses: land, mortgages, and the ancestors in Western Kenya', *Africa*, 62 (3), 1992, pp 357–388.
63 Okoth-Ogendo & Oluoch-Kosura, *Final Report on Land Tenure and Agricultural Development in Kenya*.
64 D Hunt, 'Some outstanding issues in the debate on external promotion of land privatization', *Development Policy Review*, 23 (2), 2005, p 222.
65 Pinckney & Kimuyu, 'Land tenure reform in East Africa'.
66 MR Carter, K Wiebe & B Blarel, 'Tenure security for whom? Differential effects of land policy in Kenya', in Bruce & Migot-Adholla, *Searching for Land Tenure Security in Africa*, pp 141–168.
67 De Soto, *The Mystery of Capital*, p 45.
68 *Ibid*, p 6.
69 JP Platteau, 'The evolutionary theory of land rights as applied to sub-Saharan Africa: a critical assessment', *Development and Change*, 27 (1), 1996, pp 29–86; K Firmin-Sellers & P Sellers, 'Expected failures and unexpected successes of land titling in Africa', *World Development*, 27, 1999, pp 1115–1128.
70 L Mair, 'Modern developments in African land tenure: an aspect of culture change', *Africa*, 18 (3), 1948, pp 184–189; Shipton, *Land and the Limits of Individualism*; SF Moore, 'From giving and lending to selling: property transactions reflecting historical change on Kilimanjaro', in K Mann & R Roberts (eds), *Law in Colonial Africa*, London: James Currey, 1991, pp 108–126; Okoth-Ogendo & Oluoch-Kosura, *Final Report on Land Tenure and Agricultural Development in Kenya*; Nyamu, 'Gender, culture and property relations in a pluralistic social setting'; E Daley, 'Land and social change in a Tanzanian village 2: Kinyanambo in the 1990s', *Journal of Agrarian Change*, 5 (4), 2005, pp 526–572; and Chimhowu & Woodhouse, 'Customary vs private property rights?'.
71 Interview with Mr Justus Mwanzia, Assistant chief, Mutembuku sub-location, 18 January 1999.
72 World Bank, *World Development Report 1996: From Plan to Market*, Washington, DC: World Bank, 1996, p 49.
73 Section 27(a) Registered Land Act, Chapter 300, Laws of Kenya.
74 McAuslan, *Bringing the Law Back in*, pp 4–5.
75 Platteau, 'The evolutionary theory of land rights as applied to sub-Saharan Africa', p 50.
76 *Miao ya Mbai ya Atwii-Athunzu* (Rules of the Atwii Athunzu Clan), passed on 10 July 1948, revised August 1993, Rule No 29 (author's translation).
77 Firmin-Sellers & Sellers, 'Expected failures and unexpected successes of land titling in Africa'.
78 J Singer, 'Property and coercion in federal Indian law: the conflict between critical and complacent pragmatism', *Southern California Law Review*, 63, 1990, p 1841 (emphasis in original).
79 See Singer, *Entitlement*.
80 Chimhowu & Woodhouse, 'Customary vs private property rights?', p 363.
81 Hunt, 'Unintended consequences of land rights reform', p188; and Manders, 'Sequencing property rights in the context of development'.
82 Manders, 'Sequencing property rights in the context of development'.
83 HWO Okoth-Ogendo, 'The imposition of property law in Kenya', in B Harrel-Bond & S Burman (eds), *The Imposition of Law*, New York: Academic Press, 1979, pp 147–166; AO Pala, 'Women's access to land and their role in agriculture and decision-making on the farm: experiences of the Joluo of Kenya',

*Journal of Eastern African Research and Development*, 13, 1983, pp 69–85; Shipton, *Land and the Limits of Individualism*; S Lastarria-Cornhiel, 'Impact of privatization on gender and property rights in Africa', *World Development*, 25 (8), 1997, pp 1317–1333; R Meinzen-Dick, L Brown, HS Feldstein & A Quisumbing, 'Gender and property rights: overview', *World Development*, 25 (8), 1997, pp 1299–1302; and A Whitehead & D Tsikata, 'Policy discourses on women's land rights in sub-Saharan Africa: the implications of the re-turn to the customary', *Journal of Agrarian Change*, 3 (1), 2003, pp 67–112.

84 C Dickerman, 'Security of tenure and land registration in Africa: literature review and synthesis', *Land Tenure Center Paper No 137*, Madison, WI: University of Wisconsin-Madison, 1989; R Barrows & M Roth, 'Land tenure and investment in African agriculture: theory and evidence', *Land Tenure Center Paper No 136*, Madison, WI: University of Wisconsin-Madison, 1989; McAuslan, 'Making law work', p 540; McAuslan, *Bringing the Law Back in*, pp 71–75; and Deininger & Binswanger, 'The evolution of the World Bank's land policy'.

85 Estimates place the national figure at 5%. J Davison, '"Without Land We Are Nothing": The Effect of Land Tenure Policies and Practices Upon Rural Women in Kenya', *Rural Africana*, 27, 1987, pp 19–33. In Makueni district my own calculation based on a sample of the land registers for the entire district yielded 8%. The incidence of joint registration in general is very low, let alone joint registration of spouses. In the sample, out of a total of 3183 registered parcels of land, only 69 (2%) are registered as jointly owned. Of those 69 only 45 had a woman as one of the joint owners.

86 P Karanja, 'Women's land ownership rights in Kenya', *Third World Legal Studies*, 1991, pp 109–135; F Butegwa, 'Women's legal right of access to agricultural resources in Africa: a preliminary inquiry', *Third World Legal Studies*, 1991, pp 45–57; LE Tibatemwa, 'Property rights, institutional credit and the gender question in Uganda', *East African Journal of Peace and Human Rights*, 2, 1995, pp 68–80.

87 Elizabeth Wangari Wanjohi & Elizabeth Wambui Wanjohi v Official Receiver & Interim Liquidator (Continental Credit Finance Ltd), Civil Application NAI No 140 of 1988, reproduced in *The Nairobi Law Monthly*, 14, February 1989, p 42.

88 Pala, 'Women's access to land and their role in agriculture and decision-making on the farm'.

89 Shipton, *Land and the Limits of Individualism*, p 119.

90 F Mackenzie, 'Gender and land rights in Murang'a District, Kenya', *Journal of Peasant Studies*, 17 (4), 1990, pp 609–643.

91 Nyamu, 'Gender, culture and property relations in a pluralistic social setting'; Nyamu-Musembi, 'Are local norms and practices fences or pathways?'; and Whitehead & Tsikata 'Policy discourses on women's land rights in sub-Saharan Africa'.

92 Kanji *et al*, *Research Report 1*; and Teklu, *Research Report 4*.

93 C Nyamu-Musembi, '"Sitting on her husband's back with her hands in his pockets": trends in judicial decision-making on marital property in Kenya', in A Bainham (ed), *The International Survey of Family Law*, Bristol: Jordan Publishing, 2002, pp 229–241.

94 De Soto, *The Mystery of Capital*, p 222.

# Liberalisation and the Debates on Women's Access to Land

SHAHRA RAZAVI

It is now widely recognised that the agrarian reforms implemented in the era of state-led redistributive efforts—the 'golden age' of land reform spanning from the 1910s to the 1970s—were largely gender-blind. These reforms were often based on an implicit assumption that assets allocated to households— typically to the male 'head'—would benefit all members equitably. Not only did such assumptions ignore the well-being of women and their dependents in the event of household dissolution (upon separation, divorce or widowhood), they were also blind to women's differing relationship to property and the fact that household (often male) ownership of land can more deeply exploit women's labour through heavier work loads in the form of generally unpaid family labour,[1] and adversely affect their position within the conjugal contract.[2]

In the 1990s a wide and diverse array of policy actors was able to place the reform of land tenure institutions back on the national and global policy agendas, inciting an intense debate about land reform and its potential developmental significance. At the heart of these ongoing debates are diverging views about effective routes to poverty eradication and the roles of small farm production and employment generation in the construction of the social wage, as well as broader concerns about the productivity of farming and the exigencies of accumulation and growth in developing countries.

Have the interests of diverse groups of women—in particular those from landless households, and those whose households control small and marginal plots of land—found a more secure place in this new wave of reforms than they did in the 'golden age'? While, at a certain level of generality, the principle of gender equality in access to resources, including land, has been endorsed by a diverse range of policy actors, a number of tensions and ambiguities have emerged. These include key questions about liberalisation policies *vis-à-vis* land, land markets as a vehicle for women's inclusion, and employment generation as an effective strategy for both poverty eradication and gender equality. There are also troubling implications from a gender perspective in the current endorsement of 'customary' systems of land tenure and decentralisation of land management. Women's rights advocates fear that this can play into the hands of powerful interest groups hostile to women's rights. Finally, more attention needs to be paid to the ways in which women's interests are articulated and struggled for. As has been repeatedly argued, women's and men's interests within marriage and the household are both joint and separate—an ambiguity that is well captured by the notion of 'co-operative conflict'.[3] This has important implications for how rural women's mobilisations (or lack thereof) are understood, and the kinds of policy responses that are needed to accommodate their interests.

## Recent policy and political shifts

It is no secret that, while the redistributive land reforms—in South Korea and Taiwan, for example, or even more recently the tenancy reforms in West Bengal—were successful in reducing class-based inequalities, they were strongly biased towards men deemed to be the legitimate heads of households. Admittedly the earlier reforms took place at a time when the gender question was still dormant and women's organisations lacked their current visibility and voice—an explanation that is less applicable in the case of West Bengal's *Operation Barga*, initiated in the late 1970s.[4] The historical inattention to gender inequality has been somewhat redressed by recent developments within the political and policy domains, as well as by the 'discovery' by neoclassically inclined economists of the intrahousehold arena as a realm worthy of research. We consider these factors in turn.

### *The turn to democracy and human rights*

The post-cold war developments gave women's rights agendas greater force and legitimacy. While mobilisation in opposition to authoritarian rule has not always secured women representation in formal institutional politics, it nevertheless galvanised women's movements. This helped bring women's rights into the process of constitution writing and the reform of civil codes in many countries. The Brazilian and South African 'transitions' are often held up as exemplary for legitimising women's rights agendas through constitutional and legislative reforms. In Latin America more broadly one of the main achievements of the rise and consolidation of the women's movement has been the elimination of the provision in most national civil codes which designates the husband as the legal 'head of household'. This has now been replaced by the concept of the dual-headed household, where both husband and wife jointly represent the household and manage its common property.[5]

These national-level developments were reinforced by the attention paid to rights-based approaches at the global level. The cluster of UN-sponsored conferences held in the 1990s provided women's rights advocates with a public forum and stimulated debate, both domestic and international, over policy. In these various policy arenas, women's movements and their representatives were active participants. Women lawyers, coming together through regional and sub-regional groupings, have become particularly influential as advocates demanding legal reform.

The rise and influence of the associations and groupings composed of women lawyers seem to confirm Manji's observation that the past two decades have been 'the age of land *law* reform in Africa'.[6] The context for this has been the broader 'rule of law' and 'good governance' agendas pioneered and funded by the international financial institutions, most notably the World Bank, in the aftermath of the East Asian financial crisis, as the emphasis shifted away from macroeconomic policy to the 'institutions' that undergird development and growth.[7]

But feminist lawyers in Africa as elsewhere have long been concerned with women's rights within legal systems, advocating constitutional reforms to end sex discrimination and to guarantee women's rights in all spheres, including in family laws and family relations, as well as through stronger support for women's economic security through reforms to property laws, primarily those concerning land.[8] The fact that many of these advocates speak the language of 'rights' and 'rule of law' hardly reflects their buy-in to the neoliberal agenda along the lines suggested by Manji. Indeed, following Gramsci's analysis of the way in which powerful institutions take up progressive agendas as part of their hegemonic project, one could point to the way in which concepts such as 'rights' (and 'governance'), which were initially used by social movements and women's rights advocates to critique mainstream policies, have increasingly been distorted and emptied of their meanings in the hands of powerful policy-making institutions.[9]

This is not to deny the limitations of the conceptual frameworks within which feminist lawyers operate, which tend to downplay the strength of power inequalities and institutional biases as constraints on women's ability to make effective claims on resources (on which more below). In practice these advocates take different positions on a variety of issues, and some recognise the limitations of law as a vehicle for social change, acknowledging that there may be enormous resistance to equitable practices, and severe

65

limits to law as 'an instrument of social change'.[10] Nevertheless, while the gap between formal and substantive rights is often noted, the assumption is that women's ignorance has prevented them from enforcing their rights—hence their efforts to popularise laws relevant to women's rights and to promote legal literacy.

The other overlapping stream of activism within which attention has been drawn to women's land rights is at the level of social movements, NGOs and Land Alliances. Oxfam GB has been heavily involved in supporting NGOs and coalitions in Eastern and Southern Africa for the past 10 years.[11] While the importance of building coalitions between gender advocates and other 'progressive' forces is often emphasised, divisions and tensions often render such alliances problematic and short-lived, as recent analyses of policy contestations in Tanzania have shown.[12] While in this case 'progressive' forces could be faulted for their blindness to the mechanisms that discriminate against women, the debates in Tanzania also exposed the divisions and blind spots within women's groups (see below).

Other actors have included social movements of significant political weight, most notably, the Brazilian Movimento dos Trabalhadores Rurais Sem Terra (MST). Initially some of these movements were criticised for replicating the 'male breadwinner–female dependant' bias entrenched in state-led land reform initiatives, through their bottom-up land invasions and the setting up of agrarian reform settlements. It took more than a decade of activism by feminists within the movement for women's rights to be strongly articulated by rural social movements in Brazil.[13] This is explained by the multiple and often competing venues for participation which opened up to rural women, and the many priorities of these rural social movements. It was not until the exclusion of women began to have 'real practical consequences for the consolidation of the agrarian reform settlements (the *assentamentos*) that women's land rights became an issue within the main social movement leading the agrarian reform, the MST . . . and for the state'.[14]

The South African Landless People's Movement (LPM) has yet to achieve the power and presence of MST, but early analysis suggests that race has trumped gender: 'at all levels of the movement there has been very little discussion of gender in relation to the work and struggles of the movement' even though 'there is a strand within the movement that takes gender equality seriously and seeks to build this into the work and structures of the movement'.[15] What these two examples point to is the pervasiveness of normative assumptions about the 'proper' place of women and men across policy institutions—not only in top-down bureaucratic donor organisations and patriarchal states, but also in 'progressive' social movements, NGOs and community organizations.

### Livelihoods in the era of liberalisation

Yet the recent advances in political and legal rights have not been matched by significant progress in livelihoods and social justice. Indeed, throughout the 1980s and 1990s income inequalities have been rising in most countries, while growth rates in much of the developing world (except India and China) have also been sluggish. It is important to place the 'woman and land' question that is the topic of this paper in the broader context of capitalist transformations in developing countries, and of two decades of orthodox liberalisation policies that have exacerbated the inequalities and social tensions inherent to such processes, while doing little to generate sustained economic growth and structural transformation.

The economic crisis of the early 1980s was diagnosed by the international financial institutions to stem from heavy state involvement in the economy. The agricultural sector, it was argued, was a prime victim of state-directed economic regimes marked by 'urban bias': the heavy drainage of agricultural surplus through forced indirect taxation depressed farming incomes and led to the poor performance of the agricultural sector. The 'distortions' introduced by state policy were to be corrected by letting market forces determine product and input prices and the terms of trade between agriculture and the rest of the economy, while tenure insecurity was to be tackled through land titling.[16] These standard measures, it was argued, would restore agricultural export growth and improve rural incomes and livelihoods. At the same time cutbacks in public expenditure outlays on agricultural input subsidies, marketing boards, and research and extension services were prescribed and justified on the grounds that state expenditure needed to be significantly lowered and that the benefits were, in any case, either being captured by big farmers or squandered by state officials.

There followed two decades of extensive experimentation with the liberalisation of the agricultural sector, especially in sub-Saharan Africa. Throughout the 1980s and 1990s, as liberalisation progressed, sub-Saharan Africa witnessed the steady decline of its agricultural exports as a share of world agricultural trade.[17] Meanwhile the problems surrounding food production and security were far from resolved. Deteriorating household food security in Malawi, Zambia and Zimbabwe in the late 1990s were attributed to the loss of subsidies for fertilisers and seeds and of rural credit, and to the erosion of agricultural marketing services, especially in remote areas.[18]

For much of Latin America, during the 1980s—the first reform decade—the growth rate veered widely; this crisis-ridden period also saw an overall increase in poverty, from 41% to 48% of all households. During the 1990s agricultural growth averaged only 2.2%. Poverty indices improved, but only at a laggardly pace, so that Latin America entered the new millennium with a higher proportion of poor and indigent rural people than in 1980.[19] At the same time the economic reforms tended to reinforce existing divides between regions and producers.

Given the dismal record, especially in sub-Saharan Africa, the proponents of reform have increasingly accepted that agriculture's response to liberalisation has been disappointing.[20] It has also been persuasively shown that the notion of 'urban bias' has in fact obscured more than it has illuminated the problems in developing country agriculture by reducing the problem to one simple cause outside the sector itself (namely, government policy bias), while ignoring the resource transfers into agriculture.[21] In other words, while agricultural prices may have been artificially depressed because of an overvalued exchange rate and export taxes, this was to varying degrees redressed through positive resource transfers into the sector via public investment, subsidised credit and agricultural services.[22]

Meanwhile, industrial growth, which has historically been the *sine qua non* of massive poverty reduction by absorbing the labour force that is released from agriculture, has remained anaemic in recent decades in developing countries, with the exception of East Asia.[23] Indeed, one of the remarkable features of structural change in contemporary developing countries has been the disproportionate shift of the labour force from agriculture to 'services' (rather than to industry), which is ominous, as much of this can be thinly disguised survival strategies indicative of a desperate effort to turn to anything that might be available (which happens to fall into the 'services' rubric).[24] Deflationary macroeconomic policies, the external liberalisation of developing country economies and the concomitant demonisation of industrial policies are at least partly to blame for the low rates of growth and the lack of structural transformation of these economies.[25]

## *Ideational shifts: gender and the household*

The intra-household arena has come under increasing scrutiny over the past couple of decades, initially by feminists from diverse disciplinary currents,[26] and of late by neoclassically inclined microeconomists and modellers, some of whom are associated with the World Bank and the International Food Policy Research Institute (IFPRI).

For nearly three decades the feminist literature has drawn attention to the unequal distribution of resources and power within households along gender and generational lines. Some of the literature has also documented women's greater attachment to the welfare of children (evident in women's spending priorities for example).[27] Some of these findings seem to have been taken up selectively by policy institutions: anti-poverty programmes, whether in the form of micro-credit or cash transfers, increasingly target women on the grounds that they will spend the resources under their control in ways that will enhance family and child welfare.

A different strand of thinking, very popular with neoclassically oriented economists, uses microeconomic analytical tools to argue that the structure of male and female incentives in farm households (in sub-Saharan Africa) leads to 'allocative inefficiencies' and a muted agricultural supply response.[28] These analyses have been abstracted from a set of empirical accounts of agricultural production in sub-Saharan Africa.[29] One important resource constraint to which they draw attention is women's inadequate access to land, thereby facilitating the absorption of 'the gender asset gap' into key policy documents.[30] The conclusion often drawn is that redressing gender imbalance in control of productive resources (land, labour, inputs) will enhance the efficient use of scarce resources, and reduce poverty and gender inequality. While attractive and appealing from an advocacy standpoint, recent critical analysis of this literature by feminists considers the policy conclusions that are drawn to be highly questionable, if not 'mythical', as a strategy for poverty reduction in rural sub-Saharan Africa.[31]

Interestingly there are some parallels between the above-mentioned neoclassical arguments for gender equality and arguments made by some economists for redistributive land reform as a mechanism for reducing poverty and enhancing growth and equity.[32] The argument for redistributive land reform, like the argument for gender equity, is based on the understanding that current resource allocation (to 'large landowners' versus 'small farmers', like male farmers versus female farmers) is inefficient and that the reallocation of resources (in favour of 'small farmers', as in the case of female farmers) will improve static efficiency, enhance agricultural growth and reduce poverty. Both arguments abstract from a very small number of empirical studies (Berry and Cline's 1979 work is the reference for the inverse relationship between farm size and productivity; Udry's work is the reference for the inefficiency of gender inequality), and then generalise to a 'mythical uniform terrain' (sub-Saharan Africa, the world).[33]

Even if one agrees with some of the empirical findings on which they base their more generalised arguments (the efficiency of the 'small farmer', the gender inequalities in intra-household resource allocation) it is the way in which those facts are read and interpreted which raises serious questions. For example, the efficiency of the 'small farm' (in specific contexts where it can be shown to operate) is surely a sign of distress and super-exploitation of 'family labour', most notably the labour of women, rather than being indicative of its technical superiority. In a similar way the inequalities in women's and men's access to certain resources (land, fertiliser), which neoclassical analyses of gender draw attention to, may be part of a larger and *joint* set of interests, even if these are inequitably distributed. This last point is elaborated by Whitehead and Kabeer in their critical review of Udry's work, to which I will return in final section. Last but not least, both sets of argument are ahistorical, ignoring the construction of class and gender inequalities as part of larger processes of accumulation and impoverishment in the context of foreign domination and capitalist transformation. This is inevitably linked to their methodological grounding in neoclassical economics.

## Markets as gendered institutions

Global policy guidelines *vis-à-vis* agriculture, and with respect to land more specifically, as was noted earlier, have undergone important shifts in recent years. In the landmark policy statement by the World Bank on land in 1975, formal titling was seen as a precondition of modern agricultural development, while communal tenure systems were discouraged in favour of freehold titles.[34] The argument essentially revolved not only around the efficiency- *and* equity-enhancing effects of tenure reform, but additionally land reform was seen as having wider developmental implications, given its contribution to wealth creation and accumulation. This model of state-led redistributive land reform had an uncomfortable place in the post-crisis ideological and fiscal environment, when state budgets were under severe constraint, and when redistribution was increasingly seen to be in conflict with efficiency and growth. While subsequent research both within the World Bank's Land Policy Division and beyond has led to what Whitehead and Tsikata describe as a more 'nuanced, self-critical and empirically-foregrounded' approach,[35] especially towards customary systems of tenure (this is evident in the 2003 World Bank policy statement on land), the importance of land markets and individual tenure as the essential ingredients of agricultural productivity and growth continue to be underlined.

Given the centrality of land markets to the policy advice that is given to indebted governments (many of them in sub-Saharan Africa), it is important to ask if this prescription is likely to coincide with gender equality and women's land claims. In other words, how likely are low-income women to emerge as winners in the market-based land reform model and in land market transactions more broadly?

As was noted above, gender divisions and inequalities within domestic institutions (families, households) are now increasingly being recognised by many microeconomists. Ironically, however, the attentiveness to gender structures and hierarchies does not seem to extend to other institutions, notably markets. As generations of political economists and sociologists have shown, contrary to the abstract market of neoclassical textbooks, real markets are political (and social) constructs that are infused with social norms and regulations.[36] Markets, with all their risks and variable performance, also embody gender hierarchies as they are found in society and its institutions. Although the empirical base is far from comprehensive, a judicious reading of the existing evidence points to the severe limitations of land markets as a channel for women's inclusion. It is of course important not to homogenise women as a social group; there are always groups of women, for example urban women in formal employment or women in peri-urban areas who grow food for city markets, who may have accumulated enough resources to purchase land in their own name with full property rights.[37] But for the vast majority of women smallholders, market mechanisms are not likely to provide a channel for inclusion.

For sub-Saharan Africa Lastarria-Cornhiel's examination of the continent-wide evidence for the effects of land privatisation points to women as the largest group who have had little to gain from the trend toward privatised land tenure systems.[38] In fact, the transformation of African tenure systems has tended to further weaken women's already tenuous claims to land, while other groups (community leaders and male household heads) have been able to strengthen their control over land to the detriment of women and some minority groups. Like Platteau,[39] she argues that, while previously a number of persons and community groups held different rights to a piece of land, with privatisation most of those rights are brought together and claimed by one person. In this process women have tended to lose out. The fact that women enter the market system with no property, little cash income, minimal political power, and a family to maintain, works to their disadvantage. Simple titling and land registration do not in themselves transform a customary tenure system into a freehold one—other changes are also needed for this to happen, namely the commercialisation of agriculture and the development of a land market.[40] Hence it is the general processes of privatisation and concentration that affect women's land and property rights negatively, rather than national land registration schemes *per se*.

The conclusion drawn by Whitehead and Tsikata's comprehensive review of the gender and land literature for sub-Saharan Africa, namely that in 'the development of private property regimes of any kind, sub-Saharan African women tend to lose the rights they once had…either because their opportunities to buy land are very limited, or because local-level authorities practice gender discrimination' is sobering.[41] It has become even more important to underline this statement given the extent to which policy documents across the political spectrum advocate a blanket policy mix of private property rights and land-titling not only to encourage investment and foster a more efficient land market, but as a solution to women's weak and tenuous place within land tenure institutions.

Have land markets been more inclusive of women in other regional and country settings? For six countries in Latin America, Deere and Léon provide a useful database—something that is missing for many other countries and regions—on different modes of land acquisition (through inheritance, community, state, market, other) disaggregated by sex.[42] The data show that, in these six countries, women tend to become landowners mainly through inheritance, while men do so through purchase in land markets (predictably, men are also privileged when land is acquired through the state).

Have women fared any better in so-called market-friendly land reform programmes? Here reference will be made to the recent South African experience that attempted to meld a strong commitment to the goal of social justice, including gender equality, with the principles of market-led land reform. As is by now well known, the intense negotiations around land reform led to a compromise solution or 'elite-pacted settlement': restitution and redistribution were endorsed but within the constraints of a market-led programme informed by a 'willing seller/willing buyer' principle and by protection for existing property rights. It is also widely recognised that the land reform programme was strongly influenced by the World Bank and its advisors, even in the absence of debt-related conditionalities.

There have been, as many predicted, severe constraints within this framework on effectively redistributing land, given the state's inability, within the market-friendly straightjacket, to acquire and redistribute productive land proactively and on a sufficiently large scale. Indeed, by March 2005 less than 3.5% of the area designated as 'commercial farmland' had been redistributed,[43] and random surveys of beneficiary households 'showed that their characteristics were very different to those of the average rural African household'.[44] What is perhaps not always recognised is that a strictly demand-driven programme also conflicts with the policy aim of reaching women (and other marginalised social groups), because it overlooks how power relations and divisions within communities structure 'demand'.[45]

It effectively commits the state to respond to applications from social groups that are already constituted, in which it is likely that women's role will be a marginal and dependent one. Thus in South Africa gender equality has been reflected in what Walker calls 'first tier' policy documents such as the White Paper on land. Yet, at the level of implementation, as her detailed research unravels, the commitment to gender equality has been far less evident.[46] The neglect of gender concerns at these different levels of implementation is attributed to several factors, including institutional and operational weaknesses, absence of political accountability for gender equality at the highest level, and the relative weakness of the women's movement, especially in rural areas, since 1994.

The above evidence, though far from conclusive, nevertheless seems to suggest that gender advocates should have serious reservations about land markets, both formal and informal, as an effective mechanism for women's inclusion. This is particularly the case in sub-Saharan Africa, where the introduction of exclusive (individual) ownership rights to land, sometimes spearheaded by land titling and registration programmes, under both colonial rule and after independence, have marked a setback for women and other marginalised social groups such as pastoralists and those belonging to minority tribes. Why then have women's rights advocates in some contexts fought for the rights of women to be able to inherit, purchase and own land in their own name while rejecting the customary forms of land tenure which they claim have strongly discriminated against women, in the context of recent policy efforts to liberalise land tenure institutions?

An interesting example of such advocacy comes from Tanzania, where gender advocates entered into alliance with the National Land Forum in 1998 to ensure that both gender and other equality concerns in the Land Bills were addressed. The grand coalition known as the Land Coalition soon had to face the fact that there were serious differences within it, however. There were many divisive issues, but the most relevant for the present discussion were the disagreements with respect to liberalisation policies and the risks entailed by land markets. The other issue that divided the coalition centred on discriminatory customary law rules, how they should be reformed and what powers should be vested in state and village level land management and adjudication institutions.[47] Some women's rights advocates were critical of the liberalisation agenda, given the highly adverse implications of private property regimes for resource-constrained women. Others, however, did not share this dim view of land markets. In fact, some of the most influential gender advocacy groups supported the liberalisation of land markets and land titling as opportunities for women to purchase land on an individual basis.

In this process accusations were directed at women's rights advocates for being 'middle class', 'aid-dependent' and influenced by their 'Western sponsors'. However, as Tsikata rightly points out, such assertions ignore the fact that the majority of civil society advocacy groups in Africa, as in many other regions, share these characteristics. The issue about class composition of the dominant women's groups raised by Manji, namely that the middle class position of women's rights advocates limits their capacity to engage with an issue which concerns poorer women most and also creates a conflict of interest because they stand to gain from liberalisation in ways that resource-constrained rural women do not is also questionable. Historically one of the features of feminist movements has been their predominantly middle class composition. Yet this has rarely stopped them from advocating radical measures that often conflict with their own 'class interests'—such as better wages and working conditions for women workers, especially domestic and care workers (on whom many middle class women depend for their own professional and political advancement).

A fair probing of the positions taken by women's rights advocates in national debates on land tenure reform would have to be cognisant of the concerns that many of these groups have about how 'customary practices' are being used to undermine rather than enhance women's tenure security. Indeed, Tripp claims that in Uganda 'Purchasing land has, in effect, become a way of circumventing the traditional authorities'.[48] Other women's rights advocates point out that liberalisation of land, whatever its risks and merits, is already underway and hence women should seek to gain a place in the emerging markets—this kind of position, rather than being simply a reflection of middle class interests, may be indicative of their pragmatism.

Yet while women's rights advocates are rightly concerned about the ways in which 'traditionalist' discourses and 'customary' practices are frequently used to deprive women of equal rights, seeing the constraints that women farmers face only in terms of the legal framework is limiting. While having an enabling legal framework is no doubt important, it is far from sufficient. Women's constrained access to non-land resources (credit, extension services, labour markets) also contributes to their precarious economic situation. As Whitehead has shown for sub-Saharan Africa, even though women farmers farm much less land than men do, this is not always because women are prevented from accessing land; it is also because they lack capital to hire labour, purchase inputs and access marketing channels.[49]

How are the institutional biases in marketing channels, government extension services, credit provision going to be tackled so that women can be more equitably included? These questions are often left out in women's rights advocacy around land, while the legal requirements for land access or ownership tend to assume disproportionate attention. To address these critical issues of institutional bias and power inequalities would require a broader analytical framework—one that is not so narrowly fixated on law and legal regimes.

The evidence and debates on 'customary' law and 'decentralised' land management, including their purported biases against women, constitute a complex arena to which the paper now briefly turns.

### The turn to 'the local'

In sub-Saharan Africa much land distribution and land access is governed by locally managed systems of 'customary' rights. As was noted earlier, in the

1980s the international financial institutions identified the absence of private property rights in land as a barrier to agricultural growth, and gave full support to privatisation, titling and registration of land. Yet subsequent research carried out by the World Bank and the Land Tenure Centre at the University of Wisconsin showed insignificant differences in the productivity and investment of lands held in freehold title compared with those held under customary tenure.[50] Received wisdom within the World Bank's Land Policy Division has thus been swinging in favour of 'building on customary tenures and existing institutions',[51] even though individual land titling still routinely appears in policy documents advising borrowing governments on the need for further liberalisation.[52]

At the other end of the political spectrum, for some of the more 'progressive' donor agencies and policy advocates such as Osfam and the National Land Forum in Tanzania, subsidiarity and devolution are key objectives in current land reform policy. Given the history of political abuse and processes of land alienation and 'land grabbing' facilitated by national political elites, they claim that it is best that decisions on land management and control be taken at the lowest levels possible, 'closer to home' in the words of the Shivji Commission in Tanzania.[53] Here 'the local' is seen as a site of resistance against the state (and international capital). This approach fits the general support that many of the 'progressive' donor organisations and international NGOs provide for 'participation', 'building of local capacities', and 'local-level democracy'.

Yet from the perspective of gender equality the local state is in a very 'ambiguous position'.[54] It is the part of the state that is located closest to 'the people', as many of the advocates of decentralisation claim, facilitating its engagement with women as well. Nevertheless, precisely because of its closeness to society, the local state can also become too closely intertwined with social institutions and existing power structures, and hence subject to 'elite capture'.

There is very little discussion, however, as Whitehead and Tsikata show, among those who support decentralisation as to how the proposed local-level systems might work in practice, including their capacity to deliver more equitable (and especially gender-equitable) resource allocation. While there is ample evidence of women using social relations and local-level land management fora for making strong claims to land, 'the weight of evidence suggests that economic changes have resulted in women's diminished access to land'.[55] In Uganda, for example, women's recent mobilisation for a 'co-ownership clause' was in response to the current legislation and practices, which provide 'limited possibilities for women to own land', even if that land has been jointly acquired with her husband; a husband may still leave his wife with no land and therefore no source of subsistence.[56] Tripp argues that women's movement leaders in Uganda do not see customary law and practices 'as nearly as neutral and malleable as have been suggested at times by scholars and policymakers'.[57] In some parts of the country competition over shrinking resources has intensified the patriarchal tendencies of the lineage system, even though conditions differ across the country.

Similar concerns were voiced by women's rights advocates in the Tanzanian debates to which reference has already been made. They argued that the preservation of customary law would be at odds with women's rights because it would exclude women from inheriting clan lands as well as violating the joint property provision of the 1971 Marriage Act. A study commissioned by the Ministry of Community Development, Women's Affairs and Children, jointly with the World Bank, found that female-headed households were being excluded from access to clan lands. They also found that purchasing land was a possibility rarely exercised because of the lack of resources.[58] Women were reported to be generally unhappy with the local administration bodies 'for reasons of corruption, under-representation of women and bias against them arising from prejudices and ideologies which cast them as less reliable protectors of clan land than men'.[59]

Parallel apprehensions about local authorities are echoed in a series of consultation meetings that the National Land Committee (NLC) and the Programme for Agrarian Studies at the University of Western Cape (South Africa) held with rural communities about the Communal Land Rights Bill during 2002 and 2003.[60] Here too, many women recounted the difficulties they faced in trying to secure land allocations from traditional leaders, especially if the claimant was a single mother or a widow. Traditional leaders often justified their reluctance to allocate land to single mothers by reference to the danger of 'outside' men gaining rights in the community via marriage.[61]

This is not to suggest that 'customary' practices are bad for women, while statutory rights can further their interests. Many commentators refer to the practice of 'forum shopping'—referring to the overlaps between formal legal systems and so-called customary ones, and the fact that individuals are using different courts and other dispute-settlement fora and using arguments grounded in either 'customary' or modernist principles, whichever is to their advantage.[62] Outcomes depend not only on power dynamics on the ground, but also on the kinds of structure that are being put in place, and the role of the state as a major actor.[63] It is nevertheless difficult to insert gender-equality concerns (or broader social-equality concerns) into these processes where traditional institutions have a patriarchal character—even in a seemingly best-case scenario such as South Africa.

Women's rights advocates in South Africa have had serious apprehensions about the place given to 'traditional authorities' in rural local government. The concerns are rooted in the ANC's attempts since 1994 to accommodate some of the demands of the Inkatha Freedom Party (IFP) with its stronghold in rural KwaZulu Natal, as well as ANC's reluctance to alienate the traditional authorities, given their perceived importance in delivering rural constituencies to the party.[64] Given the fact that the 'traditionalism' that is espoused by IFP and many of its adherents in the Tribal Authorities is deeply patriarchal (and a product of colonial and apartheid policies), these political maneuverings have effectively blunted ANC's commitments to gender equity in rural affairs.[65] In 2000 the new Minister for Agriculture and Land Affairs, in notable contrast to the ministry's modernising agenda for the commercial sector, advocated building on 'existing local institutions and structures' in the communal areas.[66]

February 2004 saw the stormy passage through parliament of the long-delayed Communal Land Rights Act (CLRA), to the dismay of its critics (which included the Commission on Gender Equality as well as land-sector NGOs and community groups). The critics argued that the legislation would entrench the powers of undemocratic 'traditional authorities' over communal land, fail to secure the tenure rights of women living on this land, and ultimately undermine the significant role that common property resources play in the livelihood strategies of the rural poor.[67]

This was followed by another Act, the Traditional Leadership and Governance Framework Act (TLGFA), which deems existing tribal authorities to be traditional councils, provided they meet new composition requirements within a year. It is likely that a lasting legacy of these two Acts will be 'to bolster the power of traditional leaders relative to that of the holders and users of family or individual land rights', and to 'harden the terrain' within which rural people, and especially rural women, struggle for change.[68] There are widespread concerns that the two Acts pre-empt rural people's right to choose their own representatives on the same basis as people living in other parts of the country, and that, because women's 30% quota does not need to be elected, it could lead to the selection by traditional leaders of acquiescent females to sit on traditional councils.[69]

'Local' justice and 'custom' can indeed defy women's rights with impunity, as Khadiagala found in the case of Kigesi women in Uganda.[70] There, given the patrilocal nature of marriages, if a woman takes a marital land dispute to a Local Council court she is likely to face a court that is filled by the relatives and friends of her husband. What kind of political dynamics, then, are being unleashed by the re-turn to 'the customary', and the revival of 'traditional' authorities? As Whitehead and Tsikata rightly warn, these could have highly disempowering implications for rural African women and their claims on resources. The main problem, as they vehemently argue, is that women have too little political voice at all the decision-making levels that are implied by the land question: not only within formal law and government, but also within local-level management systems.

Questions regarding traditional authorities aside, there are many warnings across the literature that 'the local' can indeed be a site of unequal rural social relations, with crucial implications for women and other less powerful social groups. Although there can be many benefits to decentralisation, its advocates (who cut across the political spectrum) often neglect the prevalence of inequitable repressive local power structures, as well as the acute scarcity of resources in many localities, even if those available locally were equitably redistributed.[71] Pressures from local organisations such as labour unions or neighbourhood associations, where they exist, can in some circumstances bring about positive social change and hasten national reforms, but it is often a long, slow process punctuated by setbacks and violent repression.

Not surprisingly some of the social movements that are struggling for land redistribution at the local level are often more aware of the importance of having the weight of the federal government behind them, and also more attentive to the risks and dangers of local government capture by powerful vested interests. One of the initiatives of the government of Fernando Enrique Cardoso in Brazil was to decentralise agrarian reform, devolving greater responsibility for its planning and execution to state and local governments. But there was very little follow-up to this initiative, primarily because of the resistance of the rural social movements to decentralisation.[72] The rural social movements were reportedly worried that the federal government would abdicate responsibility for leading the cause of agrarian reform, and that the power of landlords at the local level would be sufficient to stop any significant redistribution of land from taking place if the initiative was left to the state and local governments.

### Land and labour in multiple and diversified livelihoods

There have been many serious questions about the 'small' or 'family' farming vision that underpins neoclassical (and neoliberal) arguments for land reform, whether articulated by the World Bank or by advocates such as Keith Griffin and colleagues. Many of the criticisms point to the weak empirical foundations on which the central propositions of these advocates rest: the so-called relative efficiency of small-farm production (the 'inverse relationship between farm size and productivity'),[73] and the alleged 'multiplier effects' of land reform (agro-industrial growth linkages), whereby small-farm agriculture is supposed to stimulate the creation of non-farm jobs within rural regions.[74] These are the building blocks of the 'win-win' scenario which are weak on the empirical and theoretical front, if not entirely 'utopian', 'populist' and 'ideological'.[75]

These justified and potent criticisms of neoclassical accounts of agrarian structures and institutions and remedies for rural poverty point to the need for *situated* analyses of different paths of capitalist transformation in the countryside. What emerges from both Marxist and non-Marxist analyses of capitalist transformation, and indeed one important requirement of successful agrarian transitions, is the shift of labour from agriculture to industry. The historical record of advanced industrialised countries, as Byres reminds us, confirms this view, even though the paths taken have been diverse. And as he goes on to show, what is striking about contemporary developing countries is the limited extent to which capitalist industrialisation, even where it is proceeding, is able to absorb labour.[76]

However, as Bernstein warns, 'The potency of "models" inspired by particular historical experiences consists in how they are generalized and applied' and, in particular, whether such application 'facilitates or hinders analysis of the dynamics of other times and places, including what may be "changing before our very eyes"'.[77]

One striking feature of agrarian change and industrialisation in contemporary developing societies to which many observers have drawn attention is the growing prevalence of what is sometimes referred to as livelihood diversification, defined as 'the process by which rural families construct a diverse portfolio of activities and social support capabilities in their struggle for survival and in order to improve their standard of living'.[78] Diversification captures several different economic processes and its blanket use to describe all forms of non-farm employment is misleading. It is particularly important, from the point of view of thinking about poverty, to distinguish between diversification as a survival strategy (which it very often is) and diversification that feeds into a process of accumulation. The fact that 'poorer countries today confront more formidable barriers to comprehensive industrialization—and *a fortiori* to the generation of comparable levels of industrial employment—than did the advanced industrial countries in the past',[79] is an important part of what drives this process. For vast sections of the population, both female and male, this means a constant search for income through wage work and 'self-employment' (often thinly disguised forms of wage work) away from the village. Thus work on the household plot (if there is one) becomes articulated with other forms of activity (paid and unpaid, formal and informal, industrial and service) and with other sources of income beyond the agricultural sector and indeed very often beyond the confines of the village.[80]

In a very insightful analysis of the South African land reform programme Hart exposed not only the spurious claims of the World Bank and its advisors about the 'efficiency of small farms' and the alleged 'non-agricultural spin-offs' from small family farms, but vehemently argued in favour of a broadly based agrarian reform that supported multiple livelihoods whereby access to land can effectively underwrite the money wage—by providing some security in times of unemployment and in old age.[81] For her, therefore, the significance of land is closely intertwined with the labour question, or the 'fragmentation of labour' as Bernstein calls it.

It is within this context that we need to place some of the contemporary demands for land 'from below'—for example through spontaneous land occupations, or in the form of collective mobilisations, or even through survivalist clamouring for land, as documented by Kandiyoti for Uzbekistan.[82] In the latter context, in a situation where collective enterprises have not been able to pay their workers' wages, rural households, and rural women in particular, have fallen back on household and subsidiary plots for self-subsistence and survival. But women's current land hunger, as Kandiyoti emphatically underscores, must be understood in the context of both a wish to reinstate the terms of their former social contract with collective enterprises (as *formal employees*, which included a wide range of social benefits) and their despair given the lack of viable employment opportunities.

There is a tendency within the literature to pose land and employment in binary opposition: are employment opportunities more important for women or access to and ownership of land? Sender and Johnson, for example, advance two sets of arguments: first, that small-scale family farming, and land reform, deliver very little employment and income benefits to low-income women; and, second, that poor women stand to benefit much more from large-scale capitalist agriculture. The issue of employment opportunities, and its terms and conditions within capitalist agriculture, are critical ones as far as low-income rural women are concerned, whether their households own some land or not. The problem, however, as the authors themselves seem to acknowledge, are the terms and conditions of much of the work on offer, even within the more modern and technologically advanced farms producing horticultural products (in countries such as Mexico and Columbia, as well as in Kenya, Uganda and South Africa).

Corporate farms use a gender-segregated workforce, within which women are overwhelmingly employed in more insecure, less well paid and lower-skilled activities, without opportunities for advancement. The work is very often seasonal, with long hours of work, poor health and safety conditions and no social protection. The use of toxic inputs without adequate training and protective clothing is identified as a major health risk. In some countries producing high-value agricultural exports (including South Africa, Chile and Argentina) there has been a notable rise in the use of contract labour, both male and female, hired by third-party contractors. This reduces labour costs and facilitates the flexibility of export production as contractors move their teams from site to site.[83] Last but not least, the numbers of workers employed in these capitalist farms vary greatly across countries, from as low as 3000 workers in Uganda to 1.2 million workers in Mexico, with South Africa falling somewhere towards the higher end of the spectrum (280 000).[84]

Sender and Johnson do not seem to dispute these largely negative trends as far as employment conditions within capitalist agriculture are concerned. For example, they point to the strategies employed by large-scale horticultural operations in the Free State and Eastern Transvaal Provinces of South Africa to recruit a workforce that is predominantly 'female, foreign and casual ... not because of any local shortage at the going wage rate in the supply of female labour with similar levels of skill and experience, but because of their relatively weak bargaining power and the ease with which they could be controlled and disciplined'.[85] Policies to promote 'decently remunerated agricultural wage employment in Africa, as elsewhere, would require far higher levels of public investment and a much more interventionist state than the current consensus is prepared to contemplate'[86]—but what is to be done in the meantime, and is it not precisely because of the absence of such conditions that those deprived of decent employment or even a living wage, poor women among them, resort to land occupations or simply 'cry for land' in the words of Kandiyoti?[87]

The other important argument advanced by Sender and Johnson concerns the supposed efficiency of idealised small family farms, because it is an institutional form that has been capable of applying huge amounts of very low productivity labour to tiny parcels of land. 'The "viability" of most small family farms in Africa', they argue, 'is predicated on compulsion, either exercised by men over the labour of women, younger men and destitute kin, or enforced by acute risks of starvation that necessitate the severe exploitation of family labour'.[88] The contested issue of 'compulsion' within family-based households, especially as an aspect of intrahousehold gender relations, deserves further attention because it is one that reverberates across otherwise very different accounts of household-based agricultural production—both neoclassical, as we saw earlier emanating from gender advocates within the World Bank, as well as in political economy analyses such as those of Sender and Johnson. We turn to this question below.

## Rethinking the agrarian household: compulsion, bargaining and connectedness

There is little consensus among gender experts as to whether individual titles or joint titles would serve women's interests better. Agarwal, for example, considers joint titles to be problematic (in the Indian context at least): they make it difficult for women to gain control over the produce, to bequeath the land as they want, and to claim their share in case of marital conflict. She sees individual titles as better able to provide women with flexibility in pursuing their own agendas. However, given some of the problems that resource-strained women smallholders with individual titles might confront—for example, their lack of investible funds, and the difficulties of investing in capital equipment if the farm is small—the optimum institutional arrangement would be some collective form of investment and cultivation that would bring women smallholders together, thereby cutting across households (rather than being based on the household unit itself).

Reflecting on the South African context, Walker admits that, even where women have been listed as independent household heads and as beneficiaries in their own right, their access to land has been mediated overwhelmingly through their membership in patriarchal households. Nevertheless, sceptical of individual rights as the solution (which is a component of the Land Redistribution for Agricultural Development (LRAD) issued in November 2000), she presses for a deeper appreciation of the importance of household membership in poor women's lives, and thus the importance of ensuring women's rights to household resources. Had the LRAD framework, with its emphasis on individual rights, been in place from the start of the land reform programme, very few, if any, of the women in the present beneficiary communities would have been able to access land through it—'they are simply too poor, too isolated and too dependent on male authority to be able to establish individual rights to land'.[89]

Moreover, many women beneficiaries endorse the household model implicit in Department of Land Affairs (DLA's) work, and some have struggled very hard to secure their household's interests. While a minority seemed interested in the idea of individual titles, de-linked from that of their husbands or families, few saw this as the solution to their problems. They were more interested in mechanisms that would secure and extend their rights to household resources, through joint titles, inheritance rights for their daughters and copies of title deeds.[90]

It is clear from the above statements that the question about joint or individual titles is in fact not as straightforward as it first appears. Implicitly it is a question about how conjugal relations and the forces that bind agrarian households together are understood. The two positions, outlined above, bring to the fore some of the tensions within the current, second-generation feminist conceptualisations of the household, where the first-generation critique has established, in both theoretical and empirical terms, serious flaws in the previously dominant unified household paradigm.[91] While gender analysis sees households as sites of struggle and inequality, there is far less agreement as to how the given inequalities and tensions, as well as common interests and co-operative behaviour, should be understood. Do conflictual and bargaining models sufficiently capture the *common* interests that all household members have in the overall economic success of their households? Do women work on their household plots because 'older men prevent them from leaving their farms in search of more productive employment' as Sender and Johnson claim?[92] What makes women and junior men stay inside the patriarchal household, even though they are allocated fewer resources, take on heavy work loads of largely 'unpaid labour' and enjoy less leisure time? Is it despotism on the part of the male household head, and 'false consciousness' on the part of the junior household members, that binds the household together?[93]

These are not questions to which any definitive answers can be given. But there are powerful arguments for seeing households as 'maximizing a *range* of utilities—these might include capacity for diversification, flexibility in the case of agro-climatic shocks, other kinds of risk spreading (against illness and death, for example), long term investments, social reproduction and so on and so forth'.[94]

Why has it been difficult for women to mobilise around individual land rights? On the one hand, in many cultural contexts access to and ownership of land is closely intertwined with male gender identities. In order to claim land, therefore, women require both support and government action that establishes the legitimacy of their claims. On the other hand, women may be reluctant to embark on either collective mobilisations or individual agitation to claim individual rights to land because membership in a household provides them with a range of material and non-material benefits, and hence they are more interested in strengthening their household's access to resources, including land.

While intra-household inequalities in access to resources are well documented, this does not mean that a woman's level of well-being is unrelated to that of her husband or partner. Women's and men's interests within marriage are both joint and separate, which is what makes gender struggles so complex. What many women seem to be saying in the case studies reviewed for this paper is that they want to redress the inequalities in gender relations that hamper their access to household resources and impinge negatively on their security, and not necessarily to opt out of the household in order to make it on their own in isolation.

## Notes

This paper partially draws on the UNRISD research project 'Agrarian Change, Gender and Land Rights'. Some of the findings of the project were brought together in a special issue of the *Journal of Agrarian Change*, 3 (1–2), 2003. See also S Razavi, 'Introduction: agrarian change, gender and land rights', *Journal of Agrarian Change*, 3 (4), 2003, pp 2–32. The present paper has benefited from the comments of an anonymous journal referee.

1 C Jackson, 'Rescuing gender from the poverty trap', *World Development*, 24 (3), 1996, pp 489–504.

2 The phrase 'conjugal contract' is taken from A Whitehead, '"I'm hungry Mum"': the politics of domestic budgeting', in K Young, C Wolkowitz & R McCullagh (eds), *Of Marriage and the Market*, London: Routledge, 1981.
3 AK Sen, 'Gender and cooperative conflicts', in Irene Tinker (ed), *Persistent Inequalities*, Oxford: Oxford University Press, 1990.
4 B Agarwal, 'Gender and land rights revisited: exploring new prospects via the state, family and market', *Journal of Agrarian Change*, 3 (1–2), 2003, pp 184–224.
5 CD Deere & M Leon, 'Who owns the land? Gender and land-titling programmes in Latin America', *Journal of Agrarian Change*, 1 (3), 2001, pp 440–467.
6 A Manji, *The Politics of Land Reform in Africa: From Communal Tenure to Free Markets*, London: Zed Books, 2006, p 52 (author's emphasis).
7 On the 'rule of law' rhetoric emanating from the international financial institutions and its intellectual origins in Weberian sociology, see F Upham, 'Ideology, experience, and the rule of law in developing societies', in M J-E Woo (ed), *After the Miracle: Neoliberalism and Institutional Reform in East Asia*, Basingstoke: Palgrave, 2007.
8 C Nyamu-Musembi, *For or Against Gender Equality? Evaluating the Post-Cold War 'Rule of Law' Reforms in Sub-Saharan Africa*, OP 7, Geneva: UNRISD, 2005.
9 T Mkandawire, 'Good governance: the itinerary of an idea', *Development and Cooperation*, 31 (10), 2004, at http://www.inwent.org/E+Z/content/archive-eng/10-2004/tribune_art1.html, accessed 30 May 2007.
10 F Butegwa, cited in A Whitehead & D Tsikata, 'Policy discourses on women's land rights in sub-Saharan Africa: the implications of the return to the customary', *Journal of Agrarian Change*, 3 (1–2), 2003, pp 67–112.
11 Whitehead & Tsikata, 'Policy discourses on women's land rights in sub-Saharan Africa'.
12 For an analysis of these issues in the recent land tenure reforms in Tanzania, see A Manji, 'Gender and the politics of the land reform processes in Tanzania', *Journal of Modern African Studies*, 36 (4), 1998, pp 645–667; and D Tsikata, 'Securing women's interests within land tenure reforms: recent debates in Tanzania', *Journal of Agrarian Change*, 3 (1–2), 2003, pp 149–183.
13 CD Deere, 'Women's land rights and social movements in the Brazilian agrarian reform', *Journal of Agrarian Change*, 3 (1–2), 2003, pp 257–288.
14 Ibid, p 259.
15 S Greenberg, *The Landless People's Movement and the Failure of Post-apartheid Land Reform*, case study for the UKZN project 'Globalization, Marginalization and the New Social Movements in Post-Apartheid South Africa', University of KwaZulu Natal, 2004, p 28.
16 World Bank, *Sub-Saharan Africa: From Crisis to Sustainable Growth*, Washington, DC: World Bank, 1989.
17 UNRISD, *Gender Equality: Striving for Justice in an Unequal World*, Geneva: UNRISD, 2005, Figure 6.1.
18 G Abalu & R Hassin, 'Agricultural productivity and natural resource use in Southern Africa', *Food Policy*, 23 (6), 1999, pp 477–490.
19 CD Deere, *The Feminization of Agriculture? Economic Restructuring in Rural Latin America*, OP No 1, Geneva: UNRISD, 2005.
20 World Bank, *Adjustment in Africa: Reforms, Results and the Road Ahead*, Washington, DC: World Bank, 1994.
21 M Karshenas, '"Urban bias", intersectoral resource flows and the macroeconomic implications of agrarian relations: the historical experience of Japan and Taiwan', *Journal of Agrarian Change*, 4 (1–2), 2004, pp 170–189.
22 M Spoor, 'Policy regimes and performance of the agricultural sector in Latin America and the Caribbean during the last three decades', *Journal of Agrarian Change*, 2 (3), 2002, pp 382–401.
23 T Byres, 'Structural change, the agrarian question and the possible impact of globalization', in J Ghosh & CP Chandrasekhar (eds), *Work and Well-being in the Age of Finance*, New Delhi: Tulika, 2003.
24 Ibid, p 200.
25 KS Jomo, *Globalization, Liberalization and Equitable Development: Lessons from East Asia*, OC Paper No 3, Geneva: UNRISD, 2003; and H-J Chang, *Kicking Away the Ladder: Development Strategy in Historical Perspective*, London: Anthem Press, 2002.
26 The literature on intra-household gender inequalities is extensive. Prominent contributions include N Folbre, 'Hearts and spades: paradigms of household economics', *World Development*, 14 (2), 1986, pp 245–255; N Kabeer, *Reversed Realities: Gender Hierarchies in Development Thought*, London: Verso, 1994; B Agarwal, '"Bargaining" and gender relations: within and beyond the household', *Feminist Economics*, 3 (1), 1997, pp 1–50; and Whitehead, '"I'm hungry Mum"'.
27 J Bruce & D Dwyer, *A Home Divided: Women and Income in the Third World*, Stanford, CA: Stanford University Press, 1988.
28 The policy documents making such arguments include M Blackden & C Bhanu, *Gender, Growth and Poverty Reduction: 1998 Africa Poverty Status Report*, World Bank for the Special Program

82

of Assistance for Africa, Washington, DC: World Bank, 1999. The argument has been further generalised beyond sub-Saharan Africa in a key policy document, World Bank, *Engendering Development Through Gender Equality in Rights, Resources and Voice*, New York: Oxford University Press, 2001.

29 Particularly important in sustaining the World Bank position on the inefficiencies of gender inequality is C Udry & H Alderman, 'Gender differentials in farm productivity: implications for household efficiency and agricultural policy', *Food Policy*, 20 (2), 1995, pp 407–423; and C Udry, 'Gender, agricultural production, and the theory of the household', *Journal of Political Economy*, 104 (5), pp 1010–1046.

30 A good example of this up-take comes from the 2003 World Bank policy statement on land. World Bank, *Land Policies for Growth and Poverty Reduction*, World Bank Policy Research Report, Washington, DC: World Bank, 2003.

31 For a critical scrutiny of these studies, see B O'Laughlin, 'A bigger piece of a very small pie: intrahousehold resource allocation and poverty reduction in Africa', *Development and Change*, 38 (1), 2007, pp 21–44; and A Whitehead & N Kabeer, *Living with Uncertainty: Gender, Livelihoods and pro-poor Growth in Rural Sub-Saharan Africa*, IDS Working Paper 134, Brighton: Institute of Development Studies, 2001. For an earlier argument, see M Lockwood, *Engendering Adjustment or Adjusting Gender? Some New Approaches to Women and Development in Africa*, Discussion Paper No 315, Brighton: Institute of Development Studies, 1992.

32 K Griffin, AR Khan & A Ickowitz, 'Poverty and the distribution of land', *Journal of Agrarian Change*, 2 (3), 2002, pp 279–330.

33 RA Berry & WR Cline, *Agrarian Structure and Productivity in Developing Countries*, Baltimore and London: John Hopkins Press, 1979; C Udry, 'Gender, agricultural production and the theory of the household'; O'Laughlin, 'A bigger piece of a very small pie', p 40.

34 World Bank, *Land Reform Policy*, Washington, DC: Land Policy Division, World Bank, 1997.

35 Whitehead & Tsikata, 'Policy discourses on women's land rights in sub-Saharan Africa', p 83.

36 K Polanyi, *The Great Transformation*, Boston, MA: Beacon Press, 1957; and H-J Chang, *Breaking the Mould: An Institutional Political Economy Alternative to the Neoliberal Theory of the Market and the State*, SPD No 6, Geneva: UNRISD, 2001.

37 S Lastarria-Cornhiel, 'Impact of privatization on gender and property rights in Africa', *World Development*, 25 (8), 1997, pp 1317–1333.

38 *Ibid.*

39 J-P Platteau, *Reforming Land Rights in Sub-Saharan Africa: Issues of Efficiency and Equity*, Discussion Paper No 60, Geneva: UNRISD, 1995.

40 Lastarria-Cornhiel, 'Impact of privatization on gender and property rights in Africa'.

41 Whitehead & Tsikata, 'Policy discourses on women's land rights in sub-Saharan Africa', p 79.

42 CD Deere & M Leon, 'The gender asset gap: land in Latin America', *World Development*, 31 (6), 2003, pp 925–947, see Table 6.2.

43 Cherryl Walker, personal communication, December 2005.

44 Deininger & May and Deininger *et al*, cited in J Sender & D Johnson, 'Searching for a weapon of mass production in rural Africa: unconvincing arguments for land reform', *Journal of Agrarian Change*, 4 (1–2), 2004, p 157.

45 C Walker, 'Piety in the sky? Gender policy and land reform in South Africa', *Journal of Agrarian Change*, 3 (1–2), 2003, pp 113–148.

46 *Ibid*, p 123.

47 Detailed analyses of these debates are provided by Manji, 'Gender and the politics of the land reform processes in Tanzania'; and Tsikata, 'Securing women's interests within land tenure reforms'.

48 AM Tripp, 'Women's movements, customary law, and land rights in Africa: the case of Uganda', *African Studies Quarterly*, 7 (4), 2004, p 4.

49 A Whitehead, *Trade, Trade Liberalization and Rural Poverty in Low-Income Africa: A Gendered Account*, Background Paper for the UNCTAD 2001 Least Developed Countries Report, Geneva: UNCTAD, 2001.

50 Mighot-Adholla *et al*, cited in Whitehead & Tsikata, 'Policy discourses on women's land rights in sub-Saharan Africa', p 82.

51 World Bank, *Land Policies for Growth and Poverty Reduction*, p 62.

52 Whitehead & Tsikata, 'Policy discourses on women's land rights in sub-Saharan Africa, p 83.

53 Tsikata, 'Securing women's interests within land tenure reform'.

54 J Beall, *Decentralizing Government and Centralizing Gender in Southern Africa: Lessons from the South African Experience*, Occasional Paper 8, Geneva: UNRISD, 2005.

55 Whitehead & Tsikata, 'Policy discourses on women's land rights in sub-Saharan Africa', p 78.

56 Tripp, 'Women's movements, customary law, and land rights in Africa', p 6. The co-ownership amendment was in fact passed by the parliament but political manoeuvering on the grounds of

technicalities led to a last-minute removal of the clause. It was the president, by his own omission, who decided to pull out the co-ownership clause because he foresaw a disaster. For details, see *ibid*.

57 *Ibid*, p 11.
58 Tsikata, 'Securing women's interests within land tenure reform', p 172.
59 Rwebangira *et al*, cited in *ibid*, p 172.
60 A Claassens, *The Communal Land Rights Act and Women: Does the Act Remedy or Entrench Discrimination and the Distortion of the Customary?*, Occasional Paper No 28, Cape Town: Programme for Land and Agrarian Studies, University of the Western Cape, 2005.
61 *Ibid*, pp 18–21.
62 Whitehead & Tsikata, 'Policy discourses on women's land rights in sub-Saharan Africa', p 95.
63 *Ibid*, p 98.
64 Beall, *Decentralizing Government and Centralizing Gender in Southern Africa*.
65 Walker, 'Piety in the sky?'.
66 Cited in C Walker, 'Women, gender policy and land reform in South Africa', *Politikon*, 32 (2), 2005, pp 297–315.
67 *Ibid*, p 297.
68 Claassens, *The Communal Land Rights and Women*, p 41.
69 *Ibid*, p 32.
70 LS Khadiagala, 'The failure of popular justice in Uganda: local councils and women's property rights', *Development and Change*, 32, 2001, pp 55–76.
71 S Barraclough, *In Quest of Sustainable Development*, OC No 4, Geneva: UNRISD, 2005, p 34.
72 CD Deere & M León, *Towards a Gendered Analysis of the Brazilian Agrarian Reform*, Occasional Paper No 16, Storrs/Amherst, MA: Center for Latin American Studies, 1999.
73 See, in particular, T Byres, 'Neo-classical neo-populism 25 years on: déjà vu and déjà passé. Towards a critique', *Journal of Agrarian Change*, 4 (1–2), 2004, pp 17–44; and Sender & Johnson, 'Searching for a weapon of mass production in rural Africa', for powerful criticisms of this genre of analysis.
74 G Hart, 'The agrarian question and industrial dispersal in South Africa: agro-industrial linkages through Asian lenses', *Journal of Peasant Studies*, 23 (2–3), 1996, pp 245–277.
75 Byres, 2004; Sender & Johnson, 'Searching for a weapon of mass production in rural Africa'; and H Bernstein, '"Changing before our very eyes": agrarian questions and the politics of land in capitalism today', *Journal of Agrarian Change*, 4 (1–2), 2004, pp 190–225.
76 Byres, 'Structural change, the agrarian question and the possible impact of globalization'.
77 H Berstein, "Changing before our very eyes".
78 F Ellis, 'Household strategies and rural livelihood diversification', *Journal of Development Studies*, 35 (1), 1998, p 4. See also DF Bryceson, *Sub-Saharan Africa Betwixt and Between: Rural Livelihood Practices and Policies*, ASC Working Paper 43, Leiden: Africa-Studiecentrum, 1999.
79 Bernstein, "Changing before our very eyes"', p 204.
80 For Africa, see Bryceson, *Sub-Saharan Africa Betwixt and Between*; and Whitehead, *Trade, Trade Liberalization and Rural Poverty in Low-income Africa*. For India, see J Breman, *Footloose Labour: Working in India's Informal Economy*, Cambridge: Cambridge University Press, 1996.
81 Hart, 'The agrarian question and industrial dispersal in South Africa'.
82 D Kandiyoti, *Agrarian Reform, Gender and Land Rights in Uzbekistan*, Programme on Social Policy and Development, Paper No 11, Geneva: UNRISD, 2002; and Kandiyoti, 'The cry for land: agrarian reform, gender and land rights in Uzbekistan', *Journal of Agrarian Change*, 3 (4), 2003, pp 225–257.
83 Deere, 2005; C Dolan & K Sorby, *Gender and Employment in High-Value Agricultural Industries, Agriculture and Rural Development*, Working Paper Series No 7, Washington, DC: World Bank, 2003; and A Barrientos & S Barrientos, *Extending Social Protection to Informal Workers in the Horticulture Global Value Chain*, Social Protection Discussion Paper Series No 0216, Washington, DC: World Bank, 2002.
84 Figures taken from Dolan & Sorby, *Gender and Employment in High-Value Agricultural Industries*.
85 Sender & Johnson, 'Searching for a weapon of mass production in rural Africa', p 154.
86 *Ibid*, p 159.
87 Kandiyoti, 'The cry for land'.
88 Sender & Johnson, 'Searching for a weapon of mass production in rural Africa', p 148.
89 Walker, 'Piety in the sky?', p 143.
90 *Ibid*, pp 143–144.
91 The distinction between first-generation and second-generation feminist conceptualisations of the household should not be confused with the distinction between first wave and second wave women's movements.
92 Sender & Johnson, 'Searching for a weapon of mass production in rural Africa', p 148.
93 Whitehead & Kabeer, *Living with Uncertainty*.
94 Whitehead, *Trade, Trade Liberalization and Rural Poverty in Low-Income Africa*, p 19.

# Social Movements and the Experience of Market-led Agrarian Reform in Brazil

LEONILDE SERVOLO DE MEDEIROS

Since the beginning of the 1990s discussion about land transfers to poor rural inhabitants through market instruments, especially via credit, in order to reduce poverty, has intensified. A model, called 'market led agrarian reform' (MLAR) has been proposed by the World Bank and tried on in different regions of the world (Latin America, Africa, Asia and Eastern Europe). The issue has been the subject of academic and political discussions and the literature on this theme has been growing, both that produced by World Bank technicians,[1] and that produced by its critics.[2]

In Brazil the experience of market-led agrarian reform implementation has been marked by an intense dispute over access to land. From this perspective one of the particularities of the Brazilian experience is the way a settlement policy (based on the distribution of land obtained through expropriation, purchase or even the use of public land) coexists with a programme providing credit to people who have no access to land, in order to buy it. Understanding this coexistence requires an effort in order to capture the complexity of the Brazilian agrarian situation, the political struggles around the fight for land and the complexity of the forces involved therein.

## The agrarian question in Brazil

The concentration of land ownership in Brazil has long historic roots dating back to the colonial period, when the Portuguese king distributed large states (called *'sesmarias'*) in order to assure control of the territory and, at the same time, to produce materials for export. During this time the territories occupied consisted of large farms, using African slaves to produce for the external market. When Brazil gained its independence from Portugal these conditions did not change. The postcolonial condition merely reaffirmed the landowners' power and the prevalence of export-oriented production. In Brazil's long history ownership of large landholdings, including those not cultivated, has been synonymous with wealth and power.

At the beginning of the 20th century, especially in South-Central Brazil, the creation of the first industries, urbanization, and the various movements for political reform led to a profound questioning of the prevailing order. Some political forces began to speak about agrarian reform as an essential condition for the democratisation of the Brazilian political process. In 1946 pressure from the Communist Party in the national parliament succeeded in introducing into the text of the Constitution the concept that 'the use of property is subordinated to social well-being', creating legal limits to property rights. The Constitution also stipulated that, in the case of expropriation for social interests, the landholder should be given fair monetary compensation in advance of the transaction. Since then, the issue of the social function of property has centralised the debate around the meaning and limitations of agrarian reform.

At the same time, different forms of conflict began to be unified through the language of the Communist Party: the demand for agrarian reform and labour rights for rural workers. Agrarian reform was defined in the same terms as it was discussed in leftist debate: a change in land possession and systems of ownership, and the elimination of the *latifundio* system and the consolidation of the peasantry. At this time *'latifúndio'* came to signify above all relations of exploitation and oppression.[3] In parallel, the large landholders advocated their own version of the agrarian crisis and demanded state support for the technological modernisation of landholdings at the same time that they defended the untouchable right of property.

The force of this debate is best seen by looking at the Latin American situation at this particular moment, marked by the Cold War and by the debate over the need to stimulate industrialisation and eliminate the structural obstacles to development, such as agriculture activities based on large properties and simple technologies. The Cuban revolution accentuated the polemic about the possible risks of persistent exploitation and misery in the countryside, as it was seen both as a model for development and, from the opposite point of view, as a threat to the dominant sectors. In this context the US government encouraged Latin American governments to implement preventive agrarian reform programmes.

In Brazil the political disputes showed that the large landholders, criticised for their 'backwardness', actually counted on the support of representatives of industry against the attempt to change landed property rights. These political conflicts were one of the most important reasons for the military coup of March 1964, which restricted liberties and repressed the struggles of rural and urban workers. Despite this, the military acknowledged the criticisms of the backwardness of agriculture and created the institutional and legal conditions to carry out transformations in land ownership. The Land Statute and a constitutional amendment allowed payment for expropriated land to be made with government bonds, suspended requirements to pay compensation in advance, stipulated the need for fair indemnification in cases of expropriation and limited the use of expropriation instruments to areas of social tension.

Highlighting the influence of those on the land, the military regime introduced agricultural policies that fulfilled the proposal for agricultural modernisation previously advocated by rural producer associations, providing them with cheap credit, fiscal incentives to occupy land along the agricultural frontier, the creation of a state agricultural research institute, the construction of roads connecting the various regions of the country, etc. In a short period of time the transformation was profound: new regions were occupied and new crops and seed varieties were introduced. Banks and industries were attracted by investment in land, especially in new areas. This process valorised land, expelled small farmers who did not manage to modernise and caused a massive exodus from rural to urban areas.

Despite the wave of technological modernisation and growth of the proletariat which resulted from these changes, the struggle for land continued, though in a relatively weakened form. In some regions of the country select rural trade unions and their national confederation, the Confederação Nacional dos Trabalhadores na Agricultura (National Confederation of Agricultural Workers—CONTAG), started to demand the expropriation of areas in conflict, in accordance with the Land Statute. This organisation played an important role in the socialisation among rural workers of the knowledge of the law that shaped agrarian reform. At the same time, and as a consequence, it was formed as a particular kind of trade-unionism, a prudent one given the worries about infringing the law.[4]

During the 1970s Catholic priests and bishops linked to the Liberation Theology movement created the Comissão Pastoral da Terra (Pastoral Land Commission—CPT), engendering the conditions for the consolidation of a powerful network of influence. The CPT gave theological legitimacy to emerging demands and to acts of resistance, provided training through the actions of pastoral agents and made space and infrastructure available for meetings and the creation of new peasants organisations and trade unions opposed to CONTAG political conceptions, in a period in which the very act of people assembling in a given place was considered suspect by the military regime.[5] With this support, struggles for land gained public attention, showing different faces of resistance: of people affected by the building of large dams; of rubber tappers, who, in the North of the country, opposed the destruction of native rubber tree groves and their conversion into pasture; of small producers excluded from the benefits of modernisation and who had either lost their farms or realised that their children would only have access to this asset with great difficulty.[6]

At the end of the 1970s, with the CPT's support, land occupation began in the south of the country, the region most affected by agricultural modernisation. In 1984 the Movement of Landless Rural Workers (Movimento dos Trabalhadores Rurais sem Terra—MST) was formally constituted. In the 1980s land occupations spearheaded by MST became the main form of struggle for agrarian reform. In the 1990s the MST became perhaps the most important social movement in Latin America.

The wide-scale rural and urban popular mobilisations which took place during the last years of military government rekindled expectations of a comprehensive agrarian reform. But the defeat in 1985 of the First National Agrarian Reform Plan revealed the continuation of landowners' power, which had previously appeared weakened by urban and industrial growth, and demonstrated the complexity of the forces which had emerged inside the different elements of the state.

The next battle to institutionalise channels which would permit the achievement of significant transformation in landholding structure took place in the National Constituent Assembly (1987–88). Despite popular pressure for the introduction of measures which would allow wide-scale agrarian reform, the interests linked to land ownership managed to prevent this. The results were contradictory. In the chapter of the Land Statute entitled 'Economic and Social Order', it was stated that property had to fulfil its social function, whose definition was inspired by the Land Statutes (rational use of available natural resources, preservation of the environment, observance of labour laws), under the penalty of expropriation. Nonetheless, expropriations could only take place in unproductive areas, after fair compensation, paid in agrarian bonds, with a clause preserving their real value, redeemable in up to 20 years after the second year, thereby even further consolidating the tendency of taking market prices as the basis for land values.

Until the 1990s only 218 534 families gained access to land, although the First National Agrarian Reform Plan (PNRA) target had been to settle 1 400 000 families between 1985 and 1989. Land ownership remained concentrated: according to the 1995–96 IBGE Agricultural Census, rural establishments over 1000 hectares represented 0.83% of total rural establishments, while their owners controlled 43.5% of the area surveyed. At the other extreme, establishments with fewer than 50 hectares represented 82.67% of the total, but held only 13.5% of the total land. The Gini index was higher than 0.8.

### Market-led agrarian reform: from 'Cédula da Terra' to 'Anti-Poverty Land Credit Programme'

During the 1990s occupations intensified, spread throughout the country, and were also adopted by rural trade unions, placing agrarian reform at the centre of the political agenda.[7] At the same time violence grew in the countryside, culminating with two massacres of landless workers

(Corumbiara and Eldorado dos Carajás in the north of the country). The political situation led President Fernando Henrique Cardoso to create an Extraordinary Ministerial Office for Land Policy in 1996, which was transformed into the Ministry of Agrarian Development a year later. INCRA, the agency charged with the operationalisation of agrarian reform, was subordinated to this ministry, escaping from the jurisdiction of the Ministry of Agriculture, which had traditionally been controlled by large rural entrepreneurs resistant to land expropriations. The new ministry was also charged with the family farm policies. With these changes, the government expected to have better control over the agrarian crisis.

Social pressure forced the intensification of expropriations and the settlement of a significant (in comparison with previous periods) contingent of families on land. Between 1995 and 2002, 579 733 families were settled. Although these data have been strongly contested by social movements and despite the fact that almost 40% of the families were settled in the north of the country[8]—and mostly on public land—there is no doubt that the volume of settlements increased. At the same time measures were taken aimed at halting occupations. The most important was the legal provision that occupied land could not be expropriated. The government also sought to change the profile of its intervention in the agrarian question, adopting the principle of MLAR that was being stimulated by the World Bank and strongly supported by the landowner organisations. This was part of the broader neoliberal agrarian restructuring in Brazil.[9]

Policies of this type had already been implemented locally by some state governments, even without the advice of the World Bank, amid intensifying land struggles. This is the case of Santa Catarina state, in the south of the country, where, at the beginning of the 1980s, the State Land Credit Programme was implemented (State Law 6288/83), aimed at financing the acquisition of land for landless rural workers.[10]

According to the defenders of this model, it leads to a more efficient use of resources and a quicker transfer of land as it is carried out with the agreement of the landholders. Also emphasised is its decentralised approach, with the substitution of the central bureaucracy by local government units that are assumed by MLAR promoters to be closer to those involved in the land transfer process and less prone to corruption.[11]

In Brazil the first MLAR experiment took place in the northeast, one of the poorest regions in the country, with the name of 'Land Reform and Poverty Alleviation Pilot Project', known as *Cédula da Terra*. At the start of 1998, without any evaluation of the pilot project results, the Land Bank was created, based on a bill written by the same senator from Santa Catarina who had written the proposal 15 years before in his own state. In defence of this programme, which covered those in the south and some parts of the southeast of the country, as well as the other northeastern states, the government highlighted the high costs of expropriations as a result of the legal actions taken by owners attempting to increase the price they would receive. It was also stated that land had become cheaper, because of the impact of the economic stabilisation plan adopted by the government.

According to one of the documents announcing it, the Land Bank was publicised as being 'agrarian reform without bureaucracy, without conflict, without the need to resort to Justice'.

## Reactions to the proposal

The more representative organisations of rural workers, like CONTAG and MST,[12] reacted strongly to the new policy, insisting on expropriation as the principal instrument for agrarian reform. Another strong source of opposition to the Land Bank was the CPT, which over the years reaffirmed its theological perspective that land is a 'gift from God' and not just a commodity. The CPT accused the government of transferring responsibility for agrarian reform into the hands of the '*latifundiários*' and local oligarchies. These criticisms gained space thanks to the central role assumed by CPT in the fight against the Land Bank, since it was responsible for the Executive Secretariat of the National Forum for Agrarian Reform and Justice in the Countryside, a loose, broad coalition of trade union entities, social movements, NGOs and church-linked bodies (such as CPT and CNBB, the National Conference of Brazilian Bishops) formed in 1995. It was the principal opponent of the MLAR proposal.

The Forum addressed its demands to the National Congress, trying to bring the debate to this space and succeeded in having public hearings called. It also presented a request to the World Bank, signed by various civil society entities, for the creation of an Inspection Panel. The arguments used to justify this demand were:

- a suspicion that there had been a progressive substitution of the expropriation mechanism by market-based mechanisms in agrarian reform;
- the fact that *Cédula da Terra* and Land Bank borrowers were unable to pay off their debts because of the loan conditions;
- that, in many cases, the associations set up by the programme were politically subordinate to the landholders;
- much of the land bought had bad conditions for agricultural production;
- the Councils created to manage the programme were controlled by local powers;
- the project was heating up the land market, reversing a declining tendency that had been observed for years;
- the representative organisations of rural workers were totally excluded from the project formulation process.

The World Bank accepted the request for the panel but, after a few visits to the regions involved, it chose not to carry out an investigation.[13] At the same time it confirmed a US$1 billion loan for the four-year project cycle of the new programme. Nonetheless, despite denying the inspection request, the Bank promised not to include in the loan areas susceptible to expropriation. The Minister of Agrarian Development also altered the conditions, increasing the length of the loan from 10 to 20 years, with the first payment only to be made after three years, favouring future borrowers.

Shortly afterwards the World Bank was again requested to set up an Inspection Panel, this time based on the preliminary programme evaluation report it had itself demanded. After a new visit of Panel representatives to Brazil and further rounds of discussions with the government and the Forum, the inspection was once again not recommended. If this initially represented a defeat for the Forum, these actions had very wide ranging impacts, both internationally and nationally. In this context the Bank sought approval from civil society organisations, accepting some criticisms about the original project. The support of CONTAG, an active participant in the Forum, became fundamental for legitimating the project, which had been coming under attack and reopened an old dispute over the right to speak for rural workers. Arguing that it had the right to negotiate what seemed best for its grassroots, CONTAG made an agreement with the Bank on a programme that only involved land that could not be legally expropriated: the Anti-Poverty Land Credit Programme (Programa de Crédito Fundiário de Combate à Pobreza Rural). This ruptured the unity of the Forum.

To understand CONTAG's position in this process, it must be acknowledged that, since the beginning of the 1990s, the demand for some type of land credit which would allow smallholders or the children of small farmers to have access to land, has appeared on the agenda of the annual mobilisations led by CONTAG, when presenting its demands to government. This demand existed alongside the struggle for expropriation and rural worker settlements, because small farmers are an important constituent of CONTAG. It had been very difficult for the children of small farmers to access land and a lot of them, marked by a tradition of respect for law and a lack of organisation, did not want to engage in militant actions like establishing camps and land occupations. Nonetheless, the trade union confederation was at first quite critical of MLAR programmes. Despite this, it sought to negotiate a change in the programme profile. According to a former CONTAG adviser, the logic of the Brazilian trade union movement is based on negotiation. In addition, the government was making gestures to guarantee resources of the programme to Força Sindical, a trade union organisation which existed mainly in urban areas, but which in the 1990s began to extend its actions to rural regions and did not support land occupations. Land credit is seen by this group as the way to get into rural areas and earn the support of some trade unions. In the absence of internal consensus CONTAG started to work with the programme in order to get concrete results for its members, trying to differentiate land credit from previous programmes through the more intense participation of trade unions in its management. Thus it sought an agreement with the World Bank that resulted in the creation of the Anti-Poverty Land Credit Programme. In this model land that could be expropriated was not included in the MLAR model, interest rates were reduced and the increased participation of trade unions in the process was guaranteed. In practice, this partly implied that, while in one municipality a trade union leader could support land credit, in the neighbouring municipality another trade union could be stimulating occupations.

Despite the criticism from CPT and MST, the programme was continued by the Lula government (which shortly after the beginning of its mandate, in 2002, abolished the Land Bank) and became part of the directives of the Second National Agrarian Reform Plan, where it was given a new format and its scope of action was expanded. In addition to land credit aimed at eliminating poverty, two new programmes were introduced: 'Our First Land' (*Nossa Primeira Terra*) to facilitate the purchase of land by young people living in the countryside and 'Family Farming Consolidation', aimed at small producers. According to the Plan, the government expected to settle 400 000 families between 2003 and 2006 through the state-led agrarian reform and 150 000 families through the different forms of land credit.

In this format the land credit programmes also counted on the support of another rural trade union faction, which is strong in the south of the country: the Southern Federation of Family Farming Workers (Federação dos Trabalhadores na Agricultura Familiar do Sul—FETRAF-Sul).[14] It was one of the main forces supporting *Nossa Primeira Terra*, since one of its main spheres of action was concerned with rural youth, who tend to abandon the countryside.

For the landowners who are the traditional defenders of market mechanisms for dealing with the national land question the MLAR theme was not new. Since agrarian reform had entered the political debate, they argued that a 'fair' price should be paid for expropriated land; in other words, the commercial market value. The 1964 Constitutional Amendment that stipulated that a fair price should be paid for land, but in agrarian bonds, had led to loud protests from the rural business sector. When the issue of agrarian reform was raised once again the mid-1980s, the business associations reacted and were once again very vocal critics of expropriations and of the progressive land tax, arguing instead for negotiated mechanisms, such as land rental. As a result of these historical positions, large landholders supported the programme. The essential point for them was that it would start from a principle distinct from the conventional state-led programme.

### The implementation of the proposal

Despite some design diversity, market-led programmes of access to land share various common aspects. According to the Operational Manual of the *Cédula da Terra*, which, in general terms, was maintained in later programmes, the beneficiaries were to be landless rural producers or owners of land classified as smallholdings, and heads, or the main breadwinners, of families, including women responsible for families. They must also have had a tradition of agricultural activity; have shown the intention of acquiring, by means of purchase through a producers' association, rural property which would allow them to undertake sustainable productive activities; and be able to indicate one or more landholders willing to sell them property, which had been previously agreed in adherence with the conditions specified by the programme. Finally, they would agree to commit themselves to repay the sum given to them for the acquisition of the landholding.[15]

The starting point was the creation of an association of small producers or landless workers in order to look for a financial agent or state land institute with a proposal for a settlement. Once the request had been analysed, resources would be provided so that it could acquire an area, the value of which was to be agreed with the owner. Next, it would return to government institutions for an evaluation of whether the quality of the land was adequate, whether the agreed price was reasonable in relation to the market for that region and, finally, whether the land deeds were legally sound. Afterwards a letter of credit would be given to the association, which, through a state financial agent, would acquire the property under market conditions. The finance provided had to be repaid, with the purchasing association initially having a period of up to 10 years to redeem the debt, with a grace period of up to three years. Later, following criticism, the period for redemption of the debt was extended to 20 years.

The general criteria guiding the land purchase were the potential for the sustainable use of natural resources, as well as the generation, with a low level of additional investment, of conditions to sustain the beneficiary families; prices compatible with those normally practised in the market and with the location, natural fertility and potential economic use of the land; compliance with all the legal requirements related to the registration and transfer of the purchase and sale of rural property; good access conditions, availability of water and a reasonable infrastructure; location distant from non-demarcated indigenous lands; absence of primary forests and a size adequate to absorb the families who had joined the association. The size of the family property could not be smaller than the minimum land division unit of the region where it was situated, although, in exceptional circumstances, the acquisition of holdings which did not comply with this requirement would be allowed, once the association had decided not to carry out the formal division of the property after the liquidation of the debt incurred in its purchase.[16]

From the point of view of the proposal design, there were no restrictions on the type of property that could be acquired. As a result, properties that should have been expropriated entered the programme. When the Land Bank was institutionalised, there was strong pressure from rural trade unions to exclude properties that could be subject to expropriation from the programme. As a result, when the Anti-Poverty Land Credit Programme was created, the agreement with CONTAG implied that only the properties that could not be expropriated could be acquired with the land credit approach.

However, according to Sparoveck,[17] in around half the cases only one property was acquired, with the price paid being close to the market price. Other research also indicates that, although these properties were not very close to the villages where the most part of the families lived (proximity is a factor that raises the price of land), neither were they very distant (proximity also acts in another manner: facilitating the obtaining of knowledge about the programme). Bruno notes that the price of land in the case of the *Cédula da Terra* tended to be apparently lower than that stipulated by the landholder, but in some situations the association actually made extra 'under the table' payments to the landholder to persuade him to accept the value set in the technical document, not because of fear of loss of access to land in general, but rather for fear of loss of the specific land with which the association already had some sort of connection.[18] To understand this behaviour, it is important to realise that, for a lot of families, access to land is not a business and its price was not the central concern. To many people, the most important thing is to stay near the family and the old neighbourhood.

Contrary to what the supporters of land credit programmes took for granted, the average time to complete the operation was very long, around 17 months.[19] This delay was partly a result of the bureaucratic processing of the proposal. Studies also show the lack of knowledge among beneficiaries of the form of payment for the land, the interest rates involved, etc. According to Bruno,[20] even presidents of associations were unaware of the programme's rules and several of the people interviewed for the research in which the author participated did not understand either the role of the association in the process nor their own responsibilities. Bruno also states that they did not know that in the case of defaulting the association would lose them the right to the land. From the point of view of the rural trade unions, this was an issue to be discussed later: how to extend the debt repayment time.

In addition to the loan for the land purchase, financial resources for community investments were also provided, in three areas: infrastructure, productive activity and social matters. In relation to infrastructure, investments which improved or renewed what already existed were to be given priority. The priority for productive investments was to increase the productive capacity of the property, to raise productivity, the level of employment and the income of the beneficiaries.

The limit established for family credit was $11 200, including expenses incurred in the acquisition and registration of land, mediation, taxes and community investments. The maximum investment subsidy was $6900 per family, including installation assistance and the land grant of $1300 dollars. In accordance with the logic of the programme, the lower the value of the land credit, the higher the subsidy conceded per family and the amount of resources aimed at community investment. With the Anti-Poverty Land Credit Programme, resources for infrastructure and community projects are not reimbursed in either the 'Anti-Poverty' or 'Our First Land' modes. The period for payment was changed to 17 years, with no payments having to be made for three years, and interest rates set at between 3% and 6.5% per year, depending on the value financed. This can amount to some US$18 000 per beneficiary, depending on the line of credit.

From the point of view of the participants and of the trade union organisations, the programmewas a state programme and not one led by market forces. The fact that the loan values, payment forms and conditions were all defined by the state and the management of the programme was in the hands of councils in which the presence of the state was very strong also contributed to this perception.

According to Buainain *et al*, Sparoveck and Department of Socio-economic Rural Studies (DESER),[21] the various types of land credit programmes focus on poor rural families: smallholders possessing land in precarious conditions, many also with non-agricultural occupations; with high levels of illiteracy or low levels of education; living in small rural villages or on big properties where they work on a daily basis; and having few assets when they join the programme. In other words, this is the same group that was being mobilised for settlements and occupations by MST, trade unions and other movements involved in the struggle for land. The question is: why did these families look for land credit programmes and not take part in occupations? The choice of one path or the other in the demand for land appears, to a large extent, to be related to the opportunities that are offered, taking into account the extent of the presence and force of leaders who back either one programme or the other.

### Programme outcomes

Taking into account the three forms of MLAR in Brazil, the results of the programme are shown in Table 1.

Both the *Cédula da Terra* and the Land Bank reached their original targets. However, Land Credit is much below its own target, set at 130 000 families, for the period of the Lula government (2003–06). We can say that the programme was not a government priority in the most recent years, but we also have to consider that land prices, which were falling in the 1990s, had begun to increase more recently, partly stimulated by the new opportunities that were opened up to agribusiness. But perhaps even more important than the target quantitative output are the qualitative results.

Among the three programmes under the Brazilian version of MLAR, the *Cédula da Terra* programme is the one for which the most qualitative evaluations are available, partly because it was the oldest of the three. One aspect mentioned in these evaluations is related to the associations, central elements in the structure of the programme. According to Navarro,[22] in a

TABLE 1. Results of market-led agrarian reform programmes

| Programme | Period | Families |
|---|---|---|
| *Cédula da Terra* | 1997–2002 | 15 267 |
| Land Bank | 2000–03 | 34 478 |
| Land Credit | 2003–06 | 35 564 |

*Sources*: www.creditofundiario.org.br/biblioteca; AM Buainain (ed), *Estudo de avaliação de impactos do programa Cédula da Terra 2001*, Unicamp/Núcleo de Economia Agrícola and MDA/NEAD, Relatório de Pesquisa, 2002; and MDA, 2003–06, at www.mda.gov.br.

study carried out in 1998 when the programme was just starting, the associations created had just a single purpose: to acquire land. Once this was achieved, they and their commitments weakened, including that of the repayment of the loan, understood as an 'offer' from the government by the majority of beneficiary farmers.

In the different evaluations available,[23] little is mentioned about associative life after the purchase of land and the settlement of families. The emphasis is instead placed on the role of associations at the time of the purchase of land. Sauer and Victor call attention to an important point: the public agencies responsible for the programme determined that in the projects there had to be an area of collective planting to be used to grow commercial crops in order to guarantee the repayment of the resources lent to purchase the land.[24] The association was to be responsible for this and, according to the authors, it has generated permanent tensions: often the payment for labour on this land was in the form of daily wages, which transforms members into the employees of their own association and discourages co-operative practices.

In general the individual areas in the projects are very small. In the southern Region of Brazil the average area (12.9 ha) was significantly inferior to the average size of the family farm (17.9 ha) in the same municipalities.[25] Buainain et al, point out that the average size in the case of the Cédula da Terra was 14 hectares, also below the level required for family subsistence, if the lot is exploited in an individual form.[26] It is also important to take into account the quality of the land, often considered to be 'bad', ie of marginal agroeconomic potential. In the case of Cédula da Terra, this is related to the fact that the lower the amount spent by the association on purchasing the land, the more that is left (out of the total resources available) for investment. This led many associations to choose cheaper land, in addition to the reasons related to the selection of land discussed above. The amount of resources provided by the programme also limited access to land close to villages and to consumer markets.

The data on technical assistance are what vary the most in the available studies. According to Sparoveck, only 39% of projects received this assistance, covering 32% of the total families interviewed.[27] Assistance was basically aimed at productive community projects with an essentially commercial nature, relegating individual subsistence plots to secondary importance. Where there was no collective farming, the rate of provision fell to 17%. Buainain et al, present a different number, stating that 41% did not receive technical assistance.[28] Of those who did receive it, half stated that visits from technical advisers were sporadic. According to DESER, in the south of Brazil 76.8% of beneficiaries received technical assistance, although one-third were tobacco producers, a crop with a high commercial value and with production integrated with the large agro-industries.[29] These data indicate that land credit programmes in Brazil have reproduced the regional differences that have accompanied the country's history.

In general, the researches show that the beneficiaries believed that their living conditions had improved. According to Sparoveck,[30] this perception resulted from having gained access to land. This perspective, however, does not exclude discontentment with the current situation, related most especially to the lack of resources for infrastructure and production which, despite being part of the project, do not always arrive.[31]

Sparovek also reports that only 35% of beneficiaries lived in the projects.[32] He attributes the external residence to the fact of having young children of school age, which leads the family to seek to remain near villages to have access to schools. Another reason is that many of those who entered the programme were previously sharecroppers who still had commitments to finalise with their former landlords. The literature also highlights the fact that, given the existing difficulties for the reproduction of families, many of them combine activities in the project with other activities outside it, working on neighbouring farms or in nearby small towns, usually either in domestic service (women) or small-scale commerce.

The income analyses produced in the different research reports show that, despite the feeling that conditions had improved, as well as there being greater access to consumer goods, beneficiaries' income still remained below the poverty line. This finding was evident in the first evaluation report made at the request of the World Bank.[33] Later studies confirmed the reproduction of precariousness within the projects.

For all this, the capacity of the beneficiaries to repay their loans is somewhat questionable. According to Sauer and Victor, 60% of interviewees declared that they were unaware of the interest rates to be paid on the loan to buy the land.[34] Only 9.8% of beneficiaries knew that the property purchased would be used as the guarantee for the land credit. Around 30% of farmers interviewed declared that they had not obtained any credit to adhere to the programme, thereby demonstrating their total lack of awareness of the rules.

As shown by Sauer and Victor, 78% of beneficiaries did not possess any other goods, such as a house or land.[35] These data, associated with the fact that 66% did not have a means of transport and that 57% did not even have any animals, show that the majority of programme beneficiaries did not have anything with which to guarantee the loan. The guarantee therefore consists of the actual land since, in the case of non-payment, it can be repossessed.

In the case of the Centre-South of Brazil, when research was being carried out by DESER, many of the interviewees still had no repayments due, but those who had declared that they could not pay. These data confirm the hypothesis resulting from a simulation by the same institution carried out in 2000, shortly after the creation of the Land Bank, in which it was concluded that the payment conditions were prohibitive for the large majority of family farmers.[36] The research carried out with beneficiaries in 2005 concluded that if family living expenses were deducted from agricultural income, almost 40% of interviewees would have a result equal to zero or negative. Not by chance, Sauer and Victor refer to the high levels of evasion in *Cédula da Terra* projects.[37]

Faced with the above, it would not be strange if these indices were repeated in the other forms of land credit.

## Final considerations: the current impasse

A general accounting of MLAR outcomes cannot be made only on the basis of the number of families benefiting, the quantity of land involved, or the resources spent. A more ample vision can also shed some light on the current impasses about agrarian reform in Brazil and its perspectives.

Brazil is a country where different types of agriculture coexist. At one extreme there is a technologically sophisticated agriculture, with little environmental sustainability, using extreme forms of exploitation of labour, which for the most part remains distant from any sort of labour rights. This is the agriculture responsible for the production of grains for the foreign market, raw material for the generation of energy and fuel or for the manufacture of paper and bulk. At the other end is family-based agriculture, with differentiated levels of insertion in the market, of relations with the agribusiness sector, of income generation, and of political participation. The struggle for agrarian reform is also a struggle for the expansion of this sector, to the detriment of the other, since it is based on the demand for the expropriation of large properties. Nonetheless, these struggles have assumed over time a series of limits imposed by the successive victories of the sector linked to large-scale business production. The latter has managed to progressively protect the right to property, at the same time as it has given itself social legitimacy through its capacity to produce exports and fuel, imposing an image of itself as the real driver of 'progress' and ' development'. It also sought to delimit the possible universe of agrarian reform, which since the 1980s has come to be seen from the point of view of public policy as a 'social compensation policy' and not as the central axis of development policy.

When MLAR was consolidated as a government proposal, despite having been presented as complementary to agrarian reform based on expropriation, it appeared to be the rehearsal of an alternative policy. It was concerned with the reduction of land occupations and settlements and aimed at weakening a specific form of land struggle that has achieved prominence through the actions of MST, but which was also shortly afterwards adopted by rural trade unionism and other organisations that were created over time through splits in the MST or as alternatives to the latter. This observation becomes even more significant if we take into account similar experiences that had been tried previously (as in the case of Santa Catarina) and also the fact that, since agrarian reform had returned to the political agenda in the mid-1980s, employers' organisations has been arguing for market-negotiated mechanisms of access to land for those who were demanding it. When MST went beyond the strict limit of where it was created, it began to attract groups of employed workers from export-orientated agriculture in crisis and people who had lived for a long time on the peripheries of small and mid-sized cities and villages. These were families which had migrated to urban centres in search of better living conditions but which had not managed to incorporate themselves in an even more selective labour market. It was these families who were considered by the employers to have 'no vocation' for agriculture.

In this concept, access to land was to be restricted to 'real' farmers, ie those who mobilised to purchase land if it was available through credit mechanisms that would facilitate this purchase.

The struggles for land since the 1970s converged on the demand for the enforcement of the Land Statutes, particularly the idea it contained that areas of conflict and properties that did not fulfil their social function should be expropriated for agrarian reform. As a result, properties with many facilities have quite an elevated expropriation cost, meaning that the preference for purchase was usually given to properties that could be acquired at a cheaper price—and which were most often located far from urban centres, difficult to access and either degraded or difficult to exploit.

During the 1980s the disputes over agrarian reform were also political struggles to define the legal terms and interpretations of the Land Statute. Questions about how to define 'just value', the 'social function of land' and 'productivity' marked political and legal debates. This involved not only technical definitions, but also interpretations of the law. During this debate the rural employers, who had a strong influence on the Ministry of Agriculture and on the legislative and judicial powers, managed to ensure the prevalence of the concept that the social function of land and productivity were equivalent and that 'fair value' meant the market price of the land. In the case of the definition of productivity, regional land use indices are calculated based on census data. The last time these indices were prepared they were based on the 1975 Agricultural Census, when the modernisation of Brazilian agricultural was only just starting. Up to the time of writing these indices, dependent on the joint administrative ruling by the Ministry of Agriculture and the Ministry of Agrarian Development, have not been updated. As a result, relatively few properties in Brazil are liable to be expropriated, since most of them appear as productive under the indices currently in force, even though they are actually not productive. As a result it is increasingly difficult, within the current parameters, to obtain land through expropriation in the Centre-South of Brazil and to meet the needs of the increasing number of families camped out there.

In relation to the land prices, if a property is expropriated and the value attributed to it does not meet with the expectations of the owner, the latter has the right to go to court asking for a revision. In the majority of cases they are successful in this. In addition to legal appeals, the law also stipulates that agrarian bonds have to be adjusted by preferential interest rate, plus 12% per year, by way of compensatory interest. In this way, as well as the market price of the land, the owner is also rewarded with compensatory interest for the expropriation of a property that was not adequately used. In other words, the way that the expropriation of land occurs nowadays in Brazil is far from having the punitive character argued for by social movements and which is seen as a condition for the expansion of the scope of agrarian reform.

Since the 1980s another expedient way used by governments to meet the strong demand for land has been commercial land purchase. This mechanism was used quite often by state governments at the end of the military regime, a moment when adopting a position in favour of the demands of landless workers and guaranteeing their access to land counted positively from the political point of view.[38] The instruments for the acquisition of land expanded when, at the end of the 1990s, the president issued decree 433/92 that permitted the purchase of land by the federal government, preferentially in areas of social tension, to be paid for in agrarian bonds. This decree was prepared at a very particular moment when, since regulations for the items related to agrarian reform in the 1988 Constitution had not yet been implemented, there were no mechanisms available to obtain land through expropriation. Even after regulations had been provided for these constitutional mechanisms, the decree remained in force and has been used with quite frequently. This instrument consolidates the concept that the obtaining of land assets by the government does not imply any punishment for landholders.

Thus the proposals from the World Bank consolidated tendencies that had already been sketched out and which pointed to the importance of the market as the definer of land prices and of the conditions to access to it. Nonetheless, since the rules of the market do not operate in a vacuum of social relations, these rules became a central space in the political dispute over the design and limits of agrarian reform.

In the Brazilian case the issue of agrarian reform has been fed by the struggles for land carried out by different social groups. These demands are at the centre of the complex game that, as it unfolds, sketches out the design of possible agrarian reform. At the same time, they create the conditions to expand the limits that at a certain moment can appear to be cast in stone. The data are eloquent in this respect: since their creation, the different land credit policies have been heavily criticised and appear to be running out of steam.

In the south and southeast, it is very difficult to expropriate land and it is increasingly difficult to gain access through market mechanisms. In relation to this, the DESER study clearly shows the difficulty of buying plots of good quality land large enough to be able to sustain a family within the financial ceiling allowed by the programme.[39] It also has to be taken into account that the clear signs of families falling into debt tend to make adherence to the programme more difficult, as knowledge of indebtedness circulates rapidly, and that even the trade unions most enthusiastic about the programme have to make renegotiation of debt an item on their agendas.

Another aspect to be pointed out is that, although the encouragement to participate is part of the directives of the World Bank, this paper has exposed the fragility of the arrangements created within the associations and the relations between the associations and public authorities. While associative fragility is also encountered in agrarian reform settlements under the conventional, land occupations-instigated approach, it is possible to see that previous experiences of struggle are producing the need for greater engagement to obtain the intended improvements. The greater presence of organisations such as MST, trade unions, etc., and the networks in which they are immersed, facilitates the creation and development of demands. An emblematic example is the struggle of MST in education which is producing rich experiences in terms of innovative pedagogical ideas.

The policy problems and operational difficulties encountered in the MLAR implementation and the situation of peasants engaged in this market-based programme show MLAR's inherent limits as a solution to Brazilian agrarian problems.

## Notes

This text updates some reflections of Medeiros (2005) and Deere and Medeiros (2007). It was translated from Portuguese by Eoin O'Neill.

1 See, among others, K Deininger & H Binswanger, 'The evolution of the World Bank's land policy: principles, experiences and future challenges', *World Bank Research Observer*, 14 (2), 1999.

2 See, among others, KT Ghimire (ed), *Civil Society and the Market Question: Dynamics of Rural Development and Popular Mobilization*, New York: Palgrave Macmillan/UNRISD, 2005.

3 R Novaes, *De corpo e alma: Catolicismo, classes sociais e conflitos no campo*, Rio de Janeiro: Graphia, 1997.

4 *Ibid.*

5 *Ibid.*

6 LS Medeiros, *História dos Movimentos Sociais no Campo*, Rio de Janeiro: Fase, 1989.

7 The rural trade union movement represented by CONTAG was opposed to land occupations in the 1980s, but in the 1990s it recognised that land occupations were the engine of land expropriations, and so in some regions it too began to organise camps and occupations. This is the way it found to dispute the representation of landless people with MST.

8 The north of Brazil is the region of Amazonian forest and from the 1970s until today it has been marked by intense struggles for land, opposing traditional occupants (Indians, *posseiros*, and so on) and the interests of economic groups that want to appropriate the land and natural resources.

9 See W Wolford, 'Agrarian moral economies and neoliberalism in Brazil: competing worldviews and the state in the struggle for land', *Environment and Planning*, 37 (2), 2005, pp 241–261.

10 L Camargo, 'O Banco da Terra em Santa Catarina: da crítica às possibilidades', master's thesis, Centro de Ciências Agrárias/Universidade Federal de Santa Catarina, 2003.

11 LS Medeiros, *Movimentos sociais, disputas políticas e reforma agrária de mercado no Brasil*, Rio de Janeiro: Editora da Universidade Rural/UNRISD, 2002; S Borras, 'Questioning market-led agrarian reform: experiences from Brazil, Colombia and South Africa', *Journal of Agrarian Change*, 3 (3), 2003, pp 367–394; and JMM Pereira, 'O modelo de reforma agrária de mercado do Banco Mundial em questão: O debate internacional e o caso brasileiro—teoria, luta política e balanço de resultados', master's thesis, CPDA/UFRRJ, Rio de Janeiro, 2004.

12 In order to understand the different points of view of these organisations, see P Houtzager, 'Collective action and political authority: rural workers, church and state in Brazil', *Theory and Society*, 30 (1), 2001, pp 1–45; G Meszaros, 'No ordinary revolution: Brazil's Landless Workers' Movement', *Race and Class*, 42 (2), 2000, pp 1–18; LS Medeiros, 'Sem terra, assentados, agricultores familiares: considerações sobre os conflitos sociais e as formas de organização dos trabalhadores rurais brasileiros', in N Giarraca (ed), *Una Nueva Ruralidad en America Latina?*, Buenos Aires: Clacso, 2001, pp 103–128; and Medeiros, 'Dimensiones de la lucha por la tierra em el Brasil contemporâneo y la conformatión de espacios públicos', in HC Gramont, *La construccion de la democracia em el campo latinoamericano*, Buenos Aires: Clacso, 2006, pp 213–242.

13 For details, see J Fox, 'O painel de inspeção do Banco Mundial: lições dos cinco primeiros anos', in Flavia Barros (ed), *Banco Mundial, Participação, Transparência e Responsabilização. A experiência brasileira com o Painel de Inspeção*, Brasília: Rede Brasil, 2001.

14 FETRAF-Sul was created in 2001. It was based on the articulation of trade unionists who since the 1980s had opposed the policy of the region's unions linked to CONTAG, which they considered to be 'welfarist' and too ready to ignore mobilisations. In 2005 FETRAF-Sul was transformed into a national federation. The social origin of its leaders is very close to that of the MST.

15 AM Buainain (ed), 'Avaliação preliminar do *Cédula da Terra*', mimeo, NEAD/MDA, 1999.

16 *Ibid.*

17 G Sparoveck (ed), *Diagnóstico dos projetos de Crédito Fundiário e Combate à Pobreza Rural*, Brasília: MDA/SRA and USP/ESALQ, Relatório de Pesquisa, 2003.

18 R Bruno, 'O programa Cédula da Terra e as associações comunitárias', paper presented at the 'Seminário Cédula da Terra/Banco da Terra', Fórum Nacional pela Reforma Agrária e Justiça no Campo e Rede Brasil sobre Instituições Financeiras Unilaterais, Brasília, 1999.

19 Sparoveck, *Diagnóstico dos projetos de Crédito Fundiário e Combate à Pobreza Rural*.

20 Bruno, 'O programa Cédula da Terra e as associações comunitárias'.

21 Buainain, 'Avaliação preliminar do *Cédula da Terra*'; Sparoveck, *Diagnóstico dos projetos de Crédito Fundiário e Combate à Pobreza Rural*; and DESER, *Capacidade de pagamento do crédito fundiário no Sul do Brasil: análise a partir do programa Banco da Terra*, Curitiba: DESER/Relatório de Pesquisa, 2005.
22 Z Navarro, *O projeto piloto Cédula da Terra: Comentários sobre as condições sociais e político institucionais de seu desenvolvimento recente*, 1998, at www.dataterra.org.br, accessed 15 December 1999.
23 Buainain, 'Avaliação preliminar do *Cédula da Terra*'; Buainain (ed), *Estudo de avaliação de impactos do programa Cédula da Terra 2001*, Unicamp/Núcleo de Economia Agrícola and MDA/NEAD, Relatório de Pesquisa, 2002; Sparoveck *Diagnóstico dos projetos de Crédito Fundiário e Combate à Pobreza Rural*; and S Sauer & AD Victor, 'Estudo sobre a política do Banco Mundial para o setor agrário brasileiro com base no caso do Programa Cédula da Terra', mimeo, 2002.
24 Sauer & Victor, 'Estudo sobre a política do Banco Mundial'.
25 DESER, *Capacidade de pagamento do crédito fundiário no Sul do Brasil.*
26 Buainain, *Estudo de avaliação de impactos do programa Cédula da Terra 2001.*
27 Sparoveck, *Diagnóstico dos projetos de Crédito Fundiário e Combate à Pobreza Rural.*
28 Buainain, *Estudo de avaliação de impactos do programa Cédula da Terra 2001.*
29 DESER, *Capacidade de pagamento do crédito fundiário no Sul do Brasil.*
30 Sparoveck, *Diagnóstico dos projetos de Crédito Fundiário e Combate à Pobreza Rural.*
31 Sauer & Victor, 'Estudo sobre a política do Banco Mundial'.
32 Sparoveck, *Diagnóstico dos projetos de Crédito Fundiário e Combate à Pobreza Rural.*
33 Buainain, 'Avaliação preliminar do *Cédula da Terra*'.
34 Sauer & Victor, 'Estudo sobre a política do Banco Mundial'.
35 *Ibid.*
36 DESER, *Capacidade de pagamento do crédito fundiário no Sul do Brasil.*
37 Sauer & Victor, 'Estudo sobre a política do Banco Mundial'.
38 Under Brazilian legislation only the federal government has the power to carry out expropriations for the social purposes of agrarian reform.
39 DESER, *Capacidade de pagamento do crédito fundiário no Sul do Brasil.*

# Eliminating Market Distortions, Perpetuating Rural Inequality: an evaluation of market-assisted land reform in Guatemala

SUSANA GAUSTER & S RYAN ISAKSON

29 December 1996 marked a watershed moment in Guatemalan history. Representatives of the Guatemalan National Revolutionary Unity (URNG) came together with government officials on the patio of the National Palace to sign a peace agreement and end a 36-year civil war that had claimed some 200 000 lives. Not only did the treaty represent the end of nearly four decades of violent conflict, but it also provided the framework for transforming the structure of Guatemalan society, addressing the extreme political, social and economic inequities that had underpinned the war.

While the civil war in Guatemala revolved around many issues, the country's highly unequal distribution of land is widely regarded as its principal axis. To redress the country's concentrated agrarian structure, the peace agreement's Accord on Socio-economic Aspects and the Agrarian Situation enlists a strategy known as market-assisted land reform. Drawing upon recent thinking at the World Bank, its basic premise is that, once distortions in land and credit markets are corrected, market forces will reallocate land from large owners to more productive small farmers, thereby advancing both efficiency and equity.

More than a decade after signing the peace accords, it has become increasingly apparent that the strategy of market-assisted land reform is a failure in Guatemala. Not only is it financially unstable, but it has also fostered corruption and inefficiency, burdened many of its purported 'beneficiaries' with debt, and redistributed only a small fraction of agricultural land. While the Socio-economic Accord was fundamental to formalising peace in Guatemala, the market-led strategy that it embraces has failed to alleviate rural poverty and correct the country's concentrated agrarian structure. The fortification of land markets has indeed facilitated market transactions, but it has done so primarily to the benefit of large landowners. Persisting conflicts over land continue to destabilise the country and have tarnished its nascent peace.[1]

### The paradigm of market-assisted land reform

The logic behind the World Bank's market-oriented paradigm arises from its critique of state-led land redistribution. The Bank focuses upon the purported inefficiencies of the traditional approach, including its inability to target the most worthy beneficiaries, the loss of economies of scale that comes with the break-up of large farms, and the corruption and rent-seeking behaviour that economists typically associate with government bureaucracy.[2] Moreover, World Bank economists Deininger and Binswanger lament, traditional state-led land redistributions are rarely supported by large landowners and, consequently, are characterised by a 'confrontational atmosphere'.[3]

Instead of top-down, state-led land redistributions that are inefficient and likely to incite protests from powerful landowners, the World Bank maintains that access to land should be mediated via market mechanisms.[4] The ideology of its market-assisted land reform is founded upon 1) the empirical observation that small farms are more productive than large farms;[5] and 2) the belief that market 'imperfections'—especially poorly defined and insecure property rights and the inability of small-scale farmers to obtain credit—prevent land from being redistributed to the more efficient smallholders. Thus the logic is that, by simply correcting the imperfections, a process can be unleashed whereby market forces will induce the redistribution of land to the more productive small-scale farmers, thereby achieving a land distribution that is more equitable *and efficient*.

The implementation of market-assisted land reform is based upon five key components. First, since poor farmers are not typically deemed 'creditworthy', the creation of a land bank that lends to peasants at subsidised rates is considered fundamental to the market-led model. Second, clearly defined property rights are also necessary to facilitate the exchange of land via market mechanisms; thus the model is dependent upon the regularisation of land tenure. Third, to ensure that beneficiaries use their newly purchased land efficiently, proponents of the market-led paradigm recommend that farmers wishing to receive credit develop a productive plan for producing market commodities that will allow them to repay their loan, and that beneficiaries receive marketing and technical assistance that will allow them to implement their productive plans. Ideally, the providers of technical and marketing assistance will be from the private sector, as this is thought to ensure accountability and minimise corruption.[6] Fourth, to reduce opportunities for corruption and ensure the co-operation of large landowners, land prices should be negotiated directly between potential sellers and buyers and landowners should be paid the full amount of the negotiated value once an agreement has been formalised. Finally, along with clearly defined and secure property rights, the theory of perfectly competitive land markets is contingent upon having a large number of buyers and sellers. World Bank economists argue that large landowners will be encouraged to participate, first, by structural adjustment programmes that undermine the profitability of farming and hence lower the price of land; and, second, by the levying of taxes on large and under-utilised landholdings.[7]

Despite promises that market-assisted land reform will improve equity while enhancing economic efficiency, the paradigm has been widely criticised. Banerjee, for example, articulates several theoretical deficiencies of the model, including the limited likelihood that it will benefit the neediest peasants, the fact that it is unlikely to achieve the optimal level of land redistribution, and that it is an unusually costly approach to agrarian reform.[8] In an empirical evaluation of market-assisted land reform in Columbia, South Africa and the Philippines, Borras documents several problems with the model. He confirms Banerjee's hypothesis that the market-led strategy tends to exclude the weakest segments of the rural population and that the extension services and overall programmes are costly. He also observes that the land that is exchanged tends to be overvalued and of poor quality; the high prices are partly a result of landlords using their power to capture a share of the loans and cash grants that are intended to assist beneficiaries.[9]

## Peace through agrarian reform

The concentration of landholdings in Guatemala is extreme, even by Latin American standards. According to the country's 2003 agricultural census, 2% of the country's farms, with an average area of 194 hectares, control 57% of the land, while 87% of all farms, with an average size of 1.2 hectares, occupy just 16% of the land.[10] With a Gini coefficient for farmland distribution of 0.84,[11] Guatemala has the dubious distinction of maintaining the second most unequal distribution of farmland in all of Latin America.

The issue of agrarian inequality has long been politically explosive in Guatemala. When President Jacobo Arbenz attempted a modest redistribution of land in 1952, he was overthrown in a US-backed military coup. In the ensuing years small-scale farmers continued to lose land to large-scale agro-exporters and mining interests. As dramatically demonstrated by the 1978 Panzós massacre and the 1980 burning of the Spanish Embassy, peasants who protested against violations of their land rights were met with violent repression. Left with no legal recourse, they increasingly turned to guerrilla activities.[12]

The strategy for addressing Guatemala's agrarian question is embodied in the Accord on Socio-economic Aspects and the Agrarian Situation. Signed on 6 May 1996, the Socio-economic Accord is the longest component of the peace agreement, and was arguably the most contentious to negotiate. Talks on the accord lasted more than a year and entailed actors from a variety of political persuasions. At one end of the spectrum the Civil Society Assembly (ASC) and the National Co-ordination of Peasant Organizations (CNOC) demanded guaranteed land ownership for the poor and the reinstatement of the principle of a social function for property, which had been established in Guatemala's 1945 constitution but was subsequently revoked by the military government that overthrew Arbenz. At the other end of the spectrum the Co-ordinating Committee of Agricultural, Industrial and Financial Associations (CACIF), representing the country's business and land-owning elite, argued for the continued sanctity of private property rights and against any significant restructuring of land ownership. Among the two principal signatories to the peace accords, the conservative Arzú government toed the line of its supporters in CACIF while the URNG believed that it would have little success if it advanced 'revolutionary positions' and took what it considered to be a more 'realistic' approach to negotiating.[13] Moreover, the United Nations facilitators had been in close contact with international financial institutions like the World Bank and the International Monetary Fund, and encouraged both parties to adopt an accord that would be consistent with their stabilisation and structural adjustment efforts in Guatemala.[14]

As a result of the conservative pressures exerted during the negotiation process, the Socio-economic Accord articulates a land reform strategy that is very much akin to the market-oriented approach that is advocated by the World Bank and has been adopted in countries throughout the so-called 'developing world'. Adopting the basic premise of the World Bank's market-assisted land redistribution, the Socio-economic accord suggests that the agrarian question in Guatemala can be answered by simply correcting for distortions in the land and capital markets that prevent market forces from reallocating land from large landowners to more productive small farmers. The political and cultural context in which those markets operate is largely ignored.

The adoption of market-assisted land reform to address one of the most volatile issues in the Guatemalan peace accords has led many experts to refer to the agreement as a 'neoliberal peace', or a peace agreement that is more focused upon the creation of a market economy than on the equitable distribution of resources and power.[15] The Socio-economic Accord's reliance upon market mechanisms to level Guatemala's highly concentrated agrarian structure and its avoidance of redistributive strategies have earned it the reputation of a 'soft' accord that is unlikely to sustain Guatemala's fragile peace. Indeed, peasant organisations were so sceptical of its market strategy that they carried out land occupations immediately following the signing of the accord. The government only exacerbated the violence by forcibly evicting the families involved in the occupations.[16] Land occupations and forcible evictions have mounted over the ensuing decade, including the widely-publicized death of 11 Guatemalans in 2004 when riot police tried to remove squatters from a ranch in the municipality of Champerico. 'In this always-sensitive area,' Jonas writes of Guatemala's market-assisted land reform, 'peace brought more new conflicts than conflict resolution'.[17]

### Fontierras and the 'accomplishments' of market-assisted land reform

To promote market-assisted land reform in Guatemala, the federal government established a land trust fund, Fontierras, in May 1997. Two years later, after long and difficult deliberations, the Guatemalan congress approved Decree 24–99, which formalised the operation of the fund and established it as a decentralised and autonomous entity with its own resources. The principal responsibility of Fontierras is to facilitate the functioning of 'transparent' land and credit markets by land regularisation and authorising credit for land purchases. In order to minimise corruption and harness the purported efficiency of market-like negotiations, the fund's mandate is not to select land for redistribution or to determine land prices, but rather to co-ordinate negotiations between willing sellers and willing buyers. In practice, these responsibilities fall to the land poor.

Although Decree 24-99 specifies that Fontierras should facilitate land purchases by individuals or organised groups of peasants, thus far the fund has only attended to applications from groups comprised of at least 25 families. Some groups are comprised of 300 or more families. One of the key motivations for working with groups is to minimise the 'transaction costs'—or the resources and energies expended in bargaining, obtaining information, and enforcing market transactions—that large landowners would incur if they had to subdivide their land and deal with multiple buyers. Instead, those costs are incurred by land-poor farmers who must organise themselves into groups appropriately sized to purchase a particular parcel of land and fall within the credit limits established by the fund.

True to its intention, market-assisted land reform has facilitated land transfers in Guatemala. Its accomplishments, however, have been relatively meagre. During its first eight years of operation (1997–2005), Fontierras financed the purchase of 163 000 hectares of land by 17 822 families. Based upon figures from the country's 2003 agricultural census,[18] the reallocated land accounts for a mere 4.3% of Guatemala's total agricultural land.

107

Fontierras' limited success in redistributing land is attributable to a variety of factors, including its basis upon a dysfunctional model, its limited funding and, ultimately, a lack of political will to level Guatemala's heavily concentrated agrarian structure. Despite the World Bank's encouragement to adopt its market-oriented land policies and the Guatemalan government's enthusiastic endorsement of the strategy, both actors have been slow to provide financial backing. The World Bank, for example, waited until April 2000—nearly three years after Fontierras began operating—to provide the first of what were to be three loans to finance market-assisted land reform in Guatemala. Moreover, the loan provided funds for regularising land tenure and technical and marketing assistance, but nothing for agricultural credit.[19] For its part, the Guatemalan government has failed to provide the $40 million for a guarantee fund that was to help finance land purchases, as stipulated by Article 27 of the Law of Fontierras.

There is a general consensus that, with its current lack of funding and resources, Fontierras will not be able to notably improve poor and landless Guatemalans' access to land. Indeed, even the World Bank acknowledged that the project 'was able to respond to only a fraction of the demand from beneficiaries'.[20] As of July 2005 the fund had received 1137 applications from groups of families wishing to purchase land. Among these, only 214 groups— or 18.8%—had received credit; 37% were still enduring the long review process, while the remaining 44.2% were closed or had fallen into inactivity. The funding shortfall is so severe that Fontierras has only been able to attend to an estimated 1% of the total demand for land.[21]

## The shortcomings of the market-oriented strategy

In addition to its inability to substantially improve the highly unequal distribution of land in Guatemala, the failure of market-assisted land reform is manifest in multiple dimensions. This section discusses the various shortcomings of the model in the Guatemalan context.

### *Failure to benefit the most marginalised peasants*

One of the most obvious shortcomings of market-assisted land reform in Guatemala is its failure to assist its intended beneficiaries. Ten years after the establishment of Fontierras the land demands of an estimated 316 000 peasant families remain unmet. Moreover, the beneficiaries of the pro- gramme have not necessarily been the most needy. Although the fund has a mandate to assist poor and landless farmers, in practice it allows beneficiaries to earn a monthly salary of up to *four times* the mandated minimum wage. Given that most rural workers do not even earn the minimum salary, the fund is allocating its scarce funds to help finance land purchases by the rural middle class.

Fontierras has no mechanism for prioritising farmers who suffer from poverty or extreme poverty. Instead, it reserves its limited financing for the most economically viable applications. Indeed, two key criteria for evaluating applications are the estimated profitability of the productive projects proposed for each piece of land and the entrepreneurial ability of the group. The fund pays particular attention to the proportion of applicants in a group who are literate or have experience in commercial activities, particularly cash cropping.[22] Since poor farmers are also the most likely to be illiterate and the least likely to have commercial experience, the practice of vetting applicants according to their entrepreneurial ability is inherently biased against the most land-deprived segment of the rural population.

In addition to its failure to acknowledge Guatemala's poorest peasants, the market-oriented strategy has done little to improve the asset base of rural women. Decree 24-99 specifically recognises the importance of attending to landless *campesinos y campesinas*—or 'peasant men and women'—but in practice the beneficiaries have mostly been men. Among the more than 5000 beneficiaries who received credit to purchase land between 2003 and 2005, only 8.5% were female-headed households. Although married and common law couples are to receive joint titles over the newly purchased land, women often lack the required documents to prove their eligibility and those who receive joint titles are rarely empowered. A review of beneficiary profiles indicated that the governing bodies for beneficiary groups were made up almost entirely of men; the handful of women who held positions were all listed as second vocal, the lowest of the five administrative positions. Women are rarely granted a legitimate voice or voting rights in group assemblies. Article 20 of the Decree stipulates that Fontierras stimulate the participation of women in group governance and projects, yet efforts rarely go beyond the formation of women's groups.

### Limited supply of quality land

In addition to its failure to attend to its most marginalised peasants, Guatemala's market-oriented agrarian reform has also suffered from an insufficient quantity of land available for purchase. Like their counterparts in Brazil, South Africa and other countries that have employed market-assisted land reform,[23] Guatemalan landowners prefer to keep their land rather than selling it on the market. Even as the fall in international coffee prices around the turn of the century undermined many Guatemalan producers, large landowners were were still unwilling to sell their land. Their reluctance can be attributed to the unique benefits that emerge with land ownership. Despite World Bank ideology, land is more than a market commodity. It is a source of power, wealth and prestige; it guarantees access to credit; and it is a defence against inflation and economic instability. The income earned from land sales is rarely enough to compensate Guatemalan landowners for the loss of such entailments. Moreover, the Guatemalan government has failed to implement the land tax that was intended to provide an economic incentive to sell under-utilised land.

Among the limited land that is available for sale, most of it is of poor quality. Most of the farms that have been purchased through Fontierras are characterised by deteriorated soil and scarce tree cover, are difficult to access, and have limited supporting infrastructure like irrigation, roads and working capital. As several Fontierras officials observed, 'Productive lands are not sold'. Many observers concur, claiming that the current agrarian strategy has simply allowed landowners to receive compensation for their most marginal lands.

There are, of course, exceptions. Not all groups have purchased poor quality land. Some beneficiaries have exerted a considerable amount of time looking for good quality land, searching up to three years to find a suitable farm for purchase. Others have contracted with intermediaries who they compensate with a portion of the benefits from their land purchase.

Despite the poor quality of most of the available farms, land-hungry peasants are often eager to purchase them. Most are desperate to acquire any land, even when it is clear that the farm has limited productive potential. As a result, most parcels purchased through the land trust fund are overvalued; in some instances sale prices are more than double the actual value of the land.[24]

In addition to their eagerness to acquire land, beneficiaries' limited understanding of Fontierras' policy has also contributed to high land prices. The fund fails to properly educate interested peasants about the responsibilities associated with receiving credit. Believing that Fontierras would cover the whole cost of their purchase, many farmers made little effort to negotiate a better price for their land. Information regarding debt, interest rates and terms of payment is typically only shared with the leaders of each group; however, in many instances even they are poorly informed. As illustrated in Figure 1, the land fund has done a poor job of communicating the terms and conditions of its loans to borrowers. In a survey of the eight communities where site visits were made, more than one-third of the beneficiaries were unsure about the amount they owed for their purchase, while nearly one-half were unaware of the interest rate that they were being charged and the schedule for their payments.

The Socio-economic Accord stipulated the implementation of two institutions to increase the quantity of land available for sale. Thus far,

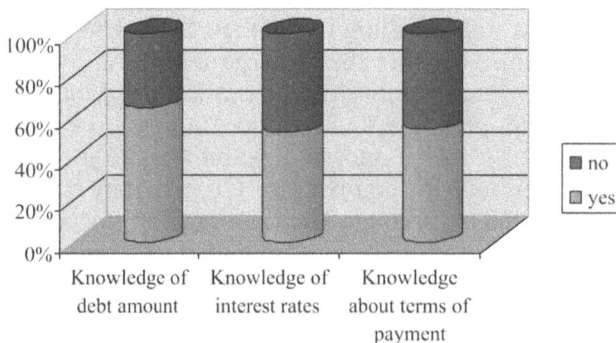

FIGURE 1. Beneficiaries' knowledge of their debt payments.

neither has been implemented. As outlined in paragraph 34 of the Accord, Fontierras was to make various forms of land accessible for purchase. In addition to private lands available from willing sellers, the fund was to be able to offer multiple types of land, including 1) unused national land-holdings and state-owned farms; 2) land that had been fraudulently acquired by the military during the civil war; 3) lands purchased by the government with national and international funds; 4) lands purchased with proceeds from the national cadastral survey; and 5) lands acquired under Article 40 of the Guatemalan constitution, which allows the government to expropriate idle land so long as it provides appropriate and timely compensation as determined by the national legislature. In a clear violation of the peace accords, none of these types of land have been made available.

Apart from making multiple types of land available for purchase, the signers of the Peace Accords also envisioned the implementation of a land tax that would provide an economic incentive for large landowners to sell their underutilised holdings. Specifically paragraph 42 of the Socio-economic Accord mandates the establishment of an easily collectable land tax upon idle or underutilised land controlled by large holders. In a move to comply with this obligation, the Guatemalan congress approved a variable-rate land tax in late 1997 that would have disproportionately affected large landowners, as rates were based upon factors such as the size of the land, its location, and the type of use. Although it was notably more progressive than its predecessor, a single-rate land tax passed in 1995, popular support for the new tax was undermined by a misinformation campaign by its opponents. With the government making no effort to clarify its provisions, the legislation was met with widespread protests. The conservative president Álvaro Arzú ultimately withdrew the legislation in February 1998, making no effort to modify it or to propose an alternative more palatable to the landed elite.[25]

*High transaction costs*

The paradigm of market-assisted land reform aims to limit the efforts and resources that large landowners must expend when selling their land, since they might otherwise lack the incentive to do so. Instead, such transaction costs are transferred to land-hungry peasants who are eager to acquire land. Peasant farmers must not only undergo the process of organising themselves into groups that are sizeable enough to purchase land through Fontierras, they must also exert considerable time and effort locating suitable plots of land for purchase and must endure the fund's increasingly cumbersome bureaucracy.

Once they have organised themselves into groups, most peasants must undergo the task of searching for land. Among the 134 groups that purchased land through Fontierras between 1998 and 2001, more than one-half looked for parcels on their own. Many engaged in long and tiresome searches that lasted up to three years. Another 18.5% already resided on the farm or had possession of it, while the same proportion found their property through intermediaries; none had acquired land from a list of available lands obtained by the fund.

After they have located a suitable piece of land, the organised groups must expend more of its resources completing socioeconomic profiles of each group member and other requisites. It must make long trips to the land trust's regional offices, purchase photocopies, notarise documents and solicit recognition as a formal group from the state. Having completed some 30 steps in all, the groups must then endure a lengthy review process by Fontierras. Table 1 shows the average amount of time that beneficiaries have had to wait for the fund to approve their loans. While the initial groups only had to wait three months to receive credit, the average wait had steadily increased to more than two years by the end of 2001.

Despite intentions to harness the purported efficiency of decentralised procedures, most beneficiaries of Guatemala's market-oriented agrarian policy have said that they incurred significant transaction costs in their quest to purchase land through Fontierras and that the process is painfully slow and bureaucratic.

### Abandonment, poor living conditions, and beneficiary debt

Despite the difficulty that they must endure to receive credit through Guatemala's market-assisted land reform, half of all beneficiaries ultimately abandon their groups.[26] Abandonment is widespread. Among the 23 groups participating in consultative workshops, more than three-quarters had members who had deserted. According to a member of the Fontierras board of directors, some 30% of the purchased farms have had high levels of abandonment.

In large part the desertions are attributable to the poor quality of the lands and their lack of basic services. The farms are often remote and inaccessible: nearly one-third of the purchased lands have insufficient road access. Even among the farms with road access, conditions are bleak. Nearly three-quarters of farms do not have access to health services while 61% lack schools. Housing conditions are also poor, as two-thirds of farms lack formal housing, 71% are without electricity and 68% have insufficient access to

TABLE 1. Number of months from initial application to receipt of credit

| Period | Credits awarded | Semester average | Annual average |
|---|---|---|---|
| 1998 Jan–June | 3 | 2.94 | |
| 1998 July–Dec | 10 | 16.00 | 12.99 |
| 1999 Jan–June | 3 | 16.73 | |
| 1999 July–Dec | 14 | 14.96 | 15.27 |
| 2000 Jan–June | 4 | 16.25 | |
| 2000 July–Dec | 41 | 20.39 | 20.03 |
| 2001 Jan–June | 36 | 21.27 | |
| 2001 July–Dec | 23 | 24.33 | 22.46 |

water. It is little wonder that one-third of the groups have not relocated to their newly purchased land.

In addition to the difficult living conditions that they face, the high rates of abandonment are also attributable to beneficiaries' fear that they will not be able to repay the large debts that they have acquired. Among the 10 742 families that received credit during Fontierras' first three years of operation, the average household incurred $2400 of debt before interest; 431 families acquired debts of $5000 or more. Meanwhile, the households on the three most successful farms identified by Fontierras earn an average of $53 per month, less than one-third of the minimum wage. As leaders from one peasant group observed, 'The high prices paid for land create an unbearable debt'. The leaders from another group concurred, 'The farms are expensive and barely productive... sometimes our colleagues get sad once they receive their land and they become aware of the debt that they must face'. Indeed, many 'beneficiaries' maintain that their economic situation was better before they acquired their land.[27] Most families are reliant upon income earned away from the farm; many have resorted to work as illegal immigrants in the USA.

Officials at the land fund are well aware of the hurdles faced by their borrowers. Among a sample of 160 farms, fund officials determined that 19% had a low probability of success while another 37% had an average probability of success.[28] Given the high debts that they face and their limited chances of success, many 'beneficiaries' determine that the actual benefits of owning a poor quality piece of land that lacks basic services are not justified by the costs, and abandon their groups.

*Corruption and lack of transparency*

Despite the dogma supporting market-based agrarian reform, its implementation in Guatemala has failed to eliminate corruption and improve transparency. During its eight years of operation Fontierras has been marred by allegations of profiteering and political manoeuvring.[29] The land fund has been criticised for the politically motivated redistribution of land, excessive payments to landowners, and for authorising the sale of lands known to be either unproductive, protected or even, in some cases, nonexistent. Employees of the fund who maintain dubious relations with landlords are said to discourage peasants from negotiating low prices for their land. Similarly, anomalies have been observed in the evaluation of land prices, including the presence of commission-earning intermediaries who maintain ties with Fontierras staff. Signs of corruption are also evident in the administration of the technical assistance intended to help beneficiaries implement productive projects on their newly purchased land. Although the peasant groups supposedly have the freedom to choose their providers of technical assistance, many claim that they have been obliged to contract with agencies that are owned by Fontierras staff or have fund employees working for them.

In addition to fraud among its lower ranks, the fund's image has been tarnished by allegations that its board of directors is often subject to political pressure. As the World Bank acknowledged in its 2006 evaluation of the project, 'a pattern of political interventions into the actions of the Fontierras Board of Directors led to accusations of non-transparent decisionmaking by the institution'.[30] According to its congressional charter, Fontierras was established as an autonomous entity governed by a board of directors representing various public interests, including representatives of peasant organisations, indigenous groups, agricultural co-operatives and agribusiness. Two of the board's seven members are representatives of the Ministry of Finance and the Ministry of Agriculture. Given that the power of the government appointees extends well beyond the functioning of Fontierras, many observers claim that the Guatemalan presidency maintains a disproportionate share of power that severely weakens the fund's purported autonomy.

The politicisation of Fontierras was illustrated in September 2004, when the board fired 40 members of its land regularisation team. Although the employees were ostensibly dismissed as part of an organisational restructuring, many—including the fired workers themselves—believe that it was because they failed to protect the interests of large landowners. The team was widely respected for its objectivity, experience and competence. Nonetheless, its actions were apparently inconsistent with the aims of the Guatemalan presidency and its loyalty to the country's wealthy elite, so it was replaced with new employees who were more sympathetic to the administration's allegiances.

*Regularization and the commodification of land*

In addition to financing land purchases by organized peasants, Fontierras also has the responsibility of regularising land tenure in the Guatemalan countryside. In theory adjudicating the landholdings of poor and indigenous farmers should enhance their property rights and improve their access to agricultural credit and other productive resources. In practice, however, the process has done little to improve the security of peasants' landholdings or to enhance their productive capacity. In fact, rather than improving smallholders' access to credit, it is thought that land regularisation in Guatemala has only increased the supply of credit available to medium-sized commercial farmers and occasioned a greater concentration of land.

Rather than empowering farmers or facilitating the progressive redistribution of land, the objective of land regularisation is to fortify the functioning of land markets. The process has privileged private property over collective ownership and other forms of holding land. Land plays an important role in the cosmology of Guatemala's predominantly Mayan rural population. Working the land is a means of expressing cultural identity and holdings are often managed by loosely bound communities, clans and extended families.[31] Privatising land via regularisation removes it from this cultural context. Moreover, the campaign has not been accompanied with the technical assistance or access to capital that would enhance the productivity of land. Instead, regularisation has converted land from a cultural and economic asset into a generic commodity that can be easily bought and sold in the marketplace.

The commodification of land via regularisation has stimulated its market exchange in Guatemala. In many regions of the country—specifically, the Petén, Alta and Baja Verapaz, and the area around Quetzaltenango—one-fifth of the land that is regularised is immediately sold. In some instances landowners use the titling process itself to transfer the land to third parties.

Most of the exchanges facilitated by regularisation are to the benefit of the landed elite and foreign capital. Faced with economic or political pressure, poor peasants are often forced to sell good quality land or parcels that are rich with minerals and other natural resources. For example, many poor peasants sell their land not because they want to abandon agriculture, but rather to acquire cash for the purchase of basic needs or to finance migration. In some areas of the country, particularly Alta and Baja Verapaz, large landholders have pressured their peasant neighbours to sell-off their most productive lands. Despite highly publicised—and paralysing—protests by Guatemala's indigenous population, the emphasis on land titling in resource-rich areas of the country has also played an important role in reopening the country to extraction of minerals and other primary products by foreign-owned capital.[32] In short, land regularisation has not secured the asset base of poor farmers. Instead, it has increased their vulnerability to losing their land. By transferring preferred lands from the weakest and most economically vulnerable segments of the rural population, the regularisation of land is not alleviating agrarian inequality, but exacerbating it.

*From land reform to land rentals*

With the many failures associated with its land access programme, Fontierras has dramatically altered its agrarian strategy in recent years. Instead of supporting market-assisted land *redistribution*, it has shifted its resources and focus to subsidised land *rentals*. Although land rentals were authorised under the 1999 Law of Fontierras, the strategy was not initiated until May 2004. Since that time land rentals have become the fund's principal means of improving access to land.

The change in Guatemala's agrarian strategy coincides with the World Bank's recent emphasis upon land rentals over land sales. The shift in focus stems from the theoretical argument that leasing land is likely to be more efficient than its outright exchange.[33] Of course, given that land rentals do not entail a full transfer of land rights, they are not as effective as land redistribution in terms of alleviating rural inequality.

The rental programme in Guatemala provides three forms of assistance, the monetary values of which have varied over the years. The principal benefits are nine months of interest-free credit and a subsidy for expenditures on working capital, agricultural inputs and food. Beneficiaries also receive two bags of chemical fertiliser, 25 pounds of hybrid corn seed, and a tool kit. Table 2 shows the amounts available for subsidies and credit in 2004 and 2005. As it illustrates, total support fell by 16.7% even as the amount of credit increased. The difference was made up with a 40% reduction in the amount of the subsidy.

In principle the land rental programme is targeted at poor and extremely poor peasant farmers who live in subsistence and below-subsistence conditions. Peasant organisations have tried to ensure that the objective is achieved by registering their poorest members. In certain areas of the country, however, the necessary forms are being distributed in the name of various members of Congress. In some instances the political representatives sell the forms for as much as $6.70, thereby discouraging many poor farmers. Anonymous informants have suggested that Fontierras staff tacitly approve of the politicisation of the rental process, once again hinting at the possibility of corruption.

Figure 2 compares the achievements of the current programmes in redistributing and renting land in Guatemala. As it demonstrates, during its three years of operation the land rental programme has benefited more than double the number of families than the strategy of subsidised land purchases. Nonetheless, it has provided access to less than one-fifth of the amount of land. Redistributing nine hectares per family, the land-purchasing programme provides the average beneficiary with nearly 12 times the amount of land accessed by the average renter (who paid for the temporary use of a mere 0.77 hectares).

TABLE 2. Benefits associated with Fontierras' land rental programme

| | | Subsidies | | |
| --- | --- | --- | --- | --- |
| Year | Total benefit | Working capital | Agricultural inputs and food | Credit |
| 2004 | $400 | $173 | $93 | $133 |
| 2005 | $333 | $93 | $67 | $173 |

*Source*: Based upon information gathered in a workshop with directors of the Coordinating Committee of Peasant Unity (CUC) and in Fontierras, *Memoria de Labores, 2004*, Guatemala: Fontierras, 2004.

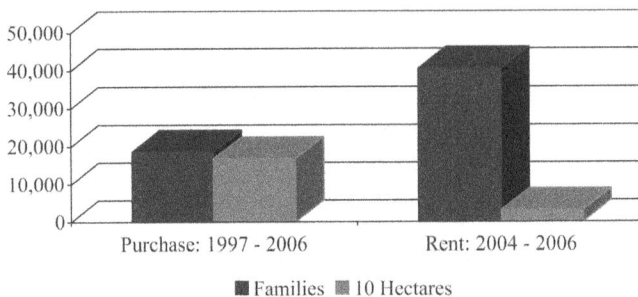

FIGURE 2. Comparison of the achievements of the land purchase and land rental programme. *Sources*: Fontierras, *Diagnostico Situacional del Fondo de Tierras*; Fontierras, 2004; Fontierras, *Memoria de Labores, 2005*, Guatemala: Fontierras, 2005; Fontierras, *Memoria de Labores, 2006*, Guatemala: Fontierras, 2006.

116

One achievement that cannot be quantified is the difference between the *ownership* that arises from purchasing land and the *access* that comes with renting. Land is more than an input for growing crops, it is also an asset. As the amount of land owned by poor farmers increases, so does their economic security, social prestige and political power. Moreover, farmers who own land have greater incentive to invest in sustainable agricultural practices like terracing, using organic fertilisers, rotating crops or intercropping, and planting trees. The land rental programme may placate demands for land in the short run, but it does little to level Guatemala's heavily tilted socioeconomic landscape. Large landlords maintain their position of power and receive income even though they do not work the land, while renters receive little more than the temporary right to use a parcel of land and only a portion of the returns from their labour.

Despite—or, perhaps, because of—the land rental programme's failure to redress Guatemala's unequal distribution of land ownership, it has become the preferred means for addressing the country's agrarian question. In 2006 Fontierras only provided credit for one group of 42 families to purchase a farm. At the same time it assisted 10 98 families to rent land, providing them with six times the amount of subsidies and credit allocated to land buyers.[34] One reason for favouring the rental programme is its relative cost. Market-assisted land reform is an incredibly expensive means of distributing land. Given their shorter time frame—one year of land use versus perpetuity of land ownership—rental programmes allow Fontierras to attend to the immediate demands of land-hungry peasants at a much lower cost. While it may not empower beneficiaries to the degree that land redistribution does, subsidised rentals provide a short-term solution to the demand for land without upsetting Guatemala's underlying power structure. Indeed, with its greater visibility and quick accomplishments, the motivation for shifting the focus to land rentals may be more political than economic.

## Conclusion

Even as the signing of the Guatemalan Peace Accords more than a decade ago raised the hope of redressing the extreme socioeconomic inequalities that had fuelled nearly four decades of violent conflict, the land reform strategy outlined in the agreement planted the seeds of its own failure. Although it promised otherwise, the market-led strategy that it is embodied in the accords has not improved poor Guatemalans' access to land and, paradoxically, rather than alleviating poverty, it has burdened many of its intended beneficiaries with debt. During its eight years of operation the strategy has facilitated the distribution of a mere 4% of agricultural land, most of it is overpriced and of poor quality and little productive potential.

By pressing for the adoption of market-assisted land reform as *the* solution to the primary source of contention during Guatemala's civil war, the World Bank and International Monetary fund have betrayed and undermined the spirit of the peace accords in the name of economic liberalisation. In a country where three-quarters of the rural population lives in poverty, Guatemala's land reform programme has prioritised efficiency over poverty alleviation and rural development. Given its dependence on the repayment of loans, market-assisted land reform does not necessarily benefit the neediest peasants. Instead, it targets farmers with the greatest entrepreneurial potential. Yet, even in its quest to transform peasants into 'new market citizens', the agrarian strategy has failed, as it does not provide farmers with the necessary training and appropriate quality of land to succeed in the marketplace. The purported 'efficiency' of the decentralised approach creates so many transaction costs for land-hungry peasants that many of them drop out of the process. Among those who see it through, many are so disappointed by the squalid conditions of their new landholdings that they abandon them.

In part, the failure of market-assisted land reform in Guatemala can be attributed to its vision of land as a commodity. While there may be plenty of willing buyers, wealthy landholders are unwilling to sell their property. Their reluctance is not because the price is too low, but rather because price does not matter. As elsewhere, land is a source of political power and social prestige in Guatemala. It also provides security against the instability of Guatemala's export-oriented economy. In short, land is an asset, the transfer of which could greatly empower the country's rural poor. Like their wealthy counterparts, Guatemala's rural poor view land ownership as a means of improving their economic, political and social well-being. For the peasantry's predominantly Mayan majority, land ownership is also a means of cultivating maize and beans for food security and, ultimately, of practising their cultural heritage.

Given the many non-market values associated with land ownership, it is foolhardy to think that market mechanisms alone are enough to spur its redistribution. Guatemalan policy makers have apparently come to this realisation. Government leaders recently refused what would have been the second of three World Bank loans to support market-assisted land reform in Guatemala. The strategy has been virtually abandoned by Fontierras. In its place has emerged a land rental programme that placates some of the immediate demand for land, but ultimately benefits the landed elite with state-subsidised land transactions. The rental programme not only fails to redress the deep economic inequalities that plague Guatemala and underpin its political instability, it exacerbates them.

Although the current Guatemalan constitution is biased towards the sanctity of private property, it also offers the possibility of a more comprehensive land reform policy. Specifically, Article 40 allows for the expropriation of land for social progress, so long as owners are justly compensated in due time. A new approach to redistributing land is necessary and warranted in Guatemala.[35] It is justified on several grounds, including the following. First, as a means for alleviating rural poverty and empowering the country's historically marginalised peasantry and indigenous population. Second, given that small farmers tend to use land more productively than largeholders, land redistribution would improve overall agricultural productivity in the country. Third, reallocating land from large agro-export plantations to small-scale farmers who tend to cultivate staple crops for domestic consumption would enhance Guatemala's national food sovereignty. Fourth, justice will only be served when Guatemala's indigenous population can reclaim the stolen land that is their heritage. Finally, Guatemala's 1996 Peace Accords call for a 'firm and lasting peace'. Such a peace will not be achieved until the inequitable distribution of land, which underpinned the civil war and continues to be the source of political conflict, is resolved.

## Notes

We are grateful for helpful comments from Saturnino M Borras, Jr and two anonymous referees. The usual disclaimers apply.

1 The findings for this evaluation of market-assisted land reform in Guatemala are based upon several years of investigation, beginning in 1999, and a variety of research methodologies. Much of the data emerged from consultative workshops that were held in four regions of the country with representatives of 23 communities who had purchased land through the market-led agrarian reform, and from field visits to a representative sample of eight communities. The study is also based upon interviews with representatives of Washington-based international financial organisations (including the World Bank and the Inter-American Development Bank), with officials from Guatemala's land trust fund and the government's Ministry of Agriculture, and with leaders of peasant groups and other civil society organisations. Additional data were gathered through documentary analysis of primary and secondary sources.

2 For a succinct summary of the market-led paradigm, see SM Borras, 'Questioning market-led agrarian reform: experiences from Brazil, Columbia and South Africa', *Journal of Agrarian Change*, 3 (3), 2003, pp 367–394.

3 K Deininger & H Binswanger, 'The evolution of the World Bank's land policy: principles, experience, and future challenges', *World Bank Research Observer*, 14 (2), 1999, pp 247–276; and K Deininger, 'Making negotiated land reform work: initial experience from Columbia, Brazil, and South Africa', *World Development*, 27 (4), 1999, pp 651–672.

4 K Deininger, *Land Policies for Growth and Poverty Reduction*, Washington, DC: World Bank/Oxford University Press, 2003.

5 A number of empirical studies has observed an inverse relationship between farm size and productivity, including RA Berry & WR Cline, *Agrarian Structure and Productivity in Developing Countries*, Baltimore, MD: Johns Hopkins University Press, 1979; and RJ Herring, *Land to the Tiller: The Political Economy of Agrarian Reform in South Asia*, New Haven, CT: Yale University Press, 1983.

6 Deininger, 'Making negotiated land reform work'.

7 Deininger, *Land Policies for Growth and Poverty Reduction*; Deininger & Binswanger, 'The evolution of the World Bank's land policy'; and Deininger, 'Making negotiated land reform work'.

8 A Banerjee, *Land Reforms: Prospects and Strategies*, Massachusetts Institute of Technology Department of Economics Working Paper 99-24, 1999.

9 Borras, 'Questioning market-led agrarian reform'.

10 Instituto Nacional Estadística (INE), *IV Censo Agropecuario: Características Generales de las Fincas Censales y de Productoras y Productores Agropecuarios*, Guatemala: INE, 2004.

11 A Gini coefficient is a measure of inequality that ranges from 0 to 1. A coefficient of 0 represents perfect equality, while a coefficient of 1 represents extreme inequality.

12 J Handy, *Revolution in the Countryside: Rural Conflict and Agrarian Reform in Guatemala, 1944–1954*, Chapel Hill, NC: University of North Carolina Press, 1994; and Handy, *Gift of the Devil: A History of Guatemala*, Boston, MA: South End Press, 1984.

13 Interview with URNG representative and signatory to the Socio-economic Accord, Pablo Monsanto, 23 May 2001.

14 S Jonas, *Of Centaurs and Doves*, Boulder, CO: Westview Press, 2000.

15 *Ibid*, pp 220–222.

16 CD Deere & M León, *Mujer y Tierra en Guatemala*, Asociación para el Avance de las Ciencias Sociales en Guatemala (AVANCSO), Serie Autores Invitados, No 4, Guatemala City: AVANCSO, 1999, p 39.

17 Jonas, *Of Centaurs and Doves*, p 182. See also J Pearce, 'From civil war to "civil society": has the end of the Cold War brought peace to Central America?', *International Affairs*, 74 (3), 1998, 587–615.

18 INE, *IV Censo Agropecuario*.

19 World Bank, *Implementation Completion Report (SCL-44320) on a Loan in the Amount of US$23 Million to the Republic of Guatemala for a Land Fund Project*, Washington, 2006.

20 *Ibid*, p 15.

21 B Garoz, A Alonso & S Gauster, *La Balance de las Políticas de Tierra del Banco Mundial en Guatemala: 1996–2005*, Guatemala: CONGCOOP, 2005.

22 Interview with an official from the Land Access Division of Fontierras, 17 December 2001.

23 R El-Ghohnemy, *The Political Economy of Market-based Land Reform*, UNRISD Discussion Paper No 104, Geneva: UNRISD, 1999.

24 Garoz *et al*, *La Balance de las Políticas de Tierra del Banco Mundial en Guatemala*.

25 Jonas, *Of Centaurs and Doves*, pp 171–176; and R Hernández Alarcón, *The Land Issue in the Peace Accords: A Summary of the Government's Response*, Guatemala: Inforpress Centroamericana, 1998.

26 B Dardón, 'Buscan dinamizar papel de Fontierras', *Prensa Libre*, 5 March 2006.

27 B Garoz & S Gauster, *Aportes a la Definición e Impulso de una Estrategia de Transformación y Desarrollo en el Area Rural de Guatemala*, Guatemala: CONGCOOP, 2006.

28 Fontierras, *Diagnostico Situacional del Fondo de Tierras*, Acta 37-2005 del Consejo Directivo del Fontierras del 6/06/05, Guatemala, 2005.

29 Land Fund Institute in Crisis, Central America Report, 33 (26), 2006; and M del Cid, 'Corrupción en Fontierras', *Prensa Libre*, 23 December 2005.

30 World Bank, *Implementation Completion Report*, p 9.

31 LR Goldin, 'Work and ideology in the Maya highlands of Guatemala: economic beliefs in the context of occupational change', *Economic Development and Cultural Change*, 41 (1), 1992, pp 103–123.

32 E Holt-Giménez, 'Territorial restructuring and the grounding of agrarian reform: indigenous communities, gold mining and the World Bank', paper presented at the Institute for Social Studies, The Hague, January 2006.

33 The theoretical argument for rentals is outlined in E Sadoulet, R Murgal & A de Janvry, 'Access to land via land rental markets', in A de Janvry, G Gordillo, JP Platteau & E Sadoulet (eds), *Access to Land, Rural Poverty, and Public Action*, Oxford; Oxford University Press, 2001.

34 Fondo de Tierras, *Resultados 2006*, at http://www.fontierras.gob.gt/?mnu=5&sec=1.

35 The National Coordination of Peasant Organizations (CNOC) has proposed a viable strategy for comprehensive agrarian reform in Guatemala. See Coordinadora Nacional de Organizaciones Campesinas, *Propuesta de Reforma Agraria Integral*, Guatemala: CNOC, 2005.

# The Politics of Peace and Resettlement through El Salvador's Land Transfer Programme: caught between the state and the market

ARIANE DE BREMOND

On 31 January 1992 representatives of the government of El Salvador and the Farabundo Martí National Liberation Front (FMLN) signed peace accords in Chapultepec, Mexico, marking the official end to almost 12 years of civil war in El Salvador. In El Salvador, a land-scarce, heavily settled country with the highest population density in the Central American region, a key issue of the civil war had been the inequitable distribution of land. Of all the Central American countries, it has been the most plagued by rural landlessness.[1] And while the peace accords articulated detailed agreements regarding reforms to the military and police apparatus, and contained provisions for some land reform, they fell far short of what leaders and the rank and file of the FMLN had hoped for in terms of socioeconomic change. In this 'negotiated revolution' land reform was a political imperative, integral to the demobilisation and reinsertion of combatants, rather than a tool for any systematic resolution of the problems of landlessness.

In the transitional period between state- and market-led land reform approaches in the policies of international development institutions, a land transfer programme not completely of the new generation but neither of the old—a state–market hybrid—was born in El Salvador. Over the six years following the signing of the accords, 10% of the nation's agricultural land (totalling over 103 300 hectares) was transferred to ex-combatants of both sides and to civilian supporters of the FMLN through the accord-mandated Land Transfer Programme known as the Programa de Transferencia de Tierras (PTT).[2] Categories of land to be transferred through the PTT included properties belonging to the state, properties exceeding the 1983 constitutional limit of 245 hectares, and private properties in delimited 'conflictive zones' offered up voluntarily for sale. Transactions were to take place at market prices in accordance with the 1980s agrarian reform terms of payment (to be made over 30 years with a four-year grace period for principal and interest, and at a fixed annual interest rate of 6%) through a Land Bank established for that purpose. Eligible beneficiaries included ex-combatants from both the FMLN and the Salvadoran military (FAES) as well as civilian supporters of the FMLN known as *tenedores* (landholders), most of whom had resided and farmed land in the conflictive zones through the war years. Although the accords stipulated that land ownership could be individual or associative, the form that property rights would take would come to constitute one of the fundamental points of contention between the two sides in the post-war years. Although the PTT retained some modes of implementation character-istic of previous state-led efforts, such as the use of a national Land Bank as financial intermediary, and initially issued associative titles, it was the voluntary, market-price approach to land transfer that defines the PTT as one of the first of the generation of market-assisted agrarian reform (MLAR) approaches now constituting the mainstay of multilateral land policy. By 2000 over 36 000 people had received land through the PTT and an additional programme had been created to parcelise and individually title all PTT lands that had formerly been deeded collectively.[3]

For ex-combatants and returned refugees throughout the ex-conflictive zones of the country, the post-war resettlement of agrarian landscapes was a process of transition with important consequences for present and future livelihoods. From where people would live, to what land they would farm, or whether they would even farm at all, the war, followed by peace, and more specifically by agrarian resettlement though the land transfer programme, were processes that profoundly shaped people's access to resources, livelihood options, and patterns of land use in resettled communities.

### A new agrarian agenda: neoliberalism and land

In the case of Central America, where civil war raged during the 1980s, land policy of the most recent decades has been intimately entwined with issues of peace building and conflict prevention. Indeed, in much of Central America today discussions of land use continue to be thoroughly enmeshed with legacies of war, peace and resettlement. Each year millions of people around the world return to their countries or regions of origin to resettle land and rebuild their lives and livelihoods. Because displacement usually occurs in response to war and civil conflict, return and resettlement often unfold in the midst or aftermath of inter- or intrastate conflict. In these situations, where political, economic and social conditions are fragile *and* contentious, land-related challenges associated with post-conflict reconstruction are often substantial.

Land issues have also become the subject of renewed attention in development policy debates. Market-based reform, in particular, has commanded much attention in recent years. The 1990s saw a great expansion of market-based land policy reforms in Latin America, as recognition in the international lending community of the centrality of land as an asset for rural livelihoods led to an expansion of support for land-related policy programming.[4] In its first public pronouncement on the land issue in 28 years, a Policy Research Report (PRR) entitled *Land Policies for Growth and Poverty Reduction*, the World Bank asserts that land policies of this new generation should emphasise growth, equity enhancement and environmental sustainability, dedicating careful attention to the diverse range of socio-economic and political contexts in which specific policies and programmes are to be embedded.

The PRR shows promising advances in the Bank's thinking on land issues and represents a departure from the ways of the past. In particular, the report emphasises the relevance of land issues to the broader contexts of social conflict and post-conflict situations and suggests that market-based approaches are less political, and thus less conflictive, than their state-led predecessors. In practice, however, implementation of market-led approaches to land reform within the World Bank's land policy portfolio are revealing different realities. Of central concern is the tendency for MLAR to treat land reform as an historical and apolitical project that can seemingly be remedied through improved technological innovation for the maintenance of private property via updated registry and cadastral systems, despite calls from within for sensitivity to political context. As has been shown in countries such as Mexico,[5] and South Africa and Colombia,[6] far from depoliticising land reform, MLAR has proven to be charged with the power and politics characterising previous state-led approaches, often falling short in its provision of even the most basic asset distribution in the form of land and of the services and support required to maintain it.

This paper describes the politics and outcomes of El Salvador's state–market hybrid land transfer. As a land reform that took place in the context of a negotiated settlement to civil war and the liberalisation of the Salvadoran economy as prescribed by the international financial institutions (IFIs) and the USA in the early 1990s, the PTT—and the ongoing contentions that occurred around it—challenge the notion that market-based approaches are inherently less political. Rather, the PTT evidences the challenges to land transfer/reform when it occurs within the context of, and according to, modalities of economic liberalization, modalities which, I argue, in the case of El Salvador fundamentally circumscribed—though did not entirely limit—the potential for reform to enhance livelihoods and support appropriate environmentally sound land use in land transfer communities. Such a critique of El Salvador's hybrid PTT provides further support for claims being made by scholars monitoring the effects of MLAR in other countries, such as the Philippines, that such an approach severely undermines efforts at needed redistributive reform by the state.[7]

The paper is organised into four sections. Section one situates the PTT in the context of El Salvador's historical political economy and civil war during the 1980s. Section two recounts the story of the long and contentious process of negotiating and implementing the terms of agrarian resettlement, demonstrating the politicised nature of land transfer in the wake of war. Section three describes the subsequent debt crisis, popular mobilisation, and parcelisation of the PTT lands that occurred on the heels of the transfer process as a means of illustrating how popular mobilization, coupled with international support of the peace process and continued commitment of agrarian activists within the FMLN, served to reshape the untenable terms of debt wrought by the market-based approach, as well as to guarantee popular participation in the parcelisation of the collectively deeded properties. Section four concludes with a discussion of the outcomes and implications of the PTT for future land reform efforts.

## Land and economy in the making of modern El Salvador

The roots of agrarian inequality in El Salvador can be traced to the introduction of a series of changes in the rules of ownership and rights to land for cultivation by the colonial Spanish in the 16th century, but the most dramatic shift in land rights and land use would not occur until much later, with the rise in world demand for coffee in the late 19th century.[8] Indian communal lands in the western highlands of the country were especially suitable for coffee. Increasing demand for land and for workers to manage burgeoning coffee plantations led the emerging elite of the state and coffee growers to abolish communal forms of tenure in the early 1880s at a time when over 40% of the land nationwide was owned by traditional peasant communities.[9] A centralised rural police force was put in place in order to enforce vagrancy laws (obligating those who owned little or no land to work for between one-third and half of the year to supply labour to the growing agricultural export economy) and to protect these now private properties.[10] Such laws forced many of these dispossessed to become *colonato*, is an institution that binds workers and families to large estates and ensuring a permanent workforce. Others became migrant labourers or squatted on smallholdings on the periphery of the coffee regions and in the northern departments of the country.

While 'regime elites' enforced conditions of labour and property rights that would guarantee the agro-export economy's smooth functioning, military hardliners provided the repressive apparatus to keep 'peace' in the countryside and guarantee access to needed land and labour.[11] This 'protection racket', whereby the military exaggerated the extent of 'communist' threats to elite interests in order to maintain military prerogatives and to justify the expansion of the coercive apparatus of the state would come to produce the social powder keg that would explode into civil war by 1980.[12]

*Too little, too late: war and land reform in the 1980s*

The land transfer negotiated through the 1992 Peace Accords was not El Salvador's first attempt at reform. In 1980, in a futile effort to stave off impending civil war, the governing civilian – military junta announced the most reaching reform to ever take place in the country. By that point, however, state-sponsored violence had intensified greatly. During that year, before overt combat between the army and the guerillas began in January 1981, it is estimated that over 10 000 campesinos had been killed, with many of those murders attributed to right-wing death squads.[13] The reform moved swiftly to expropriate hundreds of properties, taking many of the largest estates in the first phase of what would be a multi-phased process. The far right reacted strongly and, with a formal alliance between the governing Christian Democratic Party (PDC) and the military, a network of death squads was built up with the support of hard-line military factions that brought escalating violence in the form of targeted assassinations, interrogations and torture throughout the country.[14] Hoping to pre-empt a popular-leftist victory in El Salvador and to create and perpetuate instead a moderate reformist government, the USA pushed hard to assure Salvadoran government compliance with the agrarian reform, despite major resistance.[15] While transfer of one-fifth of the nation's farmland through these reforms represented the biggest shift in El Salvador's distribution of land since the 1881 – 82 outlawing of communal lands, the degree to which the reforms had a corrective effect on landlessness was limited. Phase I had benefited only those who worked full time on the farm before the reform, by default 'omitting the poorest within the sector—the landless, the land poor and the squatter',[16] while Phase II was never implemented. Phase III did, to a limited extent, benefit tenants, sharecroppers and squatters. Overall, however, very few of those without prior access to land gained land through the 1980s reforms.[17]

*What's the market got to do with it? Peace in the era of economic liberalisation*

By the late 1980s El Salvador's economy had undergone profound transformations; external shocks and internal political strife combined to decimate the Salvadoran economy.[18] Partly thanks to the 1980s land reforms and partly as a result of the shift in economic interests within the ruling classes that had occurred during the war period, with a move from agriculture to a more diversified portfolio of economic interests that emphasised non-traditional agricultural and industrial exports, the powerful elite, linked to the traditional agro-export based model, had been significantly weakened.[19] The economic model which had guided El Salvador through the previous 100 years had been fundamentally altered.[20]

It was the alternation of this economic order that in part provided the possibility of peace. As the new business elite gradually came to realise that they did not have to depend on the military to advance their political interests but could do so themselves, the power of the armed forces to intervene in politics further weakened.[21] By the end of the 1980s the FMLN offensive on the capital, the subsequent murder of six Jesuit priests, their housekeeper and her daughter, and the resultant outrage and sharp cut in aid to the Salvadoran government from the US Congress made room for a compromise that would result in the negotiation of peace agreements over the next several years. This culminated in the signing of the final set of accords in January 1992.

The newly elected rightist ARENA administration under the leadership of Alfredo Cristiani moved rapidly to open the Salvadoran economy. With the rise of the ARENA to power, the USA had secured a government partner willing to implement US neoliberal economic policy in El Salvador.[22] The peace accords and associated land transfer programme would unfold within this context of economic austerity wrought by adjustment and economic liberalisation, posing major obstacles to peace.

### The Salvadoran peace accords: the terms of a negotiated revolution

The final agreement signed by the parties at the beginning of 1992 embodied a set of commitments for both the government and the FMLN. Assembled through six principal agreements, the accords included provisions for the demilitarisation of the country, the transformation and reduction of the FAES, the substitution of the former military police by a new National Civil Police, the Policía Nacional Civil (PNC), judicial reform, electoral reform, the demobilisation of the FMLN and, lastly, economic and social measures that included the provisions for the reintegration of combatants into civilian life, with the most significant of these being land.[23] Under the series of agreements signed in the lead-up to the signing of the formal overall peace agreement the UN would provide substantial assistance in verifying the implementation of the agreements embodied in the peace accords through its verification mission, the United Nations Observer Mission in El Salvador (ONUSAL).[24]

The foremost priority of the negotiation process for the FMLN was to secure a post-war environment that would allow their transition from an insurgent organisation to a viable political party. Dismantling the oppressive police apparatus, undertaking military reform, and securing guarantees for FMLN participation in the political process were all reforms that were seen by the FMLN as critical foundations for peace. In coming to the negotiating table, the FMLN had agreed not to challenge the basic economic foundations of the country in exchange for ARENA's willingness to significantly reduce the power of the armed forces.[25] This strategy, added to the fact that the negotiation of these issues had absorbed most of the timetable of the negotiations—leaving the socioeconomic components until last—is the reason why the socioeconomic aspects of the accords—and, more specifically, the transformation of agrarian property rights—turned out, in the end, to be so limited.[26]

## The socioeconomic accords and the terms for land transfer

However tiny (Graciana del Castillo)[27]

While the conclusion of the negotiations left many of the socioeconomic issues undefined, the agreement did specifically include the land transfer to former combatants and civilian supporters of the FMLN, along with the extension of credits for agriculture and micro-enterprise.[28] As for measures to address the broader issues of socioeconomic inequity, the accords mandated the creation of a forum for labour, business and government for public debate to discuss measures to alleviate the social cost of structural adjustment programmes—a weak tool given the scope of the challenge. A National Reconstruction Plan, or Plan de Reconstrucción Nacional (PRN), was created to target the conflicted zones and to carry out programmes to help members of the FMLN re-enter civilian life.

According to the agreements, credit was to be provided to beneficiaries in order to purchase land, with additional credits available for agricultural production and technical assistance. Short-term (agricultural training, distribution of agricultural tools, basic household goods, and academic instruction) and medium-term (credit for production purposes and technical assistance) programmes would also complement the land programme. But many significant challenges lay ahead: some issues in the text of the accords were overly specific, while others lacked definition, creating a series of constraints for implementation. Under New York Agreement II, embodied in the final text of the accords, private lands to be acquired by the government and transferred through the Land Bank to beneficiaries would be those lands 'voluntarily offered for sale by their owners through transactions at market prices'.[29] The terms of financing meant that beneficiaries would repay government loans in accordance with the agrarian reform terms of payment (to be made over 30 years with a four-year grace period for principal and interest, and a fixed annual interest rate of 6%).

The stipulation that owners had to offer their land for sale voluntarily was a significant departure from past modalities of agrarian reform, such as those employed by the 1980s state-led reform, where land was expropriated and owners were usually paid with government bonds. In this respect, the land programme of the peace accords became one of the first generation of the MLAR approaches now constituting the mainstay of multilateral land policy. While still a hybrid in that the land transfer was mandated through the peace accords, the market-based character of implementation remained an essential factor shaping the way that reform would affect landscapes and people. The voluntary nature of land sales made the land agreements instantly more difficult to implement—land became harder to acquire and to finance because of the complexity involved in finding appropriate matches between sellers willing to sell in locations desired by ex-combatants, and because of the post-war hike in land prices driven by speculation.[30] Additionally, the repayment terms (the same as in the agrarian reform) also created difficulties for financing: since the government had not honored past bonds of the agrarian reform, further bond financing became infeasible.

*The (long and contested) road to implementing the land-related components of the peace accords*

The signing of the Chapultepec agreement marked the beginning of the difficult and contentious process of implementing the post-conflict transition. At the time of the signing of the Accords most of the framework of the land related components, including even the most central parameters such as the total number of potential beneficiaries, the amount and quality of land to be received, and the terms and amount of credit that would be offered by the government, were undefined. In addition, the term 'conflict zone' used in the accords was loosely defined, resulting in a great degree of ambiguity in terms of understanding which parcels of land were to qualify for the programme.[31] The issues of quantity and quality of land received remained highly contested terrain in the struggle to implement the peace accords. The FMLN hoped that, by securing decent conditions for development in the ex-conflictive zones, the political base of support could be secured, with the thick networks and organisational structure that still existed from the war transitioning to become the organisational networks needed to create alternative rural agrarian organisation and livelihood improvements.

By September 1992 the inability to resolve differing expectations in determining the shape of the programme had produced a widening gulf between the parties. By October the FMLN had halted the third of its five phases of demobilisation (with 20% demobilising in each phase) as a protest against the delays in the land programme. The struggle underlying these delays had to do with the desire of each side to achieve its respective political goals for the programme. For the government this meant turning over the least amount of assets (in terms of land quality, value and size) both for economic reasons as well as to deny the FMLN the political clout which it clearly hoped to derive from successful land transfer to its supporters. The specifics of the disagreements at this point pivoted on acreage to be transferred, which, the government argued, should be determined by availability (of both land and financing), with a ceiling in the domestic currency of the *colón* to be imposed on the amount paid for the lands acquired. The FMLN rejected this plan, claiming that such a ceiling would have the effect of reducing the size of plots that could be acquired, either as a result of rising land prices or of the depreciation of the *colón* over time. This was the first crisis since the signing of the peace accords that threatened to unravel the overall process. With the FMLN refusing to demobilise, the government responded by refusing to implement its commitments to armed forces purification, as these were linked to demobilisation of the FMLN. The peace process ground to a halt.

*A UN proposal: The 13 October Agreements*

On 13 October 1992, nearly 10 months after the formal signing of the accords in Mexico, the United Nations stepped in and presented what would become the terms of implementation of the PTT. According to this agreement, the form of ownership could be individual or associative, a decision to be made by the beneficiaries themselves. A form of joint land ownership known as *proindiviso* would be issued initially. The figure of *proindiviso* land titling was done largely to appease both sides. The FMLN, on one hand, hoped that joint ownership and production could be established in *unidades productivas* (UPs) and serve as a model of alternative organisation of development in the ex-conflictive zones, while the government and USAID, referring to the joint provisional *proindiviso* title status as an 'artifact' required to meet the Peace Accord implementation commitments, pushed for individual modes of productive organisation and land ownership.[32] In a letter to the General Command of the FMLN, UN Secretary-General Boutros-Ghali writes:

> I am conscious that the enclosed proposal will fully satisfy neither the FMLN nor the Government. Extensive discussions with both sides have confirmed that wide differences exist between them, especially concerning the size of plots to be transferred and the number of potential beneficiaries. The views of both sides, as well as those of outside experts from the IMF, the World Bank, and FAO, have all been given careful consideration in preparing the proposal.[33]

The 13 October agreement marked a turning point in efforts to advance the land transfers. Under the agreement 47 500 beneficiaries—7500 combatants from the FMLN, 15 000 from the armed forces and 25 000 *tenedores* in the ex-conflictive zones—were eligible under the agreement. The amount of land that would be received by each beneficiary would be determined by the soil type criteria employed by Salvadoran Institute for Agrarian Transformation (ISTA) for the previous agrarian reform (Table 1). There were concessions on both sides. For the FMLN the size of plots that beneficiaries would receive was smaller than what they had aimed for. As Shafik Hándal,

TABLE 1. 13 October UN proposal for the transfer of land per beneficiary (in hectares/*manzanas*)

| Soil type (based on ISTA Land Capability Classification System) | UN proposal |
|---|---|
| | Ha (mz) per beneficiary (ex-combatant and *tenedor*) |
| I and II | 1.4 (2 mz) |
| III and IV | 2.1 (3 mz) |
| V and VI | 3.6 (5 mz) |
| VII and VIII | 5.0 (7 mz) |

*Source*: *The United Nations and El Salvador 1990–1995*, UN Blue Books Series, Vol IV, New York: Department of Public Information/United Nations Publications, 1995.

of the General Command of the FMLN responded in a letter to the Secretary-General:

> As you yourself expected, we find the proposal unsatisfactory especially with regard to point #5 [the size of lots], which if applied rigidly, would leave no option to individual beneficiaries but to remain at their current levels of subsistence and in conditions of poverty.[34]

Noting that the government, the European Economic Community, which had a project in the department of Usulután, and the Land Bank had all advanced proposals based on larger plot sizes depending on soil categories, Hándal accepted the UN proposal on behalf of the FMLN, recognising the UN for its efforts to find a solution acceptable to all the parties and professing a desire to 'strengthen the viability of the peace process'.

The government, for its part, agreed to the terms of the UN proposal, which eliminated ceilings on land credits. For *tenedores* there were different size requirements: if the landowners of the occupied land were willing to sell, the landholders could remain on plots with a maximum size of land equal to that of the ex-combatants and a minimum size of half that amount.

The newly agreed-upon Land Transfer Program, or PTT, would take place in three phases. The first phase would address the emergency cases where state lands would be provided by the government and USAID would finance the purchases for over 15 000 beneficiaries. A second phase was added into the programme because, during the same period, the EU provided a separate set of funding that imposed different conditions for implementation. The EU requirement was to benefit FMLN and armed forces combatants in equal numbers and would focus on a particular geographic area of the country. As it did not include *tenedores*, it was planned to take place simultaneously with the first phase, so that *tenedor* landholders could be given legal status alongside ex-combatants. The third phase would transfer land to the remaining 60% of beneficiaries who did not come under the first two phases. At the time that the plan was drawn up, however, the third phase had no timeline for initiation or completion; both the financing and land would need to be found for 28 000 more beneficiaries before this phase could be implemented.[35] While some of the issues surrounding the conditions and form of the land transfer programme were determined through the October agreement, not all the challenges to implementing the accords were addressed: the agreement, for example, still failed to define the conflict zones, and lacked specifics on many of the procedural aspects of the programme. As will be shown in the next section, these lacunae, coupled with the lack of political will on the part of the government, would still make for a rocky road to implementation.

*Continued problems with implementation*

Many administrative, technical and logistical problems contributed to the long delays in implementation of the land transfer programme.[36] According to the timeline that was set in the October agreements, the land transfer programme would be implemented between October 1992 and October 1993, a timeframe that would prove to be utterly insufficient. Instead, the land transfer programme would take almost seven years to complete and require repeated negotiations between the government and the FMLN in addition to the repeated good offices on the part of the ONUSAL mission to keep the PTT moving forward.

Among the most significant of these problems were the issues of how delayed implementation affected reinsertion more broadly. Under the Chapultepec agreement, landholders were to be given agricultural credit before their land tenure was fully legalised, yet in practice very little agricultural credit was disbursed because of the high risk to the bank. Both the 1993 and 1994 planting seasons were hindered by lack of access to productive credit, resulting in the need for higher levels of food assistance from the international community. The steps for land transfer were extremely time-consuming and bureaucratic and were made no less so because of the need to conduct land transactions through voluntary sale at 'market values', which encouraged many owners to consolidate their holdings and sell off more marginal lands. The initial legal procedure for transfer of land involved 17 steps with the Land Bank (Banco de Tierras) acting as both an intermediary between buyer and seller and as a financing agency.[37]

Along with the additional problems related to measurement, appraisal and price negotiations, as well as other bureaucratic errors, another more significant set of problems had to do with the determination of who, in addition to the ex-combatants of both sides, was eligible to receive land. Under the agreement, *tendores* would be entitled to credits for lands they were occupying that were part of the land inventory submitted by the FMLN. But, in practice, many landholders were left out of the final lists. This was compounded when the verification of landholders was further complicated by new requirements that required landholders to present themselves at newly opened regional offices of the government implementing agency, OCTA, to be 're-verified', something that many people did not know that they had to do nor knew how to do. While the FMLN made the problem known, they did not provide a list of names of those who had been left out until much later, when 7285 people were presented on the FMLN's list. This problem resulted in another period of delays for implementation, all but halting the process again from December 1993 to May 1994. Urgings from the UN Secretary General, coupled with renewed donor commitments to financing eventually convinced the government to accept the bulk of the non-verified. Yet, even with this agreement from the government, the programme remained stagnant until late October 1994. Meanwhile, the lack of progress on the land transfers was hindering other related insertion programmes for agricultural credit, technical assistance and housing; as land ownership was a prerequisite for many of these programmes, delays in the land programme prohibited access.

In all, many administrative, technical and logistical issues, as well as a lack of political will on the part of government agencies responsible for specific aspects of the transfer programme, contributed to the long delays in implementation. But by 1998 the programme had settled a total

TABLE 2. Total properties titled to PTT beneficiaries (FMLN and FAES)

| Property type | Total properties | Total mz | Total beneficiaries | Millions of *colones*/US$ |
|---|---|---|---|---|
| Private | 3187 | 120 691 | 30 496 | 812.3/11.2 |
| State | 118 | 26 971 | 5593 | 11.2/1.28 |
| Total | 3305 | 147 662 | 36 089 | 923.5/105.5 |

*Source*: Adapted from A Alvarez & J Chavez, *Tierra, Conflicto y Paz*, San Salvador: CEPAZ, 2001; and *Acta de evaluación final del PTT*, GOES, FMLN, UN, October 1998.

of 36 089 beneficiaries at a cost of US$105.5 million (Table 2).[38] However, with the joint-provisional tenure status (*proindiviso*) of the majority of the properties set to expire within five years of the date of issue, a new round of tenure-related changes had only just begun.

## Debt crisis, popular mobilisation and parcelisation of the PTT lands (1995–2000)

By the mid-1990s El Salvador was poised on the verge of yet another series of transitions for the PTT sector that were, once again, very much in line with the new orthodoxy in land policy. The early post-war stages of demobilisation and reinsertion had been completed but, as a significant portion of the PTT remained, international observers of the peace process began sounding alarms. Economic liberalisation and peace were proving irreconcilable. Over the remainder of the 1990s the inability of the beneficiaries to pay the debt created through the market character of the programme would spark the largest popular mobilisation since the end of the war, further evidencing the flaws of the market-oriented elements of the PTT. The parcelisation of the PTT lands would also come to reveal how the overall liberalisation of the Salvadoran economy had rendered any other form of tenure but individual almost entirely untenable for the programme's beneficiaries.

### *Policy harmonization*

One of the key issues that became a point of contention of note to members of the international community was the issue of policy harmonisation, the relationship between peace-building measures, such as judicial, police and electoral reform, and the wider context of economic policy.[39] Leading UN officials, most notably Álvaro de Soto, the former chief mediator on behalf of the UN for the peace talks, spoke out publicly about the lack of harmonisation between structural adjustment programmes implemented by Bretton Woods institutions such as the World Bank and the IMF and peace agreements negotiated under the auspices of the UN. A subsequent study commissioned by the UN Development Programme (UNDP) further cautioned that the focus on formulaic economic policies based on macroeconomic stabilisation and structural adjustment that were being applied in the post-war period were at odds with the needs of a nation emerging from civil war and asserted that that the consolidation of peace was actually being hampered by the pursuit and application of World Bank- and IMF-mandated policies.[40] According to the study, improved co-ordination was required between strategies to implement the peace and strategies for promoting economic policy reforms. One such strategy—dubbed 'peace conditionality'—was for international lenders to make assistance to the government conditional on specific measures to implement the accords and consolidate the peace as a way to encourage the government to extend the required political will for implementation of the accords.

### New national agrarian policy and the World Bank

In addition to the challenges faced by the PTT sector from delays inherent to the process, the agricultural sector as a whole was suffering, with the smallholder sector facing ever more severe barriers to its viability.[41] Government policies for agriculture were virtually non-existent during the early half of 1990s but by 1994 a new government agricultural policy had begun to develop, largely in connection with two projected World Bank loans.[42] The two loans were designed to support an agricultural 'policy matrix' consisting of six principal objectives: finalising the transfer of properties under the terms of the Peace Accords; guaranteeing juridical security of property in land; modernising the institutional apparatus concerned with the agrarian question; consolidating and restructuring the agrarian debt; stimulating a market in land; and implanting an efficient system of rural finance.[43]

The timing of the policy matrix's development coincided with a period of intense debate within the country on the future of the 1980s agrarian reform beneficiaries as well as that of the PTT. Specifically, the method through which the agrarian debt was to be consolidated was a critical issue with implications for the survival of the co-operatives as well as the PTT sector. The World Bank had been influential in arguing for loan extensions by the Agricultural Development Bank (BFA), to be issued at commercial rates. The fear and, indeed, the possibility—for there were already plans under discussion that contemplated debt reduction combined with debt 'privatisation'—was that these new interest terms would be applied to reform and to PTT beneficiaries, forcing massive foreclosures, or at the very least, pre-emptive sales by debtors.

The second main concern regarding the policy matrix was its bias towards parcelisation.[44] Critics argued that, while it was important for land reform beneficiaries to have choices with regards to the forms of tenure (within the spectrum of individual freehold to collective), the absence of supportive policies for peasant agriculture created a climate that was severely biased against successful smallholder agricultural production.

There was much public protest and several rounds of controversy in policy circles including the US treasury, USAID and the World Bank concerning both the terms of the policy matrix as well as the largely non-participatory manner in which it had been developed. After this debate had gone on for some time, the Bank issued a policy statement disassociating the loan from any conditionality and 'committing the Bank to a fully participatory process in its conversations with the government about a new policy'.[45] In the end, almost all components of the second loan that did not have direct connection to land administration tasks were dropped. Agreeing that El Salvador needed assistance in surveying and registering rural properties, opponents of the overall policy matrix renewed support for the revised project and supported its approval. The policy matrix and subsequent lending from the Bank remained consistent with Bank land policy for the Latin American region overall. Promotion of land tenure security (primarily through individual title) has remained the mainline of policy support for property rights, along with 'land market stimulation' and some investment in alternative rural finance options.[46]

### The debt crisis and popular mobilisation

The policy matrix also recommended consolidation of the agrarian debt that had accumulated both from the 1980s reforms and the PTT (Table 3). The largest share of this $400 million debt was owed by the Phase I agrarian reform co-operatives to the implementing agency, ISTA. Additional debt from loans used to finance production was also owed to the banking system, which, stood at $228 million, with a large portion of this from accumulated interest.[47] As most of the reform beneficiaries from Phase III were small producers who financed production through family savings or private lenders (known as *coyotes*), few had accumulated large bank debts, but many had not completed payment for their land, owing an estimated $6.5 million to state financial institutions in 1995. The third major group of debtors were the PTT beneficiaries who, thanks to escalating land prices following the end of the war, were faced with much higher land debts than those of Phase III. These beneficiaries owed $72 million of accumulated land debt, with credit debt constituting an additional amount. In February 1996, in accordance with the policy matrix, the government began to work out a proposal that contemplated partial forgiveness coupled with 'privatisation' of the remainder of the debt.

TABLE 3. Agricultural sector debt (US$)*

| Lending agency | Amount |
| --- | --- |
| ISTA and Land Bank | 367 200 000 |
| FOSAFFI** | 87 680 000 |
| BFA and Fedecredito | 60 845 714 |

*Notes*: *Conversion from Salvadoran *colon* @ 1997 exchange rate of US$1 = 8.755 *colones*; **FOSAFFI (Fondo de Saneamiento y Fortalecimiento del Sistema Financiero)
*Source*: Fusades, Informe Trimestral de Coyuntura, Segundo Trimestre de 1997, Banco Central de Reserva and Ministerio de Agricultura y Ganadería, San Salvador.

By March the ARENA government had presented its proposal for debt recovery to the Legislative Assembly. Peasant organisations responded to the presentation of the proposal by asserting that its implementation would result in a reversal of agrarian reform through a rollback of gains made in the 1980s and through the PTT in providing the poor with access to land. In the following months peasant organisations grew more active in pressing for a complete cancellation of the *deuda agropecuaria* (agrarian debt) with marches of up to 5000 people convening on the Legislative Assembly to present these demands. The movement that arose to campaign for debt cancellation was an effort to defend the implemented phases of past reforms from government plans to dismantle them.[48]

In May 1996 the government passed a series of laws which reflected minor accommodation of peasant demands. Under the decrees the government would forgive 70% of the debt owned by the government (a further discount from the original proposal of 65%) in exchange for the prompt payment of the remainder within a one-year period. For the PTT beneficiaries the 30% remainder would be financed by USAID. And yet the debt movement, together with FMLN members in the legislature, pressed for further reform. By now a newly established peasant coalition, whose mission focused almost entirely on the forgiveness of the agrarian debt, the Foro Agropecuario, or Agrarian Forum, led the active national campaign. Protests continued throughout 1997, with four major marches and rallies held between July and August 1997, — the biggest peasant marches that the country had seen since the end of the war.[49]

In October the FMLN, in alignment with other factions within the legislature, passed two bills (Decrees 135 and 136) which mandated total forgiveness of all debts under 500 000 *colones* (roughly US$57 000) and 93% forgiveness of the agrarian and bank-related debt above this, with payments rescheduled on favourable terms. By November these decrees had been vetoed by President Calderón Sol. The conservative research organisation Fusades lobbied heavily against condemnation of the debt, arguing in a section of its 1997 second trimester report entitled, *Por que no condonar?* (Why we should not forgive?) that debt forgiveness was against the constitution, would be unfair to the non-reformed agricultural sector that had also suffered during the war, that this sector had already received benefits in terms of debt discounting, and that these amounted to nothing less than free transfers from the state to these producers. It further asserted that such a benefit to the reformed sector represented an unfair distribution of resources to the rural poor. At a popular level, however, the veto was largely interpreted as a sign that agriculture had been truly abandoned by the government. It was thought that, without some resolution to the debt crisis, the agricultural sector would be unable to recover. Four months later, in March 1998, a new law was passed forgiving 85% of the agrarian debt for the agrarian reform co-operatives and the total remainder of the PTT beneficiaries' debt from land and credit, bringing to a close the most significant mobilisation of popular forces since the end of the war.

*Parcelisation of the PTT lands*

With the debt forgiveness process concluded and the timeline running out on the provisional (five year) *proindiviso* status awarded to groups of beneficiaries receiving land through the PTT, the issue of parcelisation of the PTT lands again resurfaced. As discussed, the vague coverage of land-related agreements in the peace accords led to subsequent struggles between competing visions for agrarian 'reintegration' of ex-combatants and their supporters. And, in a sense, also to the failure to consider resettlement processes in terms of their implications for future livelihoods, let alone the land use and ecologies of their new environs. Whether or not land would stay in collective title or be parcelised into individual properties constituted a key piece of this puzzle.

Although plans for parcelisation were an explicit part of the establishment of the Land Transfer Programme from the beginning, there were no set terms for how it would be done and who would pay for it. *Proindiviso* titles were otherwise commonly used in cases of disputed inheritance, with each person deeded a certain fraction of the asset, leaving undefined which piece belongs to whom. For the PTT this meant that each beneficiary appeared on the group title, but without any delimitation of *where* each beneficiary's land was located within the larger parcel. Although the FMLN had originally envisioned the maintenance of cohesion in the post-war period through some sort of co-operative/communal productive integration in the PTT sector, there was also widespread recognition that such integration was not practically feasible given the larger macroeconomic and sectoral policy context.

For many the problem of the *proindiviso* status was that land belonged to 'everyone and no one'. By parcelising the UPs or land within the 'communities' the FMLN expected to foster an increased sense of security and ownership of the land by project beneficiaries. Following the assumed linkages according to a market approach to land regarding ownership security and land management, individualisation of tenure through a government-sponsored programme was expected to promote the sort of ownership security that would lead to increased investment in productive activities and, by extension, to better conservation of natural resources on farm. The parcelisation process began as a pilot called Convivir in 1996 and was carried out as a national project called Proseguir lasting from 1997 to 2001.

From this first pilot phase emerged three important insights regarding the difficulties of parcelisation and titling. First, community participation and social consensus in many aspects of the parcelisation—from measurements to analysis of property to determining distribution alternatives—were instrumental to assuring a non-conflictive process. Without them the potential for renewed conflict existed. Second, the participative approach to titling employed through Convivir and later Proseguir marked a step away from some of the more traditional *modi operandi* of past titling experiences by international organisations in other countries (Nicaragua, Guatemala), and from El Salvador's history of land reform processes more generally. Lastly, it became clear that this hybrid administration of titling—where NGOs conducted most of the outreach but government channels were built into the project themselves—proved instrumental to success. Government participation allowed direct access to the appropriate legal channels and secured the necessary legal reforms in a timely manner.

One very significant change made early on in the pilot was the removal of complementary community-support initiatives that would have helped to fill the gaps of support so notable in the reinsertion programmes connected with the peace accords. Progressive NGOs and the FMLN fought for the add-in of such initiatives, which were still considered crucial to the re-establishment of community stability, especially as some production structures functioning on the basis of collective management or organisation were broken down and reconstituted to reflect the new individual tenure arrangements. This component was tested in two communities and removed, according to USAID El Salvador staff, because of lack of funding. According to a USAID official interviewed in 2001, the agency had already given much to the peace process, and was in the process of significantly reducing its commitment levels.[50]

## Parcelisation Phase II: the Proseguir experience

By 1997 the national phase of parcelisation of the PTT farms, dubbed Proseguir, was underway. Three Salvadoran NGOs two of them, FUNDESA (Fundación para el Desarrollo (Foundation for Development)) and REDES (Fundación Salvadoreña para la Reconstrucción y Desarrollo (Salvadoran Foundation for Reconstruction and Development)) with strong ties to the popular movement and aligned with particular factions of the FMLN collaborated in the implementation of PROSEGUIR. FUNDESA, PROESA (Fundación Promotora de Productores) and REDES—were now contracted to carry out the promotion and parts of the measurement components for the 'rompimiento' (break-up) of the proindiviso properties, while the government counterpart in the Proseguir project, the Institute of Liberty and Progress (ILP) would expedite titling procedures. In addition to Fundesa and ILP, the international NGO, CARE, whose principal role it was to facilitate co-operation between collaborating organisations with often conflicting ideologies and tendencies, was involved.

Designed as a five year project from 1997 to 2001, Proseguir would attend to the parcelisation of some 2209 properties, equivalent to 84 360 hectares for 29 643 then co-property owners.[51] One of the main project objectives was to increase legal tenure security over land for beneficiaries of the PTT, assuring that each property owner possessed a title registered in the National Registry Center (CNR). The main components of Proseguir consisted of community promotion, engineering (measurements, agro-ecological soil studies), and the legalisation of property holdings. The degree of successful integration of these components by participating organisations was later evaluated by the organisations involved as the key factor that allowed for adequate participation and organisation by communities and for efficient and effective partitioning, titling and registration of properties.

Promoters were often chosen from among the ranks of the demobilized, frequently coming from within the communities or regions where parcelisation was happening. The parcelisation process involved 12 action steps (requiring almost as many visits to property owners). One of these steps involved the presentation of a number of different formulas for ownership. The most popular choice, a patchwork of individual homesteads, reflected little interest in collective production arrangements.

### The PTT: the importance of popular mobilisation in '(a)political' land transfer

Unsurprisingly, the cessation of armed conflict far from implied an end to the power struggles over access to material and symbolic resources. As this account shows, the peace process was equally laden with the politics of land that have characterised El Salvador since its founding, with the Land Transfer Program, debt forgiveness and the parcelisation process becoming the new theatres of struggle between the FMLN and the Salvadoran government over what livelihood futures might be possible and for whom.

### Notes

This paper is dedicated to the memory of Antonio Alvarez, who tirelessly dedicated his life to improving the lives of rural people throughout El Salvador.
1 WC Thiesenhusen, *Broken Promises: Agrarian Reform and the Latin American Campesino*, Boulder: Westview Press, 1995. The relative importance attributed to agrarian inequality as a root cause of civil war is a subject of debate among scholars of El Salvador. See MA Seligson, 'Agrarian inequality and the theory of peasant rebellion', *Latin American Research Review*, 31 (2), 1996, pp 140–157; M Diskin, 'Distilled conclusions: the disappearance of the agrarian question in El Salvador', *Latin American Research Review*, 31 (2), 1996, pp 111–126; and JM Paige, 'Land reform and agrarian revolution in El Salvador: comment on Seligson and Diskin', *Latin American Research Review*, 31 (2), 1996, pp 127–139.
2 The earlier land reforms of the 1980s transferred roughly one-fifth of the farmland of the country to roughly 10% of the country's population. MA Seligson, W Thiesenhusen *et al*, *El Salvador Agricultural Policy Analysis: Land Tenure Study*, USAID-El Salvador/Agricultural Policy Analysis Project, Phase II (APAP II), Bethesda, MD: United States Agency for International Development, 1993; H van Heijningen, 'Land reform and land transfers in El Salvador', in R Ruben & J Bastiaensen, *Rural Development in Central America: Markets, Livelihoods and Local Governance*, Basingstoke: Macmillan, 2000, pp xiv, 252; and M Foley, G Vickers *et al*, *Land, Peace and Participation: The Development of Post-War Agricultural Policy in El Salvador and the Role of the World Bank*, Washington, DC: Washington Office on Latin America (WOLA), 2000, p 18.
3 Exact numbers total 27 481 FMLN combatants and *tenedor* supporters and 8519 government soldiers. A Alvarez & J Chavez, *Tierra, Conflicto y Paz*, San Salvador: CEPAZ, 2001.
4 K Deininger & H Binswanger, 'The evolution of the World Bank's land policy: principles, experience, and future challenges', *World Bank Research Observer*, 14 (2), 1999, pp 247–276; A Zoomers & G van der Harr (eds), *Current Land Policy in Latin America: Regulating Land Tenure Under Neo-Liberalism*, Amsterdam: Royal Tropical Institute/KIT Publishers and Iberoamericana/Vervuert Verlag, 2000; and World Bank, *Land Policy and Administration: Lessons Learned and New Challenges for the Bank's Development Agenda*, Washington, DC: World Bank, 2001, p 114.
5 A Bobrow-Strain, '(Dis)accords: the politics of market-assisted land reforms in Chiapas, Mexico', *World Development*, 32 (6), 2004, pp 887–903.
6 SMJ Borras, 'Questioning market-led agrarian reform: experiences from Brazil, Colombia, and South Africa', *Journal of Agrarian Change*, 3 (3), 2003, pp 367–394.
7 SMJ Borras, 'Can redistributive reform be achieved via market-based voluntary land transfer schemes? Evidence and lessons from the Philippines', *Journal of Development Studies*, 41 (1), 2005, pp 90–134.
8 D Browning, *El Salvador: Landscape and Society*, Oxford, Clarendon Press, 1971.
9 R Menjívar, *El Salvador: The Smallest Link*, Contemporary Marxism #1: Strategies for the Class Struggle in Latin America, San Francisco: Synthesis Publications, 1979, pp 19–28.
10 EJ Wood, *Forging Democracy from Below: Insurgent Transitions in South Africa and El Salvador*, Cambridge: Cambridge University Press, 2000.

11 EJ Wood, *Insurgent Collective Action and Civil War in El Salvador*, New York: Cambridge University Press, 2003; and Wood, *Forging Democracy from Below*.

12 WD Stanley, *The Protection Racket State: Elite Politics, Military Extortion, and Civil War in El Salvador*, Philadelphia, PA: Temple University Press, 1996.

13 *Ibid.*

14 Abundant evidence links the paramilitary death squads to human rights abuses during the 1980s. See H Byrne, *El Salvador's Civil War: A Study of Revolution*, Boulder, Co: Lynne Rienner, 1996; and Stanley, *The Protection Racket State*.

15 Walter K & PJ Williams, 'The Military and Democratization in El Salvador', *Journal of Interamerican Studies and World Affairs*, 35 (1), 1993, pp 39–88, cited in Thiesenhusen 1995 *op cit.*

16 *Ibid.*

17 The new economic model that was followed by Cristiani's administration was based in a proposal developed by FUSADES, a private sector research institute created in 1983 with US financing to promote an economic model that has been developed and promoted by USAID since the first Reagan administration for the 1989 presidential elections Segovia, A. (2002). Transformación Estructural y Reforma Económica en El Salvador: El Funcionamiento Económico de los Noventa y sus Efectos Sobre el Crecimiento, la Pobreza y la Distrubución del Ingreso. Guatemala, F&G editores. For a detailed account of El Salvador's 1980s agrarian reforms, see A de Bremond, 'Regenerating conflicted landscapes: land, environmental governance, and resettlement in post-war El Salvador', *Environmental Studies*, Santa Cruz, CA: University of California Press, 2006, p 342.

18 JK Boyce, *Economic Policy for Building Peace: The Lessons of El Salvador*, Boulder, CO: Lynne Reinner, 1996.

19 For a detailed account of the role of the USA in promoting and funding Fusades, see also WD Stanley, 'El Salvador: state-building before and after democratisation, 1980–95', *Third World Quarterly*, 27 (1), 2006, pp 101–114.

20 A Segovia, *Transformación Estructural y Reforma Económica en El Salvador: El Funcionamiento Económico de los Noventa y sus Efectos Sobre el Crecimiento, la Pobreza y la Distrubución del Ingreso*, Guatemala: F&G editores, 2002.

21 Stanley, 'El Salvador'.

22 *Ibid.*

23 For a complete description of the accords, see T Wilkins, 'The El Salvador Peace Accords: using international and domestic law norms to build peace', in MW Doyle, I Johnstone & RC Orr (eds), *Keeping the Peace: Multidimensional UN Operations in Cambodia and El Salvador*, Cambridge: Cambridge University Press, 1997, pp xx, 428.

24 United Nations, *The United Nations and El Salvador 1990–1995*, UN Blue Books Series, Vol IV, New York: Department of Public Information/United Nations Publications, 1995, p 611.

25 Stanley, 'El Salvador'.

26 Wood, *Forging Democracy from Below*; and J Spence, *War and Peace in Central America: Comparing Transitions Toward Democracy and Socal Equity in Guatemala, El Salvador and Nicaragua*, Brookline, MA: Hemisphere Initiative 2004, p 100.

27 G del Castillo, 'The arms-for-land deal in El Salvador', in Doyle *et al*, *Keeping the Peace*, pp xx, 428.

28 J Spence, *War and Peace in Central America*.

29 Chapultepec Agreement, 16 January 1992, in United Nations, *The United Nations and El Salvador 1990–1995*.

30 de Bremond, 'Regenerating conflicted landscapes'.

31 The term 'conflict zone' was mainly used by the FMLN to refer to the geographic areas that had been identified by them as ones of significant political and military strength. Such a definition also served to emphasise the reality that these were, in fact, zones that had been the loci for a disproportionate amount of suffering by the local population associated with the war and therefore also zones that merited special attention in the peace process.

32 USAID, *Assistance to the Transition from War to Peace: Evaluation of USAID/El Salvador's Special Strategic Objective*, Washington, DC: USAID/El Salvador, 1996, p 154.

33 Letter dated 13 October 1992 from the Secretary-General to the General Command of the FMLN concerning a United Nations proposal for a solution to the problem relating to the land transfer programme, in United Nations, *The United Nations and El Salvador 1990–1995*.

34 Letter dated 15 October 1992 from Mr Shafik Handál, in the name of the FMLN, to the Secretary-General, in *ibid.*

35 del Castillo, 'The arms-for-land deal in El Salvador'.

36 This section draws from analysis in *ibid.*

37 Del Castillo, 'The arms-for-land deal in El Salvador', p 351.

38 Alvarez & Chavez, *Tierra, Conflicto y Paz*.

39  S Baranyi, 'Political missions, in TS Montgomery (ed), *Peacemaking and Democratization in the Western Hemisphere*, Coral Gables, FL: North–South Center Press, University of Miami, 2000, pp iii, 334.

40  JK Boyce, C Acevedo *et al*, *Adjustment Toward Peace: Economic Policy and Post-war Reconstruction in El Salvador*, San Salvador: Commissioned by the United Nations Development Program, 1995, p 172.

41  The 1997 report by the Washington Office on Latin America (WOLA) provides a detailed review of the politics of Salvadoran agricultural policy during the mid-1990s. M Foley & G Vickers, *Land, Peace and Participation: The Development of Post-War Agricultural Policy and the Role of the World Bank*, Washington, DC: WOLA, 1997.

42  *Ibid*, p 18.

43  *Ibid*.

44  *Ibid*.

45  *Ibid*.

46  Financiera Calpía is one such example of post-war microfinance efforts in El Salvador. For a detailed description, see S Navajas & C Gonzalez-Vega, *Innovative Approaches to Rural Lending: Financiera Calpía in El Salvador*, Rural Finance Program Department of Agricultural, Environmental, and Development Economics, Ohio State University, 2000.

47  PJ Hernandez & OD Hutt, *El Programa de Transferencia de Tierras*, San Salvador: Fundción Nacional para el Desarrollo (FUNDE), 1996.

48  L Kowalchuk, 'Peasant struggle, political opportunities, and the unfinished agrarian reform in El Salvador', *Canadian Journal of Sociology—Cahiers Canadiens De Sociologie*, 28 (3), 2003, pp 309–340.

49  L Kowalchuk, 'Asymmetrical alliances, organizational democracy and peasant protest in El Salvador', *Canadian Review of Sociology and Anthropology/Revue Canadienne de Sociologie et D'Anthropologie*, 40 (3), 2003, pp 291–309.

50  Personal interview, Ana Luz de Mena, USAID, San Salvador, May 2001.

51  Instituto Libertad y Progreso (ILP), *Programa de Seguridad Jurídica Rural, Proseguir*, San Salvador: Instituto Libertad y Progeso, 2000, p 25.

# Anti-poverty or Anti-poor? The World Bank's market-led agrarian reform experiment in the Philippines

SATURNINO M BORRAS, JR, DANILO CARRANZA &
JENNIFER C FRANCO

To speak of the Philippine land problem is to refer to one of the most entrenched legacies of colonialism and to recall a long, bloody history littered with half-hearted land reform laws. Nowhere else in Asia has the land problem endured so deeply and for so long—or produced so many failed attempts at land reform.

Yet, as a result of a particular confluence of social and political factors in the 1980s–90s, it is the Philippines that generated one of the more successful government land redistribution programmes in the contemporary era, known as the Comprehensive Agrarian Reform Programme (CARP). Much has been written elsewhere on CARP's accomplishments and its failures, and it is not our intention to address this question again here. Instead, our aim is to examine what is considered by some as a potential alternative to the CARP: the Community-Managed Agrarian Reform and Poverty Reduction Program (CMARPRP).

To say that CARP was *relatively* successful in land redistribution or, in the words of James Putzel, in 'partial reform',[1] is *not* to say that either the

Philippine state or Philippine society was (is) exceptional. The Philippine state is not exceptionally powerful or progressive; neither is Philippine society. Instead, what made CARP moderately successful during one historical juncture, 1992–2000, was the way in which currents of pro-reform forces in society linked up with pockets of pro-reformists within the agrarian reform bureaucracy.[2] This pro-reform alliance was critical to overcoming anti-reform resistance and to converting less-than-ideal openings for reform into actual redistribution of land *at specific times and places*. But this linking up across the state–society divide did not just happen without conflict. Rather, CARP's compromise character, itself the outcome of changes in the prevailing balance of power, in turn bred mixed results: hard-won successes in land redistribution occurred alongside tragic failures.

It is against this backdrop that we consider the World Bank's market-led agrarian reform (MLAR) experiment. This is not the Bank's first foray into the turbulent waters of Philippine land reform or the Philippines more generally.[3] World Bank representatives first attempted to recruit the government to the MLAR model in 1996, after suggesting that the Philippines ought to halt CARP land distribution implementation because it was 'distorting' the land market and financially expensive.[4] The then Department of Agrarian Reform (DAR) leadership rejected the proposal and joined forces instead with rural social movements to launch protests to defend CARP and discredit the Bank's initiative. Their efforts paid off and the Bank retreated.

In 1999, amid a creeping shortage of public funds and with CARP implementation heating up in the highly contentious commercial banana farms and the large private land categories, the Bank came back.[5] This time it succeeded in pressuring a new DAR leadership to agree to a small pilot project to explore a 'complementary land reform approach'. A series of desk-bound macro-policy studies produced several papers favourable to the pro-market policy model. Esguerra predicted economic viability, but warned of institutional, organisational and financial factors that might prevent a demand-driven process.[6] Edillion predicted MLAR's financial viability, but warned of unpredictability in the field.[7] Mamon also endorsed the project, but underscored the role of autonomous social preparation.[8] The study produced an operational manual,[9] and renamed the project, 'Community-Managed Agrarian Reform Program' (CMARP). In 2003 it became the CMARPRP.

This article examines CMARPRP. Our analysis draws on fieldwork conducted in six of its nine pilot provinces, and on an interrogation of project documents. We show how CMARPRP has involved anomalous transactions and juridically 'crooked' processes that have benefited local elites rather than the rural poor. Wealth and power transfers in the communities where it was carried out have followed four patterns—all flowing in one direction: intra-elite/elite-to-elite, state-to-elite, foreign donor-to-elite, and poor-to-elite. Judging from its outcomes, the project is best described as anti-poor, rather than anti-poverty.

142

## Background

The Philippine agricultural sector remains a pillar of the national economy, contributing one-fifth of the coutnry's GDP. It is host to 50% – 60% of the country's active labour force. The country's agrarian structure has been marked by the dominance of the land-owning classes. In 1988, the year CARP began, the Gini-coefficient for land ownership was at 0.64—suggesting a high degree of inequality in land ownership distribution.[10]

*CARP implementation*

CARP aimed to redistribute 10.3 million hectares of land to four million peasants. But it was a compromise law, accommodating demands from the landowning classes and agribusiness, as well as the peasantry. It resulted from the balance of forces in Philippine society that prevailed during the regime transition in 1986 – 88, which, as explained by Jennifer Franco,[11] involved a three-way political battle between the central state, local elite and democratic opposition for control of the nature and direction of the post-dictatorship regime. CARP was thus marked by what Francisco Lara called 'landmarks and loopholes',[12] the 'institutional avenues' or 'policy currents' that can lead to either positive or negative poles of gravity.[13] Over the years 'birthmarks' in the land reform law have offered both opportunities for *and* obstacles to land rights claim making. But where these 'avenues' have led has depended in part on how real people have acted and interacted in and around them *en route*. This is because, ultimately, state laws are neither self-interpreting nor self-implementing, but rather they are *made authoritative* in society by virtue of the contingent, concerted and contending efforts of a variety of state and non-state actors.[14]

From 1988 to 1993 the CARP process was dominated by anti-reform policy currents resulting in dismal outcomes. The process was marked by nepotism, corruption and repression, and the non-participation of rural social movements. The situation changed after 1992, however, when a reformist leadership took control of the CAR. The leadership sought out and positively interacted with rural social movements that had tentatively decided to link up with state reformers to try to maximise the programme's potential. The improved climate lasted roughly eight years; it was marked by a dynamic state – society pro-reform alliance serving to push forward the land reform process.[15] Two-thirds of the total reported CARP land redistribution output to date was achieved during this period, and a good portion of this involved real redistribution.

The positive momentum, however, ground to a halt in 2000 after the Macapagal-Arroyo administration took over. Nepotism, corruption and repression returned with a vengeance. Meanwhile, anti-reform manoeuvres by landlords via market-oriented land transfer modes, which had been part of CARP since its inception, had expanded and accelerated. This latter trend coincided with a number of political processes on the agrarian front that appeared to be converging in one basic direction—the displacement of state-led expropriatory land reform by neoliberal land sales schemes.

Inspired by the writings of Hernando de Soto,[16] who became an economic adviser to President Macapagal-Arroyo, the government attempted to legislate a law that would remove existing 'land size ceiling laws' and transform land reform certificates into negotiable financial instruments ('collateral'). A series of mobilisations by peasant movements forced it to back down, at least for the time being.

Then, in 2005, the government announced plans to convert 2.4 million hectares of upland, affecting a million peasant households, into agribusiness plantations tied to multinational companies. The announcement sparked protests by civil society groups, who argued that this would inevitably lead to land grabbing in public lands where property rights were not clear,[17] and where forest resource 'plunder' by domestic and international capital had been established historically.[18] Critics believed that it would also encourage further encroachment into already vulnerable indigenous people's territories. But the plan was boosted in early 2007 by a bilateral agreement with the Chinese government allocating a whopping 1.4 million hectares of land to production of food and biofuel destined for China.

Meanwhile, the government declared its adoption of 'non-confrontational' land transfer mechanisms involving commercial plantations, especially in the banana and sugarcane sectors, and has pushed for more exclusions in the coverage of land reform (eg taking out cattle ranches from land distribution coverage).[19]

The shift towards a market-led framework has coincided with escalating rural violence, where the state has increasingly become involved in the repression of peasants claiming land rights.[20] The murder in 2006 of Eric Cabanit, national leader of the main peasant movement struggling for land reform (UNORKA), is a case in point. It is widely understood that his assassination was punishment for his consistent opposition to the 'market-friendly' land transfer scheme in one of the banana plantations owned by the powerful Floirendo family (see below).[21] The Cabanit case is among the most prominent, but certainly not the only one. Indeed, it came just months after a bloody massacre in Hacienda Luisita (see below) of farm workers calling for revocation of the market-oriented Stock Distribution Option (SDO) contract.[22]

It is at this juncture that the Bank returned to push for a pilot MLAR. Part of this move has involved the launch of the CMARPRP experiment. However, part of it has also involved placing greater emphasis on the pre-existing provisions in CARP implementation that resonate with a neoliberal approach, namely, the various non-expropriatory modes of land acquisition already available under CARP.

## CARP's non-expropriatory provisions

One of CARP's features is its expropriation mode for land acquisition, the Compulsory Acquisition (CA) which, by definition, can be used by the state despite landlord opposition. Predictably its actual exercise by government authorities is even more contentious. The Operation Land Transfer (OLT) used for private land and corn lands is akin to CA. Combined, the CA and OLT land transfers have accounted for around 45% of total land transfers in private lands.[23]

In addition to CA and OLT, a variety of non-expropriatory land acquisition options are available under CARP. Three of these 'voluntary options' are the Voluntary Land Transfer (VLT), the SDO and leaseback. The VLT allows for the direct transfer purchase of land by peasants. The SDO was designed for corporate farms, and involves exemption of lands from redistribution if the owner opts for corporate stock sharing with beneficiaries. The leaseback option is where arrangements can be made for beneficiaries to lease out awarded lands to an investor.[24] Taken together, these different 'landlord-friendly' options integral to CARP also provided a legal framework for the Bank model. Three examples are presented below.

The elite used VLT in various ways for anti-reform purposes, the most common of which was to subdivide lands to family members and declare such act as in compliance with the law. Key informants within top levels of the DAR have confirmed what many have suspected: that this practice is widespread. According to former DAR undersecretary Conrado Navarro, 'the majority [of VLT-based land transfers], maybe as much as 70 percent, were resorted to by the landowners... to evade coverage.' Another former DAR undersecretary, Gerardo Bulatao, explains that 'VLT is often a transaction between family members' ('*malimit na transaksyon ng magkakamag-anak*'). And, as Lorenzo Reyes, a member of the national DAR Adjudication Board, puts it, 'You will have serious doubts because these VLT schemes are mostly on cash basis. How can a poor tenant afford to pay 100 per cent spot-cash for the land? It is most likely that these are just stage-managed, especially where the landowners are politically strong enough to control their tenants.'[25]

The Floirendo family is one of the biggest landlords in the country. In 1997 the Floirendos tried to evade reform by asking a prohibitively high price for their banana land, PhP750 000 ($15 000)/hectare (against the government's assessed value of only $5500/hectare). In 2001 a local court declared a nearby banana plantation to be valued at $26 000/hectare. It was odd, then, when in 2002 the Floirendos sold the land to a section of the plantation's workers for just PhP92 000 ($1900)/hectare. The sale was made via VLT tied to a *leaseback* contract, with terms including: 1) the workers would buy the land directly from the Floirendos; 2) the beneficiaries would lease the land back to the Floirendos for 30 years, renewable for another 30 years at the sole option of the Floirendos; 3) beneficiaries would amortise payment for 30 years, deducted from the yearly lease rental; 4) the lease rental would be PhP5000 ($100)/hectare/year. The VLT-leaseback scheme constituted an evasion of the land reform, prompting one observer to dub it an 'anti-reform pre-nuptial agreement'.[26]

The most telling experience with SDO involves Hacienda Luisita, the 6400-hectare sugarcane plantation, with 4000 workers, owned by the family of former President Corazon Cojuangco-Aquino. The family used SDO to evade land redistribution, using dubious 'creative accounting methods', according to Putzel.[27] Specifically, the Cojuangcos created a series of spin-off corporations related to sugarcane production, transportation, milling and marketing. The entity created to settle with the farm workers on the land issue was called Hacienda Luisita, Incorporated (HLI). Only 4900 of the 6400 hectares of the hacienda were declared an HLI land asset; the rest, which included the more expensive portions of land located near roads and residential or commercial areas, was segregated and declared the property of the other corporations. The Cojuangcos depressed the cost of the farmland to one-third of the total HLI value, so the beneficiaries ended up owning only one-third of the corporation. They then inflated the value of the non-land assets to two-thirds of HLI's value.[28] Today, the results are clear: there is no evidence that the socioeconomic condition of the beneficiaries has improved, and plenty of evidence of destitution.[29]

*Lessons*

The examples narrated here are not isolated cases; across the country similar VLT, leaseback and SDO arrangements have been forged and undertaken. The results suggest the vulnerability of market-friendly land transfer modes to landlord interests, whether that vulnerability was intended or not. They also indicate that such market-friendly modes are little more than landlord-driven schemes. But regardless of how they may have been originally intended by policy makers, there is little doubt that, in the Philippine case, they have actually—and successfully—been used by landlords, often in alliance with anti-reform state actors, to undermine potentially redistributive land reform. Past experience with market-friendly modes of land transfer calls into question any optimistic assumptions about the salutary advantages or benefits of putative 'voluntary negotiation' processes and dispute settlement mechanisms involving landlords and peasants, or more generally, those involving rich and poor disputants (the latter are explained elsewhere by Franco[30]).

The critical literature on land reform supports this finding and helps to explain it. First, landlords give not only monetary value, but also social and political weight to land, which explains why they are loath to relinquish it even when monetary compensation is possible. This runs counter to an assumption by proponents of neoliberal land reform that the value of land is essentially economic.[31] Second, a significant portion of what is today *de facto* elite-controlled, privately farmed agricultural land in the Philippines, is still classified on paper as 'public land'. Here, as in Indonesia,[32] Thailand,[33] and Bolivia,[34] this *de jure* status masks established inequitable social relations that ought to be reformed. Technical and ahistorical approaches to settling competing land claims in such situations are likely to benefit the elite, to marginalise the poor and to legitimise elite (public) land grabbing, as shown elsewhere by Razavi[35] and Toulmin and Quan.[36] Third, decentralising the process of land reform in settings marked by persistent 'local authoritarian enclaves' tends to empower the landed elite even further and at the same time to increase conflict within local communities. This warning was made much earlier by Griffin,[37] has been re-echoed more recently by Herring[38] and Peluso,[39] and has been validated in a variety of national contexts by Barros et al,[40] and Rosset et al.[41] Fourth, land redistribution is in fact power redistribution, while decentralisation is a development process that inherently involves power. The market-led policy model in land reform is a prime example of what John Harriss calls 'de-politicizing' development, a framework propagated by neoliberal-dominated institutions like the World Bank.[42] Past experience suggests that development interventions pursued from within this framework are likely to lead to elite capture and anti-poor outcomes. Finally, land redistribution cannot be separated from the broader, macro-policies such as (inter)national development policies.[43] Against this backdrop, we now turn to consider in depth the CMARPRP initiative itself.

## Overview of the World Bank's CMARPRP

The CMARPRP initiative evolved out of a political process that began with World Bank lobbying of DAR officials and led first to agreement to conduct a feasibility study project involving two community-based test cases.[44] An overview of the feasibility study is provided below.

### The pre-project feasibility study

The first site (in Misamis Occidental province, northern Mindanao) was a tenanted 178-hectare area of (provincial) government-owned land: 48 hectares lay idle, 130 hectares were planted with subsistence crops. In this case there were 178 potential buyers, chosen through CARP, ie by the DAR. The original price of PhP31 000/hectare, set by the seller (the provincial government), was rejected by the beneficiaries and other parties in the arrangement. The seller's final offer was PhP16 000/hectare payable in 10 years,[45] with the buyers shouldering the cost of the land.[46]

The second project site (in Quezon province, southern Luzon) was a tenanted 48-hectare plot of marginal private land planted with subsistence crops. The land had been for sale since 1989 and was in the process of being sold to the DAR when discussions about the CMARP project began. The landlord asked for PhP35 000/hectare payable through a 25% down-payment, with the balance payable in 10 years. Nineteen potential buyers were chosen through the CARP process. The relatively organised potential buyers rejected the landlord's asking price, and a final price was set at PhP6000/hectare, with the buyers shouldering the cost of the land, to be paid in cash through a loan from the government at commercial interest rates.[47]

In the first case the key lesson seems to be that even a government entity can be tempted to overprice land slated for sale to peasants under the direct sale process. The second case is interesting with regard to how the land price was bargained down, although it cannot be taken as representative, because the balance of power was overwhelmingly in favour of the peasants thanks to the direct assistance of national, provincial and local government and of NGO actors in pressuring the landlord to adhere to the appropriate land price. Such concerted intervention appeared to be crucial, yet was unlikely to be replicated on a wide scale.

Despite, or because of, the limited insights that could be derived from the feasibility study, the Bank decided to continue and to expand it into a small pilot programme. The pilot programme was inserted into the second phase of the Bank's project for CARP, ie the Agrarian Reform Community Development Programme (ARCDP-2), at a total cost of $2 million.[48] It aspired to carry out a textbook MLAR project in nine provinces involving 1000 hectares of land and 1000 households, starting in 2003, for completion in April 2007. It was at this point that CMARP was repackaged as the 'Community-Managed Agrarian Reform and Poverty Reduction Program' (CMARPRP).[49]

*CMARPRP*

Officially CMARPRP aims to: 1) 'empower [beneficiaries] so that they may actively participate in land market transactions'; and 2) 'contribute to poverty reduction in rural areas by introducing land tenure improvement modalities in agrarian reform that are faster'.[50] To achieve these goals, CMARPRP adopts the following MLAR principles: a negotiated willing seller-willing buyer scheme; a demand-driven approach; integrated land transfer and support services delivery; and centrality of income generation goals via farm productivity enhancement and credit financing. By April 2007, CMARPRP had reached 972 hectares of land, 650 beneficiaries, 68 landowners, and 17 villages. A total of $2 million has been spent or fully committed, not including the land purchase cost. The project fund distribution, by component, has been: 17.6% for social preparation; 4.8% for technical assistance and services; 71.4% for technical services and financing (demand-driven small-scale rural infrastructure and on-farm investment); and 6.2% for project monitoring and evaluation.[51] The pilot project was declared near-complete, with only the related infrastructure projects pending. New land titles had been issued for 785 hectares of land and the project had been declared a success.

The Bank's local project office has summarised the CMARPRP achievements, 'lessons learned' and recommendations as follows.

1. There was a quick land transfer process and production of land titles.
2. The willing seller-willing buyer land transfer scheme should be adopted more widely.
3. Government should adopt the CMARPRP land purchase repayment scheme for its national land reform strategy in order to increase the beneficiary repayment rate (45% of buyers were fully paid in less than four years, the rest have made partial payments; one site declared 100% full repayment upon land purchase).
4. The programme should provide lessons on the need to 'retool' the regular government land reform bureaucracy.

5. There is a need to force beneficiaries to pay their land taxes after receiving lands.
6. The programme gives the 'multi-stakeholder' committee (local government, lines agencies, landlord and peasant representatives) a central role in agrarian reform.[52]

This is a very rosy picture indeed, justifying its subsequent recommendation to mainstream the programme nationwide. But what is the real story?

### CARP versus CMARPRP

Standard criticism of the market-led model[53] suggests two ways of comparing the government's CARP and CMARPRP: 1) accomplishment in terms of land area and number of beneficiaries; and 2) the cost.

Looking at Tables 1 and 2, we conclude the following. First, CARP has delivered far greater land redistribution output, both in absolute terms (seven million hectares) and in yearly average (368 421 hectares), and it has benefited a greater number of people (3.5 million households; or 184 211 households/year). This compares to CMARPRP's meagre 785 and 196 hectares, and 656 and 164 households, respectively (see Table 1). Second, the huge difference between the two approaches in terms of accomplishment holds,

TABLE 1. Land Distribution Outcomes, CARP and CMARPRP

|  | Area in hectares | Average area per year in ha | Number of beneficiary households | No of beneficiaries/year | Start year |
|---|---|---|---|---|---|
| Government CARP land transfer plus leasehold reform | 7 million | 368 421 | 3.5 million | 184 211 | 1988 |
| World Bank CMARPRP land transfer output | 785 | 196 | 656 | 164 | April 2003 |

*Sources*: For data on CARP, S Borras, 'The Philippine land reform in comparative perspective: conceptual and methodological implications', *Journal of Agrarian Change*, 6 (1), 2006, pp 69–101; for CMARPRP, DAR-ARCDP 2, 'Community-managed agrarian reform and poverty reduction project (CMARPRP)', internal project document, Quezon City, 2006; DAR-ARCDP 2, 'The community-managed agrarian reform and poverty reduction project (CMARPRP): an impact analysis', internal project document, Quezon City, 2007; DAR-ARCDP 2, 'The community-managed agrarian reform and poverty reduction project (CMARPRP)'; DAR-ARCDP 2, 'The community-managed agrarian reform and poverty reduction project (CMARPRP): an impact analysis—household level assessment', internal document, Quezon City, 2007; and DAR-ARCDP 2, 'The community-managed agrarian reform and poverty reduction project (CMARPRP): an impact analysis—integrative report', Quezon City, 2007. For for the World Bank data, Borras, 'The Philippine land reform in comparative persepctive'; DAR-ARCDP 2, 'Community-managed agrarian reform and poverty reduction project (CMARPRP)'; DAR-ARCDP 2, 'The community-managed agrarian reform and poverty reduction project (CMARPRP)'; DAR-ARCDP 2, 'The community-managed agrarian reform and poverty reduction project (CMARPRP): an impact analysis—household level assessment'; and DAR-ARCDP 2, 'The community-managed agrarian reform and poverty reduction project (CMARPRP): an impact analysis—integrative report'.

TABLE 2. Costs, CARP and CMARPRP

|  | Cost/hectare | Cost/beneficiary |
|---|---|---|
| Government CARP | US$357 | US$714 |
| Land transfer plus leasehold reform | PhP14 285* | PhP28 571* |
| World Bank's | US$2547 | US$3049 |
| CMARPRP | PhP137 283** | PhP164 341** |

*Notes*: These are rough but arguably close estimates. *exchange rate: US$1 = PhP40, 1990–April 2007 (average); ** exchange rate: US$1 = PhP53.90, January 2003–April 2007 (average).
*Sources*: For the CARP data, S Borras 'The Philippine land reform in comparative perspective: conceptual and methodological implications', *Journal of Agrarian Change*, 6 (1), 2006, pp 69–101; for the World Bank project data, DAR-ARCDP 2, 'Community-managed agrarian reform and poverty reduction project (CMARPRP)', internal project document, Quezon City, 2006; DAR-ARCDP 2, 'The community-managed agrarian reform and poverty reduction project (CMARPRP): an impact analysis', internal project document, Quezon City, 2007; DAR-ARCDP 2, 'The community-managed agrarian reform and poverty reduction project (CMARPRP): an impact analysis—household level assessment'; and DAR-ARCDP 2, 'The community-managed agrarian reform and poverty reduction project (CMARPRP): an impact analysis—integrative report'.

even if we cut the government's CARP land redistribution outcome by half—assuming that a significant portion of its reported accomplishment does not represent any real reform, as explained elsewhere by Borras.[54] A significant portion of CARP's non-redistributive outcomes is comprised of the VLT transactions.[55] Third, the costs in the Bank's scheme are far greater than in the government CARP—$357/hectare and $714/household versus $2547/hectare and $3049/household for the Bank's model.

From this angle the state-led land reform appears to have delivered greater results than the Bank programme—and for less money. And yet, while relevant, even this negative balance sheet is already too optimistic, because it assumes that the CMARPRP processes and outcomes were clear and straightforward, or at least more so than those under the state-led CARP. This proves to not be the case, however. A closer look at the details of how the project was implemented in specific instances is warranted.

*Interrogating the local projects*[56]

*Quezon*. This site (around eight hours drive south of Manila) involved a contested 146 hectares of 'public' land planted to coconut. First, an absentee claimant had asserted rights to the land by paying the municipal tax on it. Second, 71 poor peasants had lived on and worked the land for their entire lifetime and most refused to pay the land rent demanded by another elite claimant. A CMARPRP document stated: 'Although the [beneficiaries] believe that they are the rightful owners of the land, they did not have any document to back up their claims'.[57] Third, this other absentee elite claimant had recently emerged and, through connections with the local government leader, had been able to impose land rent collection on a few of the peasant households. It was later confirmed that the village chief had connived with the second elite claimant to falsify legal documents. Meanwhile, a legal case between the two absentee elite claimants had been lodged in the court and at the Office of the President (OP). One of them received a favourable decision from the OP, facilitating his entry into the CMARPRP process.

When the successful elite claimant tried to sell the land for PhP30 000/ hectare, the peasants refused to buy, insisting that they were already the rightful owners. The town mayor intervened, encouraged to push for the sale of the land because there was a promise that development projects would be forthcoming. He stopped the other elite claimant from pursuing his land claim by threatening to sue him in court for earlier falsifying documents. The mayor then convinced the favoured elite claimant to sell the land for PhP10 000/hectare. Finally, the mayor asked the peasants to drop their land claim, to recognise the land ownership of the favoured elite claimant, and then to buy the land. In exchange, the road to their village would be cemented through the CMARPRP fund and they would get more livelihood projects. If they did not accept, they would be evicted from the land. The peasants relented. An internal document admitted that: 'for those farmers who used to know that the land belonged to them, it is hard for them to accept the [arrangement]; but for them, just to end a long time battle to gain ownership, it is time to cooperate'.[58]

*Mindoro.* This site is inside an indigenous people's (Mangyan) territory on the island of Mindoro (southwest of Manila). It is marked by a (sub-)- subsistence peasant economy on an isolated upland, with no paved road, no potable water system, no electricity connection. The area is part of the 74 200 hectares of land under a Certificate of Ancestral Domain Claim (CADC) that was issued before the formal enactment of the Indigenous Peoples' Rights Act (IPRA) in the mid-1990s. Since then the Mangyan claimants have been lobbying the government to convert the 'claim' (CADC) into a 'title' (Certificate of Ancestral Domain Title), considered to be a more 'secure' document under state law. Their efforts had become urgent in recent years because of the increasing encroachment of lowlanders into the territory.

By 2003 there were a dozen claims on portions of the land being made by lowlanders. One of these claims involved 110 hectares. According to the Mangyans interviewed for this study, the elite claimant in this case first staked his claim in 1964 when he was a fiscal (state prosecutor). Like other elite claimants, the affected Mangyans recall, this man started by befriending their (grand)parents and giving them goods and gifts during holidays. Returning the gesture, they agreed to let this lowlander use parts of their land for grazing livestock. Later, the lowlanders began turning their informal access into formal land claims by using their connections with the local court. Some succeeded in acquiring dubious land titles. According to the Mangyans interviewed for this study, this is probably what happened to the 110 hectares being offered to them through CMARPRP by 'owner's heirs' for PhP25 000/ hectare.

Believing the land to already be theirs, the Mangyans refused the sales offer. In a series of 'negotiations' between the Mangyans and CMARPRP staff, the seller lowered the price to PhP15 000, payable in cash within five years. For a community where the average household income is far below a dollar a day, such an amount is ridiculous. Again, the Mangyans resisted. Only the convergence of two factors broke their resolve: 1) The Mangyans say that the seller told them that if they did not enter into the land sales transaction, they would be evicted. Without the much awaited CADC, they felt that they were on shaky ground; 2) The CMARPRP staff promised them support services that could be used to indirectly pay the land cost in due time. This combination of factors—blackmail and sweet promises—broke their resolve and they agreed to join the process. Three years into it, the promised infrastructure and support services had not yet arrived, according to the Mangyans.[59]

*Bataan.* The next site is in Central Luzon, just a three-hour drive north of Manila. A CMARPRP document describes the case:

> A total of 92.87 hectares of land were acquired from nine [landowners] and distributed to 38 [beneficiaries]...The land transfer process went smoothly. All of the [beneficiaries] participated in negotiation with [landowners], all the [Certificates of Land Ownership Award, or CLOAs] have been distributed, and the [landowners] have been fully compensated and all the [beneficiaries] have fully paid amortization.[60]

Unfortunately, we were not able to visit this site. But examination of the same document suggests anomalies, however.

The report found that 'many of the [beneficiaries] are relatives of the landowner and do not reside in the [said community]. Five out of nine landowners chose their family members as the beneficiaries of the land transaction'.[61] Moreover, a beneficiary organisation was reported to have been set up, but it was discovered that none of these beneficiaries ever attended any of the meetings. The CMARPRP poured in money to construct a road and to finance agro-enterprise development and capacity-building activities. Building on our joint knowledge about this province and general VLT practices, it is likely that this is a case of a 'faked' land reform process where VLT mechanisms facilitated the nominal transfer of land to family members without any real reform in property relations. The data also suggest that some possible real estate transactions were declared instead to be 'land reform'. No wonder that three years after the so-called land purchase nobody knows where the beneficiaries are.

*Zambales.* The next site, also in Central Luzon, involved 102 hectares, 17 landowners and 81 buyers. Much of the area was untitled 'public' land (seven out of 14 properties) for which the sellers had no land titles.[62] Three of the titled seven properties were Alienable and Disposable (A&D) lands with free patents that had been given by the government only a few months before the consummation of the CMARPRP sales transactions. Legally, lands with A&D free patents cannot be sold during the first five years after the grant of the free patent. Overall 85 hectares out of the total of 102 hectares of the lands sold to

CMARPRP did not have titles. Moreover, the lands being claimed by an elite entity and being transacted in CMARPRP were also being contested by an indigenous people's community. The latter had previously indicated to the project staff that these lands were part of their ancestral territory under an existing indigenous claim (CADC).[63]

The CMARPRP staff, in collaboration with the town mayor, pushed for the land sales anyway despite the indigenous people's protestations.[64] As one CMARPRP document sighed: 'there are [indigenous peoples] in the CMARPRP area who can hardly understand or may misunderstand our intention'.[65] The mayor later 'talked' to the indigenous people's chieftain, which enabled the CMARPRP process to push forward. And so the contested landholdings, a majority of which were already claimed by an indigenous people's community and had already been government-certified as under the public domain, nevertheless were sold to an elite claimant.

Another bewildering aspect of this case was that, on the same day as the formal land sales, 76 out of the total 81 beneficiaries were declared to have fully paid for the lands they purchased, covering 97 hectares. As an external evaluation team later discovered, 'Unfortunately . . . most of the identified [beneficiaries] . . . in these landholdings are relatives of the landowners . . . other [beneficiaries] either reside outside the municipality or abroad. For example, one [beneficiary] works in [the financial district of Manila] . . . Others [9 beneficiaries] live and work in the USA'.[66] Sixteen out of 17 landowners had 'sold' their lands to family members.[67] This is a classic case of elite land claimants who tried to control public lands, and used VLT to undermine land reform and to legalise a land-grab of indigenous territory already covered by a CADC and under public domain. The anomalous transaction was further revealed when CMARPRP staff came to deliver their promised support services, such as a road, livestock dispersal and other services to the 'beneficiaries', only to discover that 'the [beneficiaries] cannot identify which lot belongs to them'.[68] It seems the buyers 'fully paid' for land they cannot even identify. Despite such disturbing signs, the CMARPRP staff pushed through the delivery of support services to the 'beneficiaries'.

*Davao.* This site (a short ferry-ride from Davao City, southern Philippines) is almost entirely within an indigenous people's territory. Our field visit to the site revealed that the CMARPRP area of 77 hectares, involving 60 beneficiaries, is upland and devoted to (sub-)subsistence farming. It is 'public land' for which the seller had no title. Some of those in the community we interviewed claimed that the said land was part of the indigenous people's domain, but that the seller was somehow able to assert his land claim anyway. Lacking title to the land, the seller's claim was legalised through an 'extra-judicial settlement' during the CMARPRP land sales negotiation.[69] Then the land was sold to the community. The CMARPRP staff triumphantly exclaimed: 'the land transfer process under VLT for untitled properties is first in Davao'.[70]

The price was PhP70 000/hectare. One of the leaders of the community that bought the land told one of the authors of this study that the value was inflated and that with their (sub-)subsistence kind of farming, he doubted if they could ever pay the amount now owed. Moreover, the seller, backed up by the CMARPRP staff, also succeeded in making the buyers reluctantly agree to paying the inheritance tax (PhP35 000). Worse still, the buyers were also forced to pay the real estate taxes, which the seller could not pay. The buyers had agreed to buy the land at the said price partly because the Samal local government had promised to pay in cash 50% of the total cost of the land as a down-payment; the buyers would then repay the government over a period of 15 years without interest.

In an interview with a key local government official, it can be deduced that one of the reasons why the government agreed to this arrangement was an unexpected windfall in their 'internal revenue allocation' (IRA) from the national government. In addition, local officials reasoned that a relatively small amount of money (PhP1.2 million) initially would bring more funds to the island in the form of road construction and support services—all in grants promised by the CMARPRP project.

The project's subsequent implementation went crooked as well. Soon another piece of land was needed for a planned water system project, and so the indigenous community was asked to 'donate' the required land from their territory not covered by the land sales. This time the community refused, prompting this condescending comment from the CMARPRP: 'Even when the benefits of the project, management, roles and obligations as owner-user of the water system were explained to them, it seemed that their minds are closed … The negotiating panel had a hard time convincing them maybe because of their culture'.[71] The beneficiaries' association fell moribund after the promised support services largely failed to materialise and conflicts arose over those that did. The staff were baffled when nobody wanted to avail themselves of the commercial loan they offered.

### Critical insights

*Questionable ownership, questionable sellers*

In most project sites the lands sold were public lands for which there were no titles, but where competing claimants already existed, including peasants claiming rightful ownership on the basis that they were the actual tillers. But instead of a land reform process that would settle competing claims in favour of poor peasants, the CMARPRP process settled the matter in favour of elite sellers. Local government officials, not particularly interested in land reform, but instead in the possible inflow of funded projects, have frequently intervened. Their actions have tended to compel peasant land claimants to drop legitimate claims in lands they have been tilling, and instead to recognise the dubious, untitled claims of elite actors and then to agree to buy 'their own land' from the elite sellers at commercial rates. Their efforts to persuade the occupant-tillers have typically been backed up by threats of eviction. Meanwhile, in at least four provinces, the land subjected to the programme carried distinct territorial claims by indigenous people's communities. And again, instead of the mandated land reform process for indigenous territories, ie IPRA, the CMARPRP facilitated a legalisation of elite land grabbing. Like their counterparts in the public land areas, and likewise under the threat of eviction if they did not comply, the affected indigenous peoples' communities were in effect robbed of their land, forced to recognise outsiders' dubious land claims, and then coerced to buy back their land at commercial prices.

## Questionable buyers, questionable beneficiaries

In all the project sites there is also the phenomenon of questionable beneficiaries, and in several sites this constituted a defining feature of the pilot. Questionable beneficiaries include those who are non-poor individuals, often family members of the seller or land speculators and often residing in nearby cities, as well as outright fictitious 'paper' beneficiaries. Ostensibly the main target beneficiaries of any purportedly 'anti-poverty' project, the poor did not end up becoming the bulk of the buyers under CMARPRP. As in other market-oriented land transfer schemes noted earlier, such a result can be seen as part of a seller's successful effort to gain (or retain), rather than forfeit (or relinquish) control of a desired piece of land. In the context of an existing land reform law (eg CARP), which, for all its weaknesses, nonetheless did threaten all agricultural lands with reform and did offer some important new legal restrictions on land use and ownership (eg land size ceiling, prioritised beneficiaries' lists, and land use restrictions), such a result constitutes an evasion, not a complementing, of land reform. Ironically, in some cases, this evasion of land reform was even amply rewarded with land sales tax exemption, free land survey provision, free land titling and registration, an influx of new infrastructure (such as roads) and aid money.

The CMARPRP-driven transfer of land to questionable beneficiaries has led to some ironic situations, such as when an external evaluation team discovered that two out of three household respondents interviewed at the beginning of the CMARPRP process could no longer be tracked down just three years later in early 2007. Probing further, the team determined that: 1) the majority had 'migrated' to other places (61%); while 2) others were 'missing' for reasons that could not be discerned (29%). Combined, these two explanations account for 90% of CMARPRP's 'missing beneficiaries',[72] making the Bank-required longitudinal comparative evaluation (before and after CMARPRP) infeasible.

## Questionable land transfers, questionable development projects

The phenomenon of coerced and missing beneficiaries suggests that an anomalous land transfer process has taken place; any ensuing farm development efforts and investments in the area will thus probably simply ratify and institutionalise the anti-reform orientation already established. Following this logical sequence, and as confirmed by our findings discussed earlier, we can safely anticipate that most of the CMARPRP-sponsored development interventions through infrastructure building and other support services served primarily elite interests, while further undermining the situation of the poor living in and around the area.

*Questionable intentions, questionable interventions*

Our findings show little reason to celebrate the role played by local government officials, who have indeed become directly involved in the project's implementation in most sites, apparently for reasons that have little to do with concern for social justice or redistributive land reform. Instead, their involvement in CMARPRP has stemmed from a calculation that minimal investment of time and seed funds can lead to significant profit, in the form of expensive infrastructure such as roads, and support services for some of their constituents. However, it is important to note too that, while this was the promise of CMARPRP, it has not always panned out, leaving local government officials in the lurch and leading to tensions and at times even open conflict between CMARPRP staff and local government officials. For instance, tensions have arisen over delays or unacceptable modifications to promised 'goodies' (eg in Samal), or over competing ideas about the project's 'co-ownership' and 'co-financing' (eg in Zambales).

Local officialdom's role in facilitating land sales and the influx of development projects has not been neutral, but selective—sidelining legitimate actors while including others whose qualifications are questionable. This role has also tended to take centre stage in the process, at the expense of community participation. As one project document reveals, more than half (54%) of the beneficiaries interviewed said that they were never involved in the land sales negotiation—and yet they were CMARPRP buyers and beneficiaries.[73] Moreover, of those interviewed, 62% said they were not aware of any CMARPRP area committee—a body that is supposed to be the main driver of the entire development process. And 71% were not aware of any 'area development plan'.[74] It would seem that, when they got involved, local government officials tended to take command of the project, to the extent of even forcing peasants and indigenous groups to drop their land claims in favour of questionable elite sellers. Indeed, they seemed to have done all that they could during the land purchase process to secure the promised funded development package, even if at the expense of poor constituents.

## Conclusion

As pointed out in our second section, a more global critique of MLAR would question the value of the CMARPRP programme on the basis that it resulted in the distribution of only a few hundred hectares of land to a few hundred peasants. Our critique of the Philippine experience takes a different tack. In our view, CMARPRP's miniscule coverage has turned out to be a blessing in disguise: it means that the project's anti-poor thrust visited its damaging effects upon just a relatively few farms and households, at least so far. Despite the clearly discouraging outcomes, there are now calls for CMARPRP to be expanded. While CMARPRP documents admit problems in the process, these were taken as 'operational in nature' (ie technical and administrative), in disregard of the underlying question of power relations among various actors involved and the political economy of resource access and control.[75] At the present juncture, when land reform is again becoming a major national political issue, and debate is taking place on whether or not to extend CARP after 20 years (or after June 2008), it is critical that CMARPRP and similar initiatives be exposed and opposed for their anti-poor and anti-reform character.

The underlying analytic issue is to determine the actual direction of wealth and power transfer in a given development intervention. At the outset there were several different possible directions in wealth and power transfer in the CMARPRP context: intra-elite/elite-to-elite, state-to-elite, foreign donor-to-elite, poor-to-elite, elite-to-poor, state-to-poor, and foreign donor-to-poor. In practice, however, it was the first four paths (pro-elite, anti-poor) that came to dominate the process.

The intra-elite/elite-to-elite/ transfer is revealed in the methods adopted by landlords to evade land reform, such as declaring family members and other 'dummy' buyers as beneficiaries, and to a limited extent in real estate land sales between non-poor, elite sellers and buyers, in speculative land purchases. The state-to-elite transfer is seen in cases where public lands were taken and privatised by elite land claim makers through dubious processes. This type of transfer can also be detected in CMARPRP processes, where anti-reform manipulations of the sellers were even rewarded through free land titling, free land sales tax, etc.—all at the government's expense. Government money was also used as a counterpart for the development projects that benefited the elite more than the poor. The foreign donor-to-elite transfer is illustrated by the logical sequence that, if the land transfer scheme benefited not the poor but the elite, and the majority of the CMARPRP beneficiaries were not the poor but the elite, then all the resources from foreign donor agencies (in this case, the World Bank) that were spent ostensibly on these types of beneficiaries were actually a net transfer of resources to the elite. The poor-to-elite transfer is partly seen by the forced resolution of competing land claims in favour of the elite. This included lands being tilled by poor peasants and lands in indigenous people's territories, but claimed by elite entities, where the CMARPRP process forced the peasants (and indigenous communities) to drop their claims, to recognise the elite's claims, and to buy the land from the latter at commercial rates.[76]

In the Philippines the scheme has been carried out at the same historical moment that the government has been trying to wind down redistributive land reform,[77] as explained at the beginning of this paper. In short, the World Bank's land transfer scheme carried out at a pilot-test scale in the Philippines has not complemented the ongoing state-led, potentially redistributive land reform (CARP), as the Bank would have it. Rather, it has clearly undermined the existing land reform process. But the MLAR experiment in the country also did not amount to any significant pro-poor reformist outcomes. Indeed, as it turns out in the Philippine case, the Bank's initiative can more accurately be described as an 'anti-poor' land transfer programme.

# Notes

We thank Robin Broad for very useful comments on an earlier version of this article.
 1 J Putzel, 'The politics of partial reform in the Philippines', in VK Ramachandran & M Swaminathan (eds), *Agrarian Studies: Essays on Agrarian Relations in Less-Developed Countries*, New Delhi: Tulika Books, 2002 and London: Zed, 2003, pp 213–229.
 2 S Borras, 'State–society relations in land reform implementation in the Philippines', *Development and Change*, 32 (3), 2001, pp 545–575.
 3 See W Bello, D Kinley & E Elinson, *Development Debacle: the World Bank in the Philippines*, San Francisco: Institute for Food and Development Policy, 1982; and R Broad, *Unequal Alliance: The World Bank, the International Monetary Fund and the Philippines*, Berkeley, CA: California University Press, 1988.
 4 World Bank, *A Strategy to Fight Poverty: Philippines*, Washington, DC: Agriculture and Environment Operations Division, Country Department 1, East Asia Pacific Region, 1996.
 5 J Franco, 'Market-assisted land reform in the Philippines: round two—where have all the critics gone?', *Conjuncture* (Quezon City: Institute for Popular Democracy), 11 (2), 1999, pp 1–6.
 6 M Esguerra, 'The community-managed agrarian reform project (CMARP): a feasibility study', unpublished study commissioned by ARCDP-DAR, Quezon City, 2001.
 7 R Edillion, 'Economic analysis of the community-managed agrarian reform pilot (CMARP)', unpublished study commissioned by the ARCDP-DAR, Quezon City, 2001.
 8 R Mamon, 'Community-managed agrarian reform project (CMARP) pilot', unpublished individual [technical adviser] report, DAR-ARCDP, Quezon City, 2001.
 9 DAR-ARCDP, *Community-managed Agrarian Reform Program (CMARP) Project Operations Manual*, Quezon City: DAR, 2001.
10 J Putzel, *A Captive Land: The Politics of Agrarian Reform in the Philippines*, London: Catholic Institute for International Relations, New York: Monthly Review Press and Quezon City: Ateneo de Manila University Press, 1992.
11 J Franco, *Elections and Democratization in the Philippines*, New York: Routledge, 2001.
12 F Lara, 'Land reform in the proposed constitution: landmarks and loopholes', *Agricultural Policy Studies* (Quezon City: Philippine Peasant Institute), 1, 1986, pp 1–25.
13 See J Fox, *The Politics of Food in Mexico: State Power and Social Mobilization*, Ithaca, NY: Cornell University Press, 1993.
14 J Franco, 'Making land rights accessible: social movement innovation and political–legal strategies in the Philippines', *Journal of Development Studies*, forthcoming.
15 Borras, 'State–society relations in land reform implementation in the Philippines'; Borras, 'The Philippine land reform in comparative perspective: conceptual and methodological implications', *Journal of Agrarian Change*, 6 (1), 2006, pp 69–101; S Borras & J Franco, 'The national land reform campaign in the Philippines', paper prepared for the 'Citizens' Participation in National Policy Processes Project' of the IDS, Brighton, and the Ford Foundation, 2006; and S Borras & J Franco, 'Struggles for land and livelihood: redistributive reform in Philippine agribusiness plantations', *Critical Asian Studies*, 37 (3), 2005, pp 331–361.
16 See also the contribution by Nyamu-Musembi in this issue.
17 S Borras, 'Redistributive land reform in public (forest) lands? Rethinking theory and practice with evidence from the Philippines', *Progress in Development Studies*, 6 (2), 2006, pp 123–145; and D Carranza, 'Dilemmas, difficulties and challenges in carrying out pro-poor property rights reforms in public lands in the Philippines', *Agrarian Notes* (Quezon City: PEACE Foundation), 2006, at www.peace.net.ph, accessed 23 October 2006.
18 R Broad & J Cavanagh, *Plundering Paradise: The Struggle for the Environment in the Philippines*, Berkeley, CA: University of California Press, 1994.
19 D Carranza & P Mato, 'Subverting peasants' land rights: the Supreme Court decision exempting livestock areas from the coverage of agrarian reform', *Agrarian Notes*, May 2006, at www.peace.net.ph, downloaded 10 July 2006.
20 See J Franco, 'Again, they are killing peasants in the Philippines: lawlessness, murder and impunity', *Critical Asian Studies*, 39 (2), 2007, pp 315–328.
21 Borras & Franco, 'Struggles for land and livelihood'.
22 Carranza 2006.
23 Borras, 'The Philippine land reforms in comparative perspective'.
24 R De la Rosa, 'Agrarian reform movement in commercial plantations: the experience of the banana sector in Davao del Norte', in J Franco & S Borras (eds), *On Just Grounds: Struggling for Agrarian Justice and Exercising Citizenship Rights in the Rural Philippines*, Quezon City: Institute for Popular Democracy and Amsterdam: Transnational Institute, 2005, pp 45–114.

25 Cited in S Borras, 'Can redistributive reform be achieved via market-based land transfer schemes? Lessons and evidence from the Philippines', *Journal of Development Studies*, 41 (1), 2005, pp 90–134.
26 De la Rosa, 'Agrarian reform movement in commercial plantations'.
27 Putzel, *A Captive Land*, pp 332–335.
28 D Carranza, 'Failing a reform: the Hacienda Luisita formula', *SENTRA Monograph* 1, 1992 Series, Quezon City: SENTRA, 1994, pp 1–35; and Carranza, 'Hacienda Luisita massacre: a tragedy waiting to happen', *Agrarian Notes*, 2005, at www.peace.net.ph, accessed 18 May 2006.
29 Based on Carranza, 'Failing a reform'; Carranza, 2006; and Putzel, *A Captive Land*.
30 J Franco, 'Peripheral justice? Rethinking "non-state justice" systems in the Philippine countryside', *World Development*, forthcoming.
31 For example, K Deininger, 'Making negotiated land reform work: initial experience from Colombia, Brazil and South Africa', *World Development*, 27 (4), 1999, pp 651–672.
32 N Peluso, *Rich Forests, Poor People: Resource Control and Resistance in Java*, Berkeley, CA: University of California Press, 1992.
33 J Sato, 'People in between: conversion and conservation of forest lands in Thailand', in M Doornbos, A Saith & B White (eds), 'Forests: Nature, People, People' (special issue), *Development and Change*, 31 (1), 2000, pp 155–177.
34 C Kay & M Urioste, 'Bolivia's unfinished reform: rural poverty and development policies', in H Akram-Lodhi, S Borras & C Kay (eds), *Land, Poverty and Livelihoods in an Era of Neoliberal Globalisation: Perspectives from Developing and Transition Countries*, London: Routledge, 2007, pp 41–79.
35 S Razavi, 'Introduction: agrarian change, gender and land rights', *Journal of Agrarian Change* (special issue), 3(1–2), 2003, pp 2–32.
36 C Toulmin & J Quan (eds), *Evolving Land Rights, Policy and Tenure in Africa*, London: DFID/IIED/NRI, 2000.
37 K Griffin, 'Economic development in a changing world', *World Development*, 9 (3), 1980, pp 221–226.
38 R Herring, 'Beyond the political impossibility theorem of agrarian reform', in P Houtzager & M Moore (eds), *Changing Paths: International Development and the New Politics of Inclusion*, Ann Arbor, MI: University of Michigan Press, 2003, pp 58–87.
39 N Peluso, 'Violence, decentralization and resource access in Indonesia', *Peace Review*, 19 (1), 2007, pp 23–32.
40 F Barros, S Sauer & S Schwartzman (eds), *The Negative Impacts of World Bank Market-based Land Reform*, Brazil: Comissao Pastoral da Terra, Movimento dos Trabalhadores Rurais Sem Terra (MST) and Foodfirst Information and Action Network (FIAN), 2003.
41 P Rosset, R Patel & M Courville (eds), *Promised Land: Competing Visions of Agrarian Reform*, Oakland, CA: Food First Books, 2006.
42 J Harriss, *Depoliticizing Development: The World Bank and Social Capital*, London: Anthem Press, 2002.
43 H Akram Lodhi, S Borras Jr, C Kay & T McKinley, 'Neoliberal globalisation, land and poverty: implications for public actions', in Akram-Lodhi *et al*, *Land, Poverty and Livelihoods in an Era of Neoliberal Globalisation*, pp 383–398; S Borras, 'Free market, export-led development strategy and its impact on rural livelihoods, poverty and inequality: the Philippine experience seen from a southeast Asian perspective', *Review of International Political Economy*, 14 (1), 2007, pp 143–175; K Griffin, AR Khan & A Ickowitz, 'Poverty and distribution of land', *Journal of Agrarian Change*, 2 (3), 2002, pp 279–330; and H Bernstein, 'Land reform: taking a long(er) view', *Journal of Agrarian Change*, 2 (4), 2002, pp 433–463.
44 Data gathering for the national level analysis of CMARPRP was carried out through a combination of research methods that included close and careful examination of nearly all programme documents, many of which are not for public consumption. This approach was combined with interviews with key informants, including: a few (in)formal discussions with Klaus Deininger of the World Bank, in 1999 and 2000 in Manila (by Borras and Franco); an interview with the director of the CMARPRP (Bert Baniqued in 2002, by Borras) and with a senior programme staff member who requested anonymity (in a series of interviews in 2001, 2002, 2003 and 2007, by Borras, Franco and Carranza). Interviews with two former CAR Secretaries (Ministers, Ernesto Garilao (in 2002, 2004) and with Horacio Morales Jr (in 2002) by Borras were also extremely useful.
45 UPSARDFI, 'Families and households in the ARC: focusing ARCDP II for greater and lasting impact in the rural countryside', manuscript prepared by the University of the Philippines (UPSARDFI), Quezon City: CSWCD, UP-Diliman and DAR, 2001, pp 94–95.
46 MUCEP, 'Proposal for the preparation of area development plan and household level farm business plans for World Bank–DAR–CMARP project in Misamis Occidental. A Project Proposal by the Misamis University Community Extension Program (MUCEP) submitted to the ARCDP-DAR', Misamis Occidental: MUCEP and Quezon City: DAR-ARCDP, 2001.
47 UPSARDFI, 'Families and households in the ARC', p 94.
48 For a background on the World Bank support for agrarian reform communities, ie ARCDP, see J Fox & J Gershman, 'The World Bank and Social Capital: Lessons from Ten

Rural Development Projects in the Philippines and Mexico', *Policy Sciences*, 33 (3–4), 2000, pp 399–419.

49 At the moment, there has been no other independent study on CMARPRP, except for a forthcoming study by De Asis which is focused on 'state–community partnership' around development projects. It evades the question of land transfer.

50 DAR-ARCDP 2, 'The community-managed agrarian reform and poverty reduction project (CMARPRP): an impact analysis', internal project document, Quezon City, 2007, p 1.

51 DAR-ARCDP 2, 'Community-managed agrarian reform and poverty reduction project (CMARPRP)', internal project document, Quezon City, 2006, p 2.

52 *Ibid.*

53 See, for example, Barros *et al*, *The Negative Impacts of World Bank Market-based Land Reform*; Rosset *et al*, *Promised Land*; and JM Pereira, 'The World Bank's "market-assisted" land reform as a political issue: evidence from Brazil (1997–2006)', *European Review of Latin American and Caribbean Studies*, 82, 2007, pp 21–49.

54 Borras, 'The Philippine land reform in comparative perspective'.

55 Borras, 'Can redistributive reform be achieved via market-based land transfer schemes?'.

56 Data gathering for the local case studies was carried out through a combination of research methods. Following the national-level research, explained in note 44, the authors were able to secure most of the available unpublished, internal documents from all the CMARPRP field sites, giving us a rare opportunity to take a close critical look at the 'un-polished project reports'. This exercise, linked to the national level analysis, provided us with a good overview of the entire project dynamics. In addition, we carried out field visits in five project sites: Isabela, Zambales, Quezon, Negros Oriental and Davao del Norte. Borras did the Davao field visit, Carranza went to Quezon. We also recruited a few trusted research assistants to gather data for us in the field, equipped with a predetermined/semi-structured set of questionnaires: Danny Gatche for Pangasinan, Bong Gonzal for Negros, Leslie Inso for Mindoro, Wendy Ludovico for Quezon, Santiago Corpuz for Isabela, and Ronita Buenaventura for Davao. These research assistants were extremely familiar with the local agrarian structures in the project sites they were assigned to visit. The field visits were carried out on various dates in 2005–06. Interviewed key informants included CMARPRP local project site staff, local government officials including mayors, municipal administrators, and village officials, as well as the CMARPRP beneficiaries. On most occasions, focused group discussions were carried out.

57 DAR-ARCDP 2, 'The community-managed agrarian reform and poverty reduction project (CMARPRP): an impact analysis—integrative report', Quezon City, 2007, p 35.

58 DAR-ARCDP 2-Quezon, 'CMARPRP in Guinayangan, Quezon', Quezon City, 2006, p 9.

59 DAR-ARCDP 2-Mindoro, 'Process documentation: CMARPRP Occidental Mindoro: second class citizens? No more!', internal project document, Quezon City, 2006, p 6.

60 DAR-ARCDP 2, 'The community-managed agrarian reform and poverty reduction project (CMARPRP): an impact analysis—integrative report', Quezon City, 2007, p 25.

61 *Ibid*, pp 19, 25.

62 *Ibid*, p 30.

63 *Ibid.*

64 DAR-ARCDP 2, 'The community-managed agrarian reform and poverty reduction project (CMARPRP)', p 22.

65 DAR-ARCDP 2-Zambales, 'Process documentation: CMARPRP against all odds', internal project document, Quezon City, 2005, p 10.

66 DAR-ARCDP 2, 'The community-managed agrarian reform and poverty reduction project (CMARPRP)', pp 21–22.

67 *Ibid*, p 7.

68 DAR-ARCDP 2-Zambales, 'Process documentation', p 5.

69 DAR-ARCDP 2-Samal, 'LGU bridge funding in Samal Island, unique and one and only in the Philippines', Quezon City, 2006, pp 6–7.

70 *Ibid*, p 7.

71 *Ibid*, p 16.

72 DAR-ARCDP 2, 'The community-managed agrarian reform and poverty reduction project (CMARPRP): an impact analysis—household level assessment', internal document, Quezon City, 2007, pp 3–6.

73 *Ibid*, p 26.

74 *Ibid*, p 30.

75 See DAR-ARCDP 2, 'The community-managed agrarian reform and poverty reduction project (CMARPRP): an impact analysis—integrative report', Quezon City, 2007, pp 35–36.

76 Borras, 'Can redistributive reform be achieved via market-based land transfer schemes?'; Carranza, 'Failing a reform'; Carranza, 2006; Franco, 'Making land rights accessible'; and Franco, 'Peripheral justice?'.

77 Putzel, 'The politics of partial reform in the Philippines'.

# 'Willing Buyer, Willing Seller': South Africa's failed experiment in market-led agrarian reform

EDWARD LAHIFF

Since its transition to democracy in 1994 South Africa has adopted a strongly pro-market approach to land reform, influenced by conservative forces within the country and international backing for market-assisted agrarian reform (MLAR), particularly from the World Bank. A slow rate of land transfer, however, has led to calls for a more radical approach that would effect a more rapid redistribution of land from the white minority to the black majority, but has not been backed up by mobilisation of the landless and has yet to deflect the state from its chosen path.

In contrast to countries such as Brazil and the Philippines, where market-led agrarian reform evolved from, and has not entirely replaced, longer-running processes of 'state-led' reform, South Africa's land redistribution programme has fallen entirely within the era and the parameters of MLAR. Factors that made South Africa a candidate for MLAR—apart from the timing of its liberation—were the extreme inequalities in landholding (particularly along racial lines), the highly commercialised nature of South African agriculture, the presence of a well developed land market and the commitment of the incoming African National Congress (ANC) government to neoliberal economic policies and 'national reconciliation'. Moreover, the historical path of agricultural development in South Africa—specifically, the dispossession or extreme marginalisation of smallholders and tenant farmers and the consolidation of production in the hands of relatively few large-scale producers—meant that a 'land to the tiller' approach was not a realistic option.[1] Land reform, to be meaningful, would have to be fundamentally redistributive, benefiting not only those currently involved in agriculture but also those who had long been dispossessed.

## From colonial dispossession to democratic reform

The extent of dispossession of the indigenous population in South Africa, by Dutch and British settlers, was greater than in any other country in Africa, and persisted for an exceptionally long time. European settlement began around the Cape of Good Hope in the 1650s and progressed northwards and eastwards over a period of 300 years. By the mid-20th century most of the county, including most of the best agricultural land, was reserved for the minority white settler population, with the African majority confined to just 13% of the territory, the 'native reserves', later known as African Homelands or Bantustans.[2]

At the end of apartheid roughly 82 million hectares of commercial farmland (86% of total agricultural land, or 68% of the total surface area) were in the hands of white people (10.9% of the population), and concentrated in the hands of some 60 000 owners.[3] Over 13 million black people, the majority of them poverty-stricken, remained crowded into the former homelands, where rights to land were generally unclear or contested and the system of land administration was in disarray.[4] These areas were characterised by extreme poverty and under-development relative to the rest of the country. On privately owned (white) farms millions of workers and their families faced tenure insecurity and lack of basic facilities. Today, South Africa has one of the most unequal distributions of income in the world, and income and material quality of life are strongly correlated with race, location and gender.[5]

The negotiated transition to democracy in South Africa (1990–94) left much of the power and wealth of the white minority, including land owner-ship, intact.[6] The international political and economic climate had also shifted decisively, and the old certainties that had informed both the nationalist and the socialist wings of the liberation movement, led by the ANC,[7] were fading fast. The new Constitution guaranteed the rights of existing property owners but also granted specific rights of redress to victims of past dispossession and set the legal basis for a potentially far-reaching land reform programme.[8]

South African agriculture is dualistic in nature, with a highly developed and generally large-scale commercial sector coexisting with large numbers of small-scale farmers on communal lands.[9] Some 82% of the total surface area of the country is available for agricultural use, but relatively low rainfall, particularly in the western parts of the country, means that the majority is suitable only for extensive grazing.[10] The scarcity of good quality land, and the domination of the agricultural sector by high-value products such as meat and fruit (much of it for export), has major implications for land reform, especially where demand is for small plots for production of staple food crops.

The white-dominated commercial sector generates substantial employment and export earnings, but contributes relatively little to GDP in what is today a highly urbanised and industrialised economy.[11] While close to half of the black (African) population continue to reside in rural areas, most are engaged in agriculture only on a very small scale, if at all, and depend largely on non-agricultural activities for their livelihood, including migration to jobs in the urban areas, local wage employment and state welfare grants. South Africa had a thriving African peasant sector in the early 20th century, but this was systematically destroyed by the white settler regime on behalf of the mines, which demanded cheap labour, and of white farmers demanding access to both land and labour.[12] Thus, a key challenge set for itself by the government of the 'new South Africa' was how to redress historical injustice, combat rural poverty and contribute to economic development, without destroying the advanced agricultural sector or alienating politically conservative white landowners.

## South Africa's land reform policy

The Constitution of the Republic of South Africa sets out the legal basis for land reform, particularly in the Bill of Rights.[13] Section 25 places a clear responsibility on the state to carry out land and related reforms, and grants specific rights to victims of past discrimination. It allows for expropriation of property for a public purpose or in the public interest, subject to just and equitable compensation, and states explicitly that 'the public interest includes the nation's commitment to land reform, and to reforms to bring about equitable access to all South Africa's natural resources'.

The policy framework for land reform was set out in the 1997 *White Paper on South African Land Policy* and identifies three broad categories of reform:[14]

- land restitution, which provides relief for victims of forced dispossession;
- land redistribution, a discretionary programme to redress the racial imbalance in landholding;
- tenure reform, intended to secure and extend the tenure rights of the victims of past discriminatory practices.

The objectives of the redistribution programme, and the preferred means of achieving them, are described in the White Paper thus:

> The purpose of the land redistribution programme is to provide the poor with access to land for residential and productive uses, in order to improve their income and quality of life. The programme aims to assist the poor, labour

163

tenants, farm workers, women, as well as emergent farmers. Redistributive land reform will be largely based on willing-buyer willing-seller arrangements. Government will assist in the purchase of land, but will in general not be the buyer or owner.

While tenure reform and restitution include an element of redistribution, it is the redistribution programme itself that is expected to make the most substantial contribution and benefit the greatest number of people. The legal basis for redistribution is the Provision of Land and Assistance Act of 1993,[15] but this is no more than an enabling act that empowers the Minister of Land Affairs to provide funds for land purchase. The details of the redistribution programme are thus contained in various policy documents, rather than in legislation.

The foundations for the South African land reform programme were laid during the negotiated transition to democracy, when the ANC (the dominant element within the liberation movement) was itself in rapid transition from a Marxist-influenced national liberation movement to a neoliberal party of government. The concept of 'willing buyer, willing seller' entered the discourse on land reform gradually during the period 1993–96. It was entirely absent from the ANC's *Ready to Govern* policy statement of 1992, which instead advocated expropriation and other non-market mechanisms, and from the *Reconstruction and Development Programme*, the manifesto on which the party came to power in 1994. By the time of the *White Paper on South African Land Policy* of 1997, however, a market-based approach, and particularly the concept of 'willing buyer, willing seller', had become the cornerstone of policy. Such an approach was not dictated by the South African Constitution, which makes explicit provision for expropriation for purposes of land reform and for compensation at below market prices, but was rather a policy choice, in line with the wider neoliberal (and investor-friendly) macroeconomic strategy adopted by the ANC in 1996.[16]

Until 2000 redistribution policy centred on the provision of the Settlement/ Land Acquisition Grant (SLAG), a grant of R16 000 available to qualifying households with an income of less than R1500 per month.[17] This phase of the redistribution programme was generally described as targeting the 'poorest of the poor', which it appears to have done with some success, but was also widely criticised for 'dumping' large groups of poor people on former commercial farms without the skills or resources necessary to engage in agricultural production.[18]

Since 2001 SLAG has been effectively replaced by a programme called Land Redistribution for Agricultural Development (LRAD), which was introduced with the explicit aim of promoting commercially oriented agriculture but claimed to cater to other groups as well. The new policy offers higher grants, paid to individuals rather than to households, and makes greater use of loan financing through institutions such as the state-owned Land Bank. Beneficiaries can access LRAD grants from R20 000 to R100 000. All beneficiaries must make a contribution, in cash or kind, the size of which determines the value of the grant for which they qualify, although this requirement is, in practice, waived for those applying at the bottom of the scale.

Most redistribution projects have involved groups of applicants pooling their grants to buy formerly white-owned farms for commercial agricultural purposes. This emphasis on group projects has largely been the result of the small size of the available grant relative to the size and cost of the typical agricultural holding and of a general hostility—among sellers of land and state officials—to the sub-division of land (see below). Under LRAD, however, there has been a move towards smaller groups, including extended family groups, because of the increased availability of finance in the form of both grants and credit. In addition, the removal of the income ceiling for applicants has facilitated the entrance of black business people into the redistribution programme, who are able to engage more effectively with officials and landowners in order to design projects and obtain parcels of land that match their needs.

Less commonly groups of farm workers have used the grant to purchase shares in existing farming enterprises, especially in areas of high-value agricultural land such as the Western Cape. While these 'share-equity schemes' are often seen as one of the more successful types of land reform in South Africa, they have also been criticised for perpetuating highly unequal relations between white owner-managers and black worker-shareholders, and for providing little by means of material benefits to workers.[19] Since 2001 state land under the control of national and provincial departments of agriculture has also been made available for purchase. Over 700 000 hectares of land have been provided in this way, much of it transferred in freehold title to existing black occupiers, including many associated with the former homeland administrations.[20] A separate grant, the Grant for the Acquisition of Municipal Commonage, has been made available to municipalities wishing to provide land for use by the poor, typically for grazing purposes.

In terms of overall achievements, land reform in South Africa has consistently fallen far behind the targets set by the state and behind popular expectations. In 1994 virtually all commercial farmland in the country was owned by white people, and the incoming ANC government set a target for the entire land reform programme to redistribute 30% of this within a five-year period.[21] The target date was subsequently extended to 20 years (ie to 2014), but, at current rates, this target is most unlikely to be met—by 2006 only 4.1% of agricultural land had been transferred under all aspects of the programme. Government has tended to attribute this slow progress to resistance from landowners and the high prices being demanded for land, but independent studies point to a wider range of factors, including complex application procedures, budgetary limitations and bureaucratic inefficiency.[22]

By July 2006 a total of 3.4 million hectares had been transferred through the various branches of the land reform programme, benefiting an estimated 1.2 million people (see Table 1). The greatest amount of land (43.8%) was transferred under the redistribution programme, with lesser amounts being transferred through restitution, state land disposal and tenure reform. The total area of land transferred is *equivalent* to 4.1% of the agricultural land in

TABLE 1. Total land transfers under South African land reform programmes, 1994–2006

| Programme | Hectares redistributed | Contribution to total (%) |
|---|---|---|
| Redistribution | 1 477 956 | 43.8 |
| Restitution | 1 007 247 | 29.9 |
| State land Disposal | 761 524 | 22.6 |
| Tenure Reform | 126 519 | 3.7 |
| **Total** | 3 373 246 | 100.0 |

*Source*: Department of Land Affairs, power point presentation to Nedlac by Mr Mduduzi Shabane, Deputy Director-General, 24 August 2006.

white ownership in 1994 but because much of the land transferred under restitution and tenure reform, as well as some of the land under redistribution and all the land under State Land Disposal, was land that was formerly under state ownership, the actual impact on white-owned land is considerably less. Missing from these statistics is the amount of 'pure' market-based redistribution (ie land sales unconnected with the official land reform programme)[23] and, more significantly, the vast number of farm dwellers (workers, tenants and their dependants) who have *lost* access to land on white-owned commercial farms since 1994. A recent study by Wegerif, Russell and Grundling found that over two million farm dwellers—including some tenant farmers engaged in independent production—had been displaced between 1994 and 2004, more than had been displaced in the last decade of apartheid (1984–94) and more than the total number of people who had benefited under all aspects of the official land reform programme since it began.[24] It must be emphasised that the precise achievements of the land reform programme are a matter of intense debate, largely thanks to a lack of detailed reporting by the state agencies involved.

The weaknesses of current policy—and the criticisms raised by land reform activists—have been increasingly acknowledged by politicians and officials of late. The National Land Summit held in July 2005 heard calls for the review or even abandonment of the 'willing buyer, willing seller' approach from activists and senior political figures, among them the deputy president and the then minister of land affairs. Government has since signalled its commitment to a more proactive approach to land purchase, and to a greater role for local government, but it appears unlikely that this will translate into any fundamental departure from the principles of market-led reform.[25]

## Competing visions of land reform

While the South African land reform programme is usually described as market-led (or market-based), it differs from other versions of MLAR in a number of important respects. It is argued here that, taken in its entirety, the South African land reform programme should be seen not as a single and coherent policy approach, but rather as the outcome of competing imperatives and contending political forces. The result is a messy compromise that has proven to be extremely slow and has failed to deliver on its key policy objectives. Part of the explanation for this must be the low levels of mobilisation (and the absence of militancy) among the rural poor and landless, which has left the design and implementation of land reform policies to be shaped by state officials and their technical advisors and, less directly, by landowners through their power to withhold land from the programme.

While land reform has never been a very prominent issue within South African politics—when compared to issues such unemployment, housing or HIV/AIDS—there has been considerable ideological contestation around the subject since the transition to democracy began in the early 1990s. Much of the debate has been pursued at a relatively abstract, rhetorical level, with recurring calls from land reform activists, politicians and others to 'speed up' the process of reform, or to 'get tough' with landowners (as a group) and to provide land for 'the poor' and 'the landless', effectively as abstract categories. This is unfolding largely in the absence of parallel struggles on the ground where identifiable groups of people might mobilise to acquire specific pieces of land for particular purposes.

A powerful lobby of both conservatives and liberals has argued for the preservation of the existing, large-scale commercial agricultural sector, albeit with varying degrees of acceptance of the need to increase black participation within the sector. This position draws support from landowners, needless to say, but also from powerful business interests and, more surprisingly, from elements within the government's Department of Agriculture and the ANC itself. Much of this loose coalition can be considered hostile to radical land reform but accepting of the need to create a more 'inclusive' commercial agricultural sector and to defuse social tensions, if only for reasons of political stability. For the big business-aligned Centre for Development and Enterprise land reform is about 'deracialising land ownership in commercial agriculture, and "normalising" the countryside'.[26] The needs of the rural poor and landless, it argues, can best be addressed within the urban and industrial sectors, and in the development of the existing black rural areas (ie the former homelands) rather than through any restructuring of landholding or of the large-scale agriculture sector.

A second body of opinion—which combines elements of neoliberalism and neo-populism—argues for reform of landholding and the agricultural sector via the market. This position—articulated most prominently by the World Bank and drawing support from a range of academics and policy analysts within South Africa and internationally—argues that South Africa's large-scale commercial sector is inefficient, thanks to decades of subsidies, protectionism and discriminatory policies and should be restructured to allow the emergence of more 'family size' farms.[27] Black people wishing to enter or expand within the agricultural sector should be provided with assistance to enter the land market and compete with large-scale commercial farmers. Within the country, this approach is most actively supported by proponents of Black Economic Empowerment (BEE), the South African version of affirmative action, who advocate redistribution to black 'entrepreneurs' but who generally oppose radical restructuring in favour of the poor. It has also been seized upon enthusiastically by landowners because of the seemingly objective arguments it presents in favour of voluntarily negotiated purchases at market prices, and by a government keen to deflect popular expectations of a more radical, interventionist, policy.

A third, broad, position articulates a more radical ('populist') version of land reform. Drawing support from the mass popular mobilisation against apartheid, in which the ANC played a central role, this position has been framed largely in terms of restorative justice—'return of the land'—and calls for direct intervention by the state to effect a widespread redistribution of land to the poor and landless, often accompanied by calls for minimal compensation to landowners.[28] This position undoubtedly enjoys widespread support among the organisations of the poor and landless, such as the Landless People's Movement, NGOs associated with the former National Land Committee and the newer Alliance of Land and Agrarian Reform Movements (ALARM), as well as the grassroots membership of the ANC.

Most attention from this loose coalition has been focussed on pressurising the state to take action against white landowners *in general*, with little mobilisation around concrete demands at a local level. Land occupations—the most direct expression of demand for land—have been rare and almost entirely restricted to peri-urban areas, where the demand is primarily for land for housing rather than for agricultural production. The negotiating power of civil society was further weakened by the collapse, resulting from internal tensions, in 2004 of the National Land Committee (NLC), a federation of provincial non-governmental organisations, which was for many years the foremost voice for land reform. An associated grouping, the Landless People's Movement (LPM), loosely modelled on Brazil's Movimento dos Trabalhadores Rurais Sem Terra (MST), emerged in various parts of the country between 1999 and 2004, but it too had collapsed by the time of the National Land Summit in 2005.[29] A new coalition, the aforementioned ALARM, has more recently emerged but, like the former NLC, it consists mainly of provincially based NGOs and lacks a mass membership base.[30]

Notably absent from the mainstream discourse is a radical, small farmer position that focuses on the provision of relatively small plots of land to poorer households for production of staple foods, within an appropriate (state-assisted) support structure. Several critiques of the dominant policy discourse, and suggestions for greater emphasis on smallholder production and poverty alleviation, have been put forward, mainly by academics and a few local NGOs, but these have had little influence on the policy process do date.[31]

In the sections that follow critical areas of land reform in South Africa are examined, looking at both the ideological factors that have shaped policy and their practical outcomes. Of these, the methods of land acquisition and compensation are the most controversial and have received the most attention from all sides in the debate to date. The other three—beneficiary selection, farm planning and post-transfer support—have been relatively neglected, both by analysts and by actors within the reform process.

### Land acquisition and compensation

The critical question of how land for redistribution is to be acquired, and the compensation (if any) to be paid, was resolved in favour of the 'willing buyer, willing seller' model in the White Paper of 1997, which effectively granted landowners absolute discretion over participation in the land reform programme. This discretion applies most directly in the areas of land redistribution and farm workers' tenure reform, but it also heavily influences the rights-based restitution process which, in theory and in law, falls outside the 'willing buyer, willing seller' paradigm.

While there is certainly an active land market in South Africa, there is reason to believe that much of the land being transacted is not available to land reform beneficiaries.[32] Good quality land that comes onto the open market tends to be sold by public auction or private contract and transfer of ownership typically takes place within a few months of the initial offer to sell. Funding applications from would-be land reform beneficiaries generally take significantly longer than this to process and must be linked to a specific property. Moreover, the size of farms in South Africa generally tends to be much larger than what would be suitable for new entrants to the agricultural sector, a problem compounded by a general unwillingness among landowners to sell off portions of their land and strong official bias against subdivision (see below).

The official approval process for grant applications requires, among other things, a written agreement to sell from the landowner, an agreed price that is confirmed as 'market-related' by an independent valuer and a detailed farm plan, all of which can take anywhere between three months and two years to assemble. Thus would-be beneficiaries cannot participate in auctions, or 'shop around', or confirm a purchase within the usual timeframe demanded by the market, and so are excluded from the great majority of land sales. The 'willing sellers' are, in practice, required to wait for an extended period for confirmation of sale, and face the risk that the application will be turned down on technical grounds or because of an absence of available funds.[33] While little firm evidence has been produced on this point to date, it seems reasonable to assume that only a landowner who is exceptionally committed to the cause of land reform, or who cannot dispose of land by other means (because of poor location or quality of land, for example), would be likely to enter into a land reform transaction.[34]

An integral part of the landowner veto is the freedom to negotiate their own price which should, in theory, be market-based, or market equivalent. Aliber and Mokoena argue that MLAR places landowners in a strong negotiating position because of the limited number of properties being offered for land reform purposes, because applicants often have a strong preference for a particular property (because of its proximity to their current residence or because of ancestral connections), and because of the additional cost that would be incurred (for government and applicants) if negotiations were to collapse and the lengthy planning process had to begin again for another property.[35] Payment of market prices has been strenuously opposed by organisations representing landless people, as demonstrated at the National Land Summit of July 2005, and has been declared 'non-negotiable' by landowners. While the land market has reacted to changes in the wider political and economic environment during the transition to democracy, the scale of the land reform programme itself has been too small to have had any discernible impact on supply or price of land.

Prices paid for land for reform purposes are, in practice, set by professional land valuers retained by the Department of Land Affairs (DLA), who generate their own estimate of 'market price' based on factors such as recent sales of comparable properties in the area. Where such an estimate falls below the asking price of the landowner, some limited negotiation is entered into between the DLA and the landowner and landowners are free to accept or reject the offer made by DLA. The intended beneficiaries have no direct role in this process, and therefore have no power to influence the price paid or the final outcome of the negotiations. Cases have been reported of deals falling through because of miniscule differences between the asking price and the amount offered by DLA, suggesting that negotiating skills may not be adequate amongst DLA officials.[36]

A specific claim of MLAR is that, by paying landowners cash prices at the time of sale, it will make itself attractive to landowners and keep prices down, but this does not appear to be the case in South Africa. Landowners and their representatives complain not only of the lengthy and cumbersome bureaucratic procedures around sale agreements, but also of delays in payment once agreement has been reached. Cases have been reported of landowners waiting up to four years for their money.[37] In a study from the Northern Cape Province, Tilley identified a perception among landowners that both land reform applicants and the DLA were 'unreliable' negotiating partners: applicants because they did not have autonomy to engage in negotiations on their own behalf and remained dependent on officials to determine the ultimate grant amount and to finalise the transaction; DLA because of 'its protracted procedures, negotiating style and phased project cycle'.[38]

Price setting thus occurs through bureaucratic processes that bear only a distant relationship to the workings of the 'real' land market. 'Willing sellers' and 'willing buyers' find themselves caught up in often-protracted and obscure processes dominated by officials attempting to apply market principles, a far cry from 'the independent encounter of willing buyers and sellers in the market' envisaged by its proponents.[39] The bureaucratic complexity of the process does not make it attractive to landowners, while limited grant sizes, limited budgets, lengthy and restrictive approval processes and landowner prejudice combine to ensure that would-be land reform beneficiaries are restricted to a small proportion of the land coming onto the market every year, and often end up with land that is of relatively poor quality and more extensive that they would wish. The failure to introduce any specific measures to increase the supply of land for redistribution—and particularly the lack of any credible threat of expropriation—not only limits the impact of reform but also fails to send a clear political message to landowners as to what, if anything, is required of them under the reform programme.

## Beneficiary targeting

In line with World Bank recommendations the South African redistribution programme is premised on the principle that the beneficiaries will 'self-select', rather than be selected by government officials. In practice, little is known about the type of people benefiting from land reform, those who apply and are rejected, and those are not being reached by the programme at all. Since its inception the South African land reform programme has been beset by a lack of basic information, arising from inadequate (and often non-existent) systems for monitoring and evaluation.[40] This results in a dearth of reliable data on the socioeconomic characteristics of beneficiaries entering the programme as well as on the impact of land reform on livelihoods and the broader economy. While some of this can be attributed to poor data management systems within the Department of Land Affairs, much of the problem—especially regarding the socioeconomic profile of beneficiaries— results from the fact that relevant data is simply not collected in the first instance. Hence there has been considerable speculation around who exactly is benefiting from the programme and how this might be changing over time.

The few studies available suggest that only a small proportion of the landless and land-hungry are gaining access to the programme; that they are predominantly literate males over 40 years of age; and, increasingly, that they are those with access to wage income (including pensions), rather than the unemployed, and have relatively good access to information.[41]

While land reform policy officially aims to reach a range of beneficiaries— including women, young people, the unemployed, farm workers and aspirant commercial farmers—there has been a discernable shift in policy in favour of the latter group in recent years.[42] This is manifested in two main ways—the size of individual grants (and loans) awarded, and the criteria used to evaluate 'business plans' (ie farm planning—see below). Since 2001 the size of grants awarded to successful land reform applicants has been determined by the size of 'own contribution' made by the applicant. Own contribution can be in cash or in kind (eg agricultural equipment or livestock). Grants can also be used to leverage loans from the state-owned Land Bank (and visa versa: loans can be used as 'own contribution' to leverage grants), further favouring those with demonstrable assets. Own contributions do not necessarily contribute to the purchase of land, especially when the contribution is in kind rather than in cash, meaning that the land is in most cases purchased entirely from the land reform grant (or less commonly, by a combination of grant and loan).[43] Far from being a 'contribution' to the farming enterprise, and thereby ensuring commitment (or 'buy-in'), as the advocates of MLAR would suggest, 'own contribution' in the South African case simply qualifies the applicant to a greater or lesser degree of financial support, as estimates of asset worth are used to 'reward' applicants with varying levels of grants and loans.

Early in the South African land reform programme Zimmerman identified a range of barriers created by the concept of 'demand-led rationing', or self-selection, that is likely to exclude poorer groups, highlighting the lack of clarity within policy on the intended beneficiaries of land reform and the likelihood that a demand-led programme would be driven largely by considerations of racial equity that assume a homogenous black popula-tion.[44] Ongoing failure to define clearly the intended beneficiaries of land reform, the lack of a specific poverty alleviation strategy, an emphasis on economic 'viability' and a chronic failure to monitor the programme suggest that this exclusion of poor and marginalised groups is likely to continue.

## Farm planning

Apart from the ways in which land is acquired, and beneficiaries selected, the South African land reform has been shaped by highly conservative farm (or project) planning. Two particularly problematic issues stand out—the general failure to subdivide large properties and the imposition of unrealistic 'business plans'.

Subdivision of agricultural holdings was legally prohibited under apartheid (in terms of the Subdivision of Agricultural Land Act of 1970) and, although the law has now been repealed by parliament, it has been waiting over four years for the presidential signature necessary to give it effect. Before the repeal of this Act subdivision of land for land reform purposes was already exempt from its provisions, but little or no use was made of this. Indeed, subdivision of land is seen as an expensive and administratively cumbersome process by landowners and is unlikely to be undertaken by them even once all legal obstacles have been removed.[45] The result is that land continues to come on to the market in relatively large holdings, and groups of would-be beneficiaries are obliged to pool their grants in order to acquire them. No assistance is provided to beneficiaries wishing to subdivide properties after acquisition. The failure to subdivide is arguably the single greatest contributor to the failure and general underperformance of land reform projects, as it not only foists inappropriate sizes of farms on people (and absorbs too much of their grants in the process) but also forces them to work in groups, whether they wish to do so or not.[46]

Efforts by official agencies to preserve the structure of South African agriculture extend from a general antipathy to subdivision to the imposition of commercially oriented business plans on beneficiaries as a condition of their land reform grant. Business plans are typically drawn up by government-appointed consultants (or, less commonly, by officials of one of the provincial departments of agriculture), who often have minimal contact with the intended beneficiaries. Such plans typically provide ultra-optimistic projections for production and profit, based on textbook models drawn from the large-scale commercial farming sector, and further influenced by past use of the land in question.[47] Production for the market is usually the only objective, and plans typically require substantial loans from commercial sources, purchase of heavy equipment, selection of crop varieties and livestock breeds previously unknown to the members, hiring of labour (despite typically high rates of unemployment among members themselves) and sometimes the employment of a professional farm manager to run the farm on behalf of the new owners. Failure to obtain loans, as is often the case, renders the business plan unworkable, yet officials usually insist that beneficiaries comply with such plans and make this a condition for the release of discretionary grants to which beneficiaries are entitled. In cases where credit has been accessed in order to implement the business plan, there have been widespread reports of defaults on loans (but no official data), leading to some threatened repossession of properties by the banks.

A central weakness of most business plans is that they assume that the land will be operated as a single entity (ie as used by the previous owner), regardless of the size of the beneficiary group.[48] As argued above, because of the lack of support for subdivision, beneficiaries are often obliged to purchase properties much larger than they need, and even to expand the size of groups to aggregate sufficient grants to meet the purchase price. This results in widespread problems of group dynamics as former single-owner farms are turned into agricultural collectives. Official policy documents are remarkably silent on the preferred forms of land use, and nowhere in the official discourse are the words 'collective' or 'group farming' used, yet attempts at collective farming have become a hallmark of land reform projects in South Africa. Legally virtually all land transferred under the land reform programme is owned by either a Communal Property Association or a Trust, on behalf of the named members (beneficiaries). These land-owning institutions have been widely criticised as dysfunctional—many are in practice inoperative—and for leaving the rights of members ill-defined and poorly protected.[49]

The official emphasis on commercial 'viability' has increased considerably since the beginning of the land reform programme. Within months of being launched as a 'sub-programme' of redistribution, LRAD had virtually replaced SLAG, with the result that the 'commercial' logic of LRAD is now applied to all land reform applicants, regardless of their resources, abilities or stated objectives.[50] Applications that propose small-scale ('subsistence') production or the break-up of existing farm units stand little chance of being approved under the current system, even though various studies suggest that such small-scale land use is the most sought-after by the rural poor and landless.[51]

Conservative elements within the country—which appear to include most of the agricultural 'establishment' of landowners, agricultural economists and officials of the Departments of Agriculture and Land Affairs – are opposed to any change in agrarian *structure*, of which subdivision would be the most obvious sign, and make extensive use of the language of 'viability'. This feeds directly into the arguments for 'deracialisation', whereby conservative and some more progressive forces agree on the need for a change in the racial profile of landownership, but reject major restructuring along class lines (ie from relatively few large units to many smaller units). Subdivision is advocated by the World Bank and those aligned to it, but the Bank appears to have had remarkably little influence over policy in this respect. Radical and populist elements have not called for subdivision of property or individualisation of production, suggesting that they do not see it as an issue, perhaps because of an ideological antipathy to private enterprise and sympathy for collectivist solutions, whether of the socialist or traditional African variety.

Thus a defining characteristic of South African land reform policy is that beneficiaries—no matter how poor or how numerous—are required to step into the shoes of former white owners and continue to manage farms as unitary, commercially oriented enterprises, while alternative models, based on low inputs and smaller units of production, are actively discouraged. This inappropriate model, and the tensions within beneficiary groups that emerge from it, are largely responsible for the high failure rate of land reform projects, as discussed below.

## Post-settlement support

A lack of support services to newly resettled beneficiaries of land reform has, of late, been identified as a major weakness in South Africa's land reform.[52] In terms of market-led reform beneficiaries are not expected to rely exclusively on the state for post-settlement support services, but to access services from a range of public and private providers. Recent studies show that land reform beneficiaries experience numerous problems accessing services such as credit, training, extension advice, transport and ploughing services, and veterinary services, as well as input and produce markets.[53]

Services that are available to land reform beneficiaries tend to be supplied by provincial departments of agriculture and a small number of non-governmental organisations, but the available evidence would suggest that these only reach a minority.[54] For Jacobs the lack of post-settlement support stems from a general failure to conceptualise land reform beyond the land transfer stage, and from poor communication between the national Department of Land Affairs (responsible for land reform), the nine provincial Departments of Agriculture (responsible for state services to farmers), and local government, responsible for water, electricity and other infrastructure.[55]

The need for additional support for land reform beneficiaries has of late been acknowledged by the Ministry of Agriculture and Land Affairs and has led to the introduction, in 2004, of a new Comprehensive Agricultural Support Programme (CASP), with a total of R750 million allocated over five years. Since 2005 a new micro-credit programme, the Micro-Agricultural Finance Schemes of South Africa (MAFISA), has also been established by the state to provide loans to small farmers, including land reform beneficiaries, but the impact of these initiatives has yet to be reported.

The well developed (private) agri-business sector that services large-scale commercial agriculture has shown no more than a token interest in extending its operations to new farmers. The principal explanation for this, of course, is that land reform beneficiaries are, on the whole, so cash-strapped that they are not in a position to exert any effective demand for the services on offer, even if these services were geared to their specific needs.

The problems of post-settlement support have been raised by various commentators and analysts but have not been a major concern for some of the radical–populist groups, which can perhaps be seen as part of a general tendency to focus on the 'headline' political issue of land acquisition rather than on the more mundane technical details of agricultural production.[56]

## Conclusion: from market-led to people-led agrarian reform

Market-based agrarian reform makes claims for positive impacts on equity and efficiency, but serious doubts can be raised around both dimensions on the strength of the evidence from South Africa. The land reform programme as a whole—including substantial programmes of restitution and state land disposal—has managed to transfer relatively little land, and far below official targets. Land reform transactions depart considerably from 'normal' market transactions, and appear to be concentrated on less sought-after land that is purchased at prices higher than it might fetch on the open market. The bureaucratic complexity of the grant-making process ensures that intended beneficiaries are not able to compete in the 'real' market, but rather operate in a parallel market dominated by state officials, where beneficiaries have little influence over the purchase negotiations or the price paid. Conservative farm planning models, based on questionable assumptions about 'economic viability' and entrenched antipathy to subdivision of land, contribute to unwieldy collectives and low productivity and effectively exclude those who require small areas of land for household food production. The envisaged private sector support for new and emerging farmers has not materialised, largely because of the low productivity and limited availability of working capital among land reform beneficiaries. This has meant continued reliance on limited state support services that are poorly co-ordinated and targeted.

There is clearly little enthusiasm within the dominant social and political forces in South Africa for a radical land reform, and MLAR has provided the ideological justification for the avoidance of more traditional state-led approaches. Populist rhetoric about the need to look 'beyond the market' continues to be used by politicians to placate the rural social movements, but this contrasts starkly with the repeated assurances given to large-scale commercial farmers and black business interests eying opportunities under BEE.[57] On the side of landowners—many of them openly hostile to the new democratic order and the land reform process—MLAR has created opportunities to sell land that they might not otherwise be able to dispose of or at prices higher than the market might offer. It has provided cash injections with little change in power or flow of benefits in the case of share equity schemes, and allowed landowners as a whole to claim to be cooperating with the land reform process.

Politically and ideologically, the persistence of MLAR represents a triumph for landowners and other conservative elements, including those within the ruling ANC and the state structures. The interests of landowners—including new black entrepreneurs—have been fully protected, while the possibility of a radical restructuring of South African agriculture in favour of small family farms has been kept firmly at bay. This has been further facilitated by the absence of significant mobilisation of the rural poor and landless, despite the persistence of extreme poverty, inequality and evictions from commercial farms. In so far as there has been a politics of agrarian reform within the country, it has been framed largely in terms of restorative justice, with little attention to the finer points of beneficiary targeting, farm planning or post-settlement support. Where these issues are addressed, it tends to be in ways that exclude the very poor and favour better-resourced applicants. Moreover, popular pressure has been directed almost exclusively at the new democratic government rather than towards land occupations or struggles at the farm level. This focus on the state can be seen as a result of the enormous political legitimacy enjoyed by the ANC as the party of liberation, especially among the black majority, but also because of the 'developmental' rhetoric employed by the state which emphasises the centrality of 'official' processes and actively discourages mobilisation by autonomous social forces—a rhetoric that sits uneasily with the promotion of market-based approaches across virtually all areas of the economy.

While MLAR in South Africa has undoubtedly had some success in terms of transferring land and in not antagonising landowners, the complexity of the process, its slow pace and its inability to effectively target the most needy households or the most appropriate land (especially in terms of plot sizes) makes it unlikely that it can ever be a means of large-scale redistribution or poverty alleviation. In practice, the policy of 'willing buyer, willing seller' as implemented in South Africa is little more than a programme of assisted purchase, masquerading as agrarian reform, under which the main beneficiaries are likely to be white landowners and a small minority of better-off black entrepreneurs.

In order to meet the multiple objectives outlined in the South African Constitution, land reform policy will require major changes in all the key areas identified here. On land acquisition, purchases on the open market—whether by individuals, groups or a pro-active state agency—should remain part of the strategy, but much more is required in order to acquire appropriate land in areas of high demand and to divide it into manageable plot sizes. This can only be achieved by a well-resourced state agency willing to use its constitutional powers of expropriation to overcome landowner resistance and to provide land for a range of users, including the very poor.

In terms of beneficiary targeting, greater clarity—and more debate—is required on who the intended beneficiaries of reform are to be, and on the strategies required to reach various categories, especially the more marginalised such as the very poor, women and farm workers. Existing procedures, based on highly bureaucratic systems of grant application, clearly discriminate against more marginal groups. Again, there is an unavoidable duty for state agencies to work proactively with such groups and to simplify the application process—ideally by scrapping the system of grants altogether and focusing on direct provision of land.

In the critical area of farm planning there is a need to move away from existing conservative models to develop solutions that meet the needs of resource-poor farmers, whether working in groups or as individuals. This will require challenging the overwhelming power of national and provincial departments of agriculture and the agricultural 'establishment' of large farmers and agricultural economists who remain wedded to orthodox models of large-scale, capital-intensive farming. A clear commitment to subdivision of large properties, and the abandonment of inappropriate notions of economic 'viability', would bring multiple benefits in terms of opening up land reform to a wider range of beneficiaries and developing land use models more appropriate to resource-poor entrants.

Post-settlement support is clearly in need of a major overhaul, although the problems being encountered lie not only with the quality of services on offer but also with the inappropriate—often unworkable—farming models being imposed by officials. MLAR has been interpreted by state agencies in South Africa as an excuse not to provide systematic support to land reform beneficiaries. The Department of Land Affairs, provincial departments of agriculture, local municipalities and NGOs all have a role to play in post-settlement support but there is a pressing need to clarify their respective responsibilities and secure commitment by them to the land reform process. Above all, there is a need for a lead agency—something that does not exist at present—to contract with beneficiaries and take overall responsibility for co-ordination of state support services.

An accelerated agrarian reform programme that redistributes substantial areas of land and provides appropriate support services to the rural poor is unlikely to emerge, however, without a significant shift at the political level. Organisations representing the rural poor and landless remain weak and marginal to the policy-making process, while rural people themselves have not mobilised on a substantial scale to push their demands for land. In this context MLAR has provided a politically expedient alternative to traditional state-led agrarian reform which, if attempted, would undoubtedly set the state on a collision course with white landowners and their neoliberal supporters—black and white, at home and abroad. The landowner veto provided under MLAR ensures that the pace and direction of reform will be dictated by one of the most conservative elements in South African society and one with a vested interest in maintaining the current—highly unequal—structure of the agrarian economy. While a small number of new black farmers may be co-opted into the farming establishment, the big losers will undoubtedly be the poor and landless in need of land for survivalist purposes. Until this class can be mobilised to challenge the interests of established landowners and agricultural capital, and to force decisive intervention by the state, there is unlikely to be any fundamental change in the conditions which recreate poverty, landlessness and inequality in rural South Africa.

## Notes

I wish to thank Ben Cousins, Saturnino Borrras Jr. and Cristobal Kay for their valuable comments on the draft article. Responsibility for the final product rests with the author.

1 H Bernstein, 'South Africa's agrarian question: extreme and exceptional?', *Journal of Peasant Studies*, 23 (2–3), 1996, p 41.

2 L Thompson, *A History of South Africa*, New Haven, CT: Yale University Press, 1985, p 109.

3 See R Levin & D Weiner, 'The agrarian question and the emergence of conflicting agricultural strategies in South Africa', in S Matlhape & A Munz (eds), *Towards a New Agrarian Democratic Order*, Amsterdam: SAERT, 1991, p 92. For 1996 the South African Census reported a total population of 40.5 million, broken down in the following terms: African = 76.7%; White = 10.9%; Coloured (mixed race) = 8.9%; Indian/Asian = 2.6%; Unspecified/Other = 0.9%. Statistics South Africa, *The People of South Africa: Population Census 1996—Census in Brief*, Pretoria: Statistics South Africa, 1998.

4 See F Hendricks, *The Pillars of Apartheid: Land Tenure, Rural Planning and the Chieftaincy*, Uppsala: University of Uppsala, 1990; B Cousins, 'Livestock production and common property struggles in South Africa's agrarian reform', *Journal of Peasant Studies*, 23 (2–3), 1996; and E Lahiff, *An Apartheid Oasis: Agriculture and Rural Livelihoods in Venda*, London: Frank Cass, 2000.

5 J May, 'Growth, development, poverty and inequality', in May (ed), *Poverty and Inequality in South Africa: Meeting the Challenge*, Cape Town: David Philip, 2000, p 2.

6 H Marais, *South Africa: Limits to Change—The Political-Economy of Transition*, London: Zed Books, 1998.

7 The African National Congress (ANC) was founded in 1912. During the struggle against apartheid (1948–94) it contained both nationalist and socialist factions, and has a long-standing alliance with the South African Communist Party and the Congress of South African Trade Unions. The ANC was victorious in the general elections of 1994 (when it formed a multiparty Government of National Unity under the leadership of Nelson Mandela) and again in 1999 and 2004 (under the leadership of Thabo Mbeki).

8 AJ Van der Walt, 'Property rights and hierarchies of power: a critical evaluation of land reform policy in South Africa', *Koers*, 2–3 (64), 1999; L Ntsebeza, 'Land redistribution in South Africa: the property clause revisited', in L Ntsebeza & R Hall (eds), *The Land Question in South Africa: The Challenge of Transformation and Redistribution*, Cape Town: HSRC Press, 2007, pp 107–131.

9 OECD, *Review of Agricultural Policies: South Africa*, Paris: OECD, 2006, p 11.

10 In 1994–95, 81.9% of the territory (85 million hectares) was used for grazing, 10.9% (13.3 million ha) for dryland cropping and just 1.2% (1.5 million ha) for irrigated cropping. Statistics South Africa, *Land Accounts—Including Land-use and Land-cover—for South Africa, 1994/1995*, Pretoria: Statistics South Africa, 2004.

11 Agriculture accounted for 10% of formal employment in 2002. Its share of GDP fell from 9.12% in 1965 to just 3.2% in 2002. N Vink & J Kirsten, 'Agriculture in the national economy', in L Niewoudt & J Groenwald (eds), *The Challenge of Change: Agriculture, Land and South African Economy*, Scottsville: University of Natal Press, 2003.

12 C Bundy, *The Rise and Fall of the South African Peasantry*, London: Heinemann, 1979.

13 Republic of South Africa, *Constitution of the Republic of South Africa (Act 108 of 1996)*, Pretoria: Government Printer, 1996.

14 Department of Land Affairs, *White Paper on South African Land Policy*, Pretoria: Department of Land Affairs, 1997, p 38.

15 Previously called the Provision of Certain Land for Settlement Act (Act 126 of 1993), until its amendment and renaming in 1998.

16 See World Bank, *South African Agriculture: Structure, Performance and Options for the Future*. Washington, DC: World Bank, 1994; Marais, *South Africa*; and R Hall, P Jacobs & E Lahiff, *Evaluating Land and Agrarian Reform in South Africa: Final Report*, Cape Town: Programme for Land and Agrarian Studies, University of the Western Cape, 2003.

17 The South African currency is the Rand (R). In April 1994, R1 was equal to roughly US$0.28 (R3.58 = US$1); by April 2007 the value of the Rand stood at roughly US$0.14 (R6.97 = US$1).

18 See K Deininger & J May, *Can there be Growth with Equity? An Initial Assessment of Land Reform in South Africa*, Policy Research Working paper 2451, Washington, DC: World Bank, 2000; E Lahiff, 'The impact of land reform policy in the Northern Province', in B Cousins (ed), *At the Crossroads: Land and Agrarian Reform in South Africa into the 21st Century*, Cape Town/Johannesburg: Programme for Land and Agrarian Studies, University of the Western Cape/National Land Committee, 2000; and S Turner, *Land and Agrarian Reform in South Africa: A Status Report, 2002*, Cape Town: Programme for Land and Agrarian Studies, University of the Western Cape, 2002.

19 For a variety of perspectives on share equity schemes, see K Deininger & J May, *Can there be Growth with Equity?*; D Mayson, *Joint Ventures*, Cape Town: Programme for Land and Agrarian Studies,

University of the Western Cape, 2003; and K Kleinbooi, E Lahiff & B Tom, 'Land reform, farm employment and livelihoods: Western Cape case study—Theewaterskloof local municipality', unpublished report, Programme for Land and Agrarian Studies, University of the Western Cape and Human Sciences Research Council, Pretoria, 2006.

20 M Wegerif, *A Critical Appraisal of South Africa's Market-based Land Reform Policy: The Case of the Land Redistribution for Agricultural Development (LRAD) Programme in Limpopo*, Cape Town: Programme for Land and Agrarian Studies, University of the Western Cape, 2004.

21 G Williams, 'Setting the agenda: a critique of the World Bank's rural restructuring programme for South Africa', *Journal of Southern African Studies*, 22 (1), 1996, p 139.

22 See Ministry of Agriculture and Land Affairs, *Delivery of Land and Agrarian Reform*, Report to the National Land Summit, Pretoria: Ministry of Agriculture and Land Affairs, 2005; and P Jacobs, E Lahiff & R Hall, *Land Redistribution*, Cape Town: Programme for Land and Agrarian Studies, University of the Western Cape, 2003.

23 MC Lyne & MAG Darroch, *Land Redistribution in South Africa: Past Performance and Future Policy*, BASIS CRSP Research Paper, Department of Agricultural and Applied Economics, University of Wisconsin-Madison, 2003.

24 M Wegerif, B Russell & I Grundling, *Summary of Key Findings from the National Evictions Survey*, Polokwane: Nkuzi Development Association, 2005.

25 Department of Land Affairs, Media briefing by Minister of Agriculture and Land Affairs, Lulu Xingwana, 7 September 2006, at http://land.pwv.gov.za/publications/news/press_releases/KEYMES~2.DOC.

26 Centre for Development and Enterprise, *Land Reform in South Africa: A 21st Century Perspective*, Johannesburg: CDE Research report 14, 2005, p 22.

27 For detailed exposition of this position, see H Binswanger & K Deininger, 'South African land policy: the legacy of history and current options', in J van Zyl, J Kirsten & HP Binswanger (eds), *Agricultural Land Reform in South Africa: Policies, Markets and Mechanisms*, Cape Town: Oxford University Press, 1996; J Van Zyl & H Binswanger, 'Market-assisted rural land reform: how will it work?', in van Zyl *et al*, *Agricultural Land Reform in South Africa*; M Lipton, 'Rural reforms and rural livelihoods: the context of international experience', in M Lipton, M de Klerk & M Lipton (eds), *Land, Labour and Livelihoods in Rural South Africa*, 2 vols, Durban: Indicator Press, 1996; K Deininger & J May, *Can there be Growth with Equity*; and R Van den Brink, G Thomas, H Binswanger, J Bruce & F Byamugisha, *Consensus, Confusion, and Controversy: Selected Land Reform Issues in Sub-Saharan Africa*, World Bank Working Paper 71, Washington, DC: World Bank, 2006.

28 See A Mngxitama, 'The taming of land resistance: lessons from the National Land Committee', *Journal of Asian and African Studies*, 41(1–2), 2006, pp 39–69; WD Thwala, 'Land and agrarian reform in South Africa', in Peter M Rosset, Raj Patel & Michael Courville (eds), *Promised Land: Competing Visions of Agrarian Reform*, Oakland, CA: Food First/Institute for Food and Development Policy, 2006; L Ntsebeza, 'Land redistribution in South Africa: the property clause revisited', in Ntsebeza & Hall, *The Land Question in South Africa*; and C Walker, 'Redistributive land reform: for what and for whom?', in Ntsebeza & Hall, *The Land Question in South Africa*.

29 S Greenberg, 'The landless people's movement and the failure of post-apartheid South Africa', in R Ballard *et al* (eds), *Voices of Protest: Social Movements in Post-apartheid South Africa*, Pietermaritzburg: University of KwaZulu-Natal Press, 2006; and Mngxitama, 'The taming of land resistance'.

30 M Andrews, 'Struggling for a life in dignity', in Ntsebeza & Hall, *The Land Question in South Africa*.

31 See R Levin, R Russon & D Weiner, 'Class, gender and the politics of rural land reform', in R Levin *et al* (eds), *"No More Tears": Struggles for Land in Mpumalanga, South Africa*, Trenton, NJ: Africa World Press, 1997; Jacobs *et al*, *Land Redistribution*; SM Kariuki, *Creating the Black Commercial Farmers in South Africa*, ASC Working Paper 56/2004, Leiden: African Studies Centre, 2004; E Lahiff & B Cousins, 'Smallholder agriculture and land reform in South Africa', *IDS Bulletin*, 36(2), 2005; B Cousins, 'Agrarian reform and the "two economies": transforming South Africa's countryside', in Ntsebeza & Hall, *The Land Question in South Africa*; R Hall, 'Transforming rural South Africa? Taking stock of land reform', in Ntsebeza & Hall, *The Land Question in South Africa*; and C Walker, 'Redistributive land reform'.

32 An average of 6.3% of rural land was transacted per year in the period 1995–2000, but this included a high proportion of inter-family transfers (inheritance). M Aliber & R. Mokoena, *The Interaction Between the Land Redistribution Programme and the Land Market in South Africa: A Perspective on the Willing-Buyer/Willing-Seller Approach*, Cape Town: Programme for Land and Agrarian Studies, 2002.

33 Insufficient budgets to fund approved projects have been a recurring problem since about 2003, leading to additional (post-approval) delays in transactions. R Hall & E Lahiff, *Budgeting for Land Reform*, Policy Brief 13, Cape Town: Programme for Land and Agrarian Studies, University of the Western Cape, 2004, p 2.

179

34 Aliber & Mokoena, *The Interaction Between the Land Redistribution Programme and the Land Market in South Africa.*

35 *Ibid*, p 27.

36 S Tilley, *Why do the Landless Remain Landless? An examination of land acquisition and the extent to which the land market and land redistribution mechanisms serve the needs of land-seeking people*, Cape Town: Surplus People Project, 2004, p 10.

37 Gert Raal, vice-chair of AgriLimpopo quoted in the *Mail and Guardian*, 22 April 2005.

38 Tilley, *Why do the Landless Remain Landless?*, 2004, p 38.

39 K Deininger, *Making Negotiated Land Reform Work: Initial Experience from Brazil, Colombia and South Africa*, Policy Research Working Paper 2040, Washington, DC: World Bank, 1999, p 12.

40 See the following for examples of monitoring and evaluation exercises and discussions of their limitations: Department of Land Affairs, *Annual Quality of Life Report, 1998*, Pretoria: Department of Land Affairs, 1998; I Naidoo, *Measuring the Impact of the Land Reform Programme: Some Issues for Consideration*, Directorate: Monitoring and Evaluation, Department of Land Affairs, 1999; J May & B Roberts, *Monitoring and Evaluating the Quality of Life of Land Reform Beneficiaries: 1998/1999— Summary Report prepared for the Department of Land Affairs*, 2000; A Ahmed, P Jacobs, R Hall, W Kapery, R Omar & M Schwartz, *Monitoring and Evaluating the Quality of Life of Land Reform Beneficiaries 2000/2001*, technical report prepared for the Department of Land Affairs, Directorate of Monitoring and Evaluation, Pretoria, 2003.

41 E Lahiff, 'The impact of land reform policy in the Northern Province'; M Wegerif, *A Critical Appraisal of South Africa's Market-based Land Reform Policy*; Jacobs *et al*, *Land Redistribution*; R Hall, 'LRAD Rapid Systematic Assessment Survey: nine case studies in the Eastern Cape', unpublished paper, Programme for Land and Agrarian Studies, University of the Western Cape, 2004; Human Sciences Research Council, 'Land redistribution for agricultural development: case studies in three provinces', unpublished report, Integrated Rural and Regional Development division, HSRC, Pretoria, 2003.

42 Jacobs *et al*, *Land Redistribution*.

43 R Hall, *Land and Agrarian Reform in South Africa: A Status Report 2004*, Cape Town: Programme for Land and Agrarian Studies, University of the Western Cape, 2004.

44 F Zimmerman, 'Barriers to participation of the poor in South Africa's land redistribution', *World Development*, 28 (8), 2000, pp 1439–1460.

45 Aliber & Mokoena, *The Interaction Between the Land Redistribution Programme and the Land Market in South Africa.*

46 Van den Brink *et al*, *Consensus, Confusion and Controversy*, p 45.

47 See Lahiff, 'The impact of land reform policy in the Northern Province'; Human Sciences Research Council, 'Land redistribution for agricultural development'; Jacobs *et al*, *Land Redistribution*; Wegerif, *A Critical Appraisal of South Africa's Market-based Land Reform Policy*; Hall, 'LRAD Rapid Systematic Assessment Survey'; and A Bradstock, *Key Experiences of Land Reform in the Northern Cape Province of South Africa*, London: FARM-Africa, 2005.

48 Lahiff, 'The impact of land reform policy'; Human Sciences Research Council, 'Land redistribution for agricultural development'.

49 Jacobs *et al*, *Land Redistribution*; C Walker, 'Piety in the sky? Gender policy and land reform in South Africa', *Journal of Agrarian Change*, 3 (1–2), 2003, pp 113–148; and Council for Scientific and Industrial Research, *Review of Communal Property Institutions*, Pretoria: CSIR, 2005.

50 Lahiff & Cousins, 'Smallholder agriculture and land reform in South Africa'.

51 M Aliber, M Roefs & M Reitzes, *Auditing the Realisation of Democracy and Human Rights in the Context of Rural Land Reform in South Africa: A Component of the Metagora Pilot Project—Final Technical Report*, Pretoria: Human Sciences Research Council, 2005; and T Marcus, K Eales & A Wildschut, *Down to Earth: Land Demand in the New South Africa*, Johannesburg: Land and Agricultural Policy Centre and Durban: Indicator Press, 1996.

52 Ministry of Agriculture and Land Affairs, *Delivery of Land and Agrarian Reform.*

53 Human Sciences Research Council, 'Land redistribution for agricultural development'; Hall, 'LRAD Rapid Systematic Assessment Survey'; Wegerif, *A Critical Appraisal of South Africa's Market-based Land Reform Policy*; and Bradstock, *Key Experiences of Land Reform in the Northern Cape Province of South Africa.*

54 Human Sciences Research Council, 'Land redistribution for agricultural development', p 72; Hall, 'LRAD Rapid Systematic Assessment Survey'; and 'Didiza offers reasons for Limpopo failures', *Farmers Weekly*, 18 November 2005.

55 P Jacobs, *Support for Agricultural Development*, Cape Town: Programme for Land and Agrarian Studies, University of the Western Cape, 2003, p 7. See also R Hall, M Isaacs & M Saruchera, *Land and Agrarian Reform in Integrated Development Plans: Case Studies from Selected District and Local*

180

*Municipalities*, Cape Town: Programme for Land and Agrarian Studies, University of the Western Cape, 2004.

56 See Jacobs *et al*, *Land Redistribution*.

57 This was most evident at the National Land Summit held in July 2005 where, in front of a large audience of land reform activists and representative of landowners, the denunciation of 'willing buyer, willing seller' was led by the Deputy President and the Minister of Agriculture and Land Affairs. Two years later the policy remained in place.

# Politics, Power and Poverty: twenty years of agricultural reform and market liberalisation in Egypt

RAY BUSH

This article examines the impact of economic reform in Egypt's countryside. It explores the 20-year history of market liberalisation, the consequence of change in land tenure and the contemporary drive by the International Financial Agencies (IFIs) and the Egyptian government to promote export-led growth. Egypt has had two stormy political years. The state's promise of political reform that conveniently coincided with a presidential election (coronation) ran alongside ferocious political violence waged by the government and its agents of law and disorder to arrest, detain and frustrate secular and Islamic opposition. Worker unrest and the escalation of factory and industrial disputes are now on an unprecedented scale.[1]

Agreement with the World Bank for structural adjustment began after the first Gulf War in 1991. Liberalisation of the agricultural sector started in 1987. Agricultural liberalisation was facilitated before Gamel Abdul Nasser's death in 1970: it was certainly driven by his successor Anwar Sadat in a process of de-nasserisation that Hosni Mubarak accelerated. Yet there is a contradiction and a failure at the heart of Egypt's agrarian reforms. Market reform in the countryside has ended state provision of inputs and marketing, legal requirements for cropping, and credit supply. But the reforms have failed to deliver sustained growth and poverty reduction, returning some regions in the Nile Delta to the power of big landlords. The reforms have accelerated poverty, the legal frameworks for markets in land have been shaped by the powerful rather than providing the declared universal security for tenants and smallholders. Labour regimes, moreover, have not 'liberated' the near-landless to work as wage labourers but have become more coercive and added to processes of impoverishment amid rhetoric that market reform generates growth, opportunity and security for all.

After 20 years of failed reforms the IFIs are on a renewed mission to promote 'agricultural competitiveness'.[2] Egyptian policy makers are prevailed upon to promote export-driven growth in horticultural commodities and cotton. This is a familiar edict and one that has proved singularly unsuccessful.[3]

Egypt's agricultural sector accounts for about 15% of GDP, industry 34%, services 51%. Agriculture accounts for probably around 36% of overall employment and 22% of commodity exports. Over half of Egypt's more than 70 million live in the countryside and farming is restricted to about 5% of the land area—more than 90% of farming centred in the north of the country in the Nile Delta. Land reclamation in desert areas has been a feature of Egypt's agricultural strategy since before Nasser but there are now developments in what might be called the 'new, new' lands. These are desert areas along the northern coast together with large ambitious development projects like Toshka in what has been labelled the New Valley in the desert west of the Aswan Dam. These are part of plans to double cultivable area.[4] Until recently, when market reform began jeopardising historical patterns of crop rotation in the Nile Valley and Delta, a farmer using a three-year cotton rotation cycle divided land into three parts. The winter fodder of clover or short berseem was replaced in summer by cotton, after two cuttings of fodder were taken. A second portion of land might be used to grow long berseem, and a third wheat. In summer the land would then be sowed for maize, rice or sorghum. Regional variation to this pattern of rotation included the cultivation in summer of rice, followed by winter cereals and legumes in the northern part of the Delta, and maize in the summer; and in the winter wheat and legumes in the southern part of the Delta and middle Egypt. In southern Egypt sorghum is normally the main summer crop and in Upper Egypt sugar cane is the cash crop that replaces cotton.

The IFIs and the government are now trying to maximise the production of high-value low nutritious foodstuffs for export markets. In doing this they focus on developing new land, reclaiming deserts and investing in capital-intensive machinery that only large landowners and investors can afford. The neglect of smallholders and rural development in the old lands is a key feature of the dispossession of the *fellahin*.[5] Before we look at the counter-revolution, however, it is important to trace aspects of what the government has turned its back on.

## The revolution

One of the reasons behind the Free Army Officer's seizure of power in 1952 and the abolition of the monarchy was the persistence of rural poverty and the mounting wealth of Egypt's landowning Pasha class.[6] Nasser introduced the most famous agrarian reform in the Middle East. It was enacted initially very swiftly and then over a number of years. Egypt's countryside at the start of the 20th century was marked by declining standards of living and insecurity for smallholders and landless people.[7] The countryside was dominated politically and economically by large-scale owners who also had links with urban industry. Land reform legislation in 1952, 1961, 1963 and 1969 redistributed 12% of the country's land. The redistribution intended to give landless and near landless farmers' rights to land for the first time in the country's history.

Table 1 indicates the scale of unequal land holdings before and after Nasser's agrarian reforms. The reforms tried to break the political and economic power of large owners. Holders with fewer than five *feddans* (1 feddan = 1.038 acres or 0.42 hectares) increased and so too did their overall proportion of land. Estates bigger than 200 *feddan* disappeared. Although large ceilings on land holdings held by individuals were lowered to 100 *feddan*, families could still own 300 *feddan*.

A major dimension to the reforms was the introduction of secure tenure for tenants. About 60% of total cultivable land was worked by tenants and rental values were set at seven times the agricultural land tax—determined in relation to soil fertility and location. For the first time tenants received a lease and new legislation gave tenants rights of inheritance in perpetuity. Yet by 1980 only 14% of the total cultivated land had been redistributed to fewer than 10% of agricultural households. Dispossessed landowners received compensation, private property persisted, large landowners found ways of retaining their land: there was ultimately very little fundamental shift in the balance of political and economic power.

Disparities in land holding and rural inequality continued but they ran alongside dramatic improvements in rural standards of living, income distribution, diets and agricultural productivity. Probably as many as 350 000 families benefited from the agrarian reform laws, accessing 700 000 *feddans*.[8] Poverty reduction and economic growth was helped by a regional oil boom and surge in the number of Egyptian labour migrants working in neighbouring oil-producing states.[9] The reforms were also an attempt to drain surplus from agriculture to subsidise urban growth and industrialisation.[10] One of the main dimensions of Nasser's initiative in doing this was the reform of agricultural credit co-operatives that had previously been dominated by large landowners. After the revolution the position of landlords in co-ops were replaced by state appointees. The co-ops also acted as a major break on political activities of rural producers perceived to challenge state policy. The co-ops determined cropping patterns, input supplies, credit provision and marketing.

The hallmark of Nasser's presidency was an authoritarian populism that promoted Arab nationalism and delivery of improved conditions for Egypt's middle classes and poor.[11] Nasser promoted a social contract: political repression and limited political participation among the working class and peasantry in return for the state's delivery of basic services. The challenge the

TABLE 1. Distribution of land ownership before and after agrarian reform laws, 1952–61

| Feddans | Landowners pre-reform | Landowners post-reform | Holding size pre-reform | Holding size post-reform | Landowners (%) pre-reform | Landowners (%) post-reform | Area owned (%) pre-reform | Area owned (%) post-reform |
|---|---|---|---|---|---|---|---|---|
| <5 | 2 642 000 | 2 919 000 | 2 122 000 | 3 172 000 | 94.3 | 94.1 | 35.4 | 52.1 |
| 5–10 | 79 000 | 80 000 | 526 000 | 516 000 | 2.8 | 2.6 | 8.8 | 8.5 |
| 10–20 | 47 000 | 65 000 | 638 000 | 648 000 | 1.7 | 2.1 | 10.7 | 10.6 |
| 20–50 | 22 000 | 26 000 | 654 000 | 818 000 | 0.8 | 0.8 | 10.9 | 13.5 |
| 50–100 | 6000 | 6000 | 430 000 | 430 000 | 0.2 | 0.2 | 7.2 | 7.1 |
| 100–200 | 3000 | 5000 | 437 000 | 500 000 | 0.1 | 0.2 | 7.3 | 8.2 |
| 200+ | 2000 | | 1 177 000 | | 0.1 | | 19.7 | |
| Total pre-reform | 2 801 000 | | 5 984 000 | | 100.0 | | 100.0 | |
| Total post-reform | | 3 101 000 | | 6 084 000 | | 100.0 | | 100.0 |

*Source*: Adapted from MS Sallam, 'Agrarian reform in Egypt', paper presented to the Land Reform Conference, Cascavel, Brazil, April 1998.

regime faced was doing this without dependence upon foreign loans to pay for service provision and industrialisation.

Egypt's GDP more than doubled between 1961 and 1970, schools were built at an average of one a day from 1952 to 1966 and the numbers receiving free primary education rose by 1.3 million to 3.4 million, of which more than half were girls. The development hallmarks of Nasser's presidency became the land reforms, the building of the Aswan High Dam and other industrial projects. At the time of his death in 1970, Egypt's civilian debt was $1.7 billion. More significantly Nasser failed to recover from the defeat of the 1967 war with Israel, the 600% increase in military expenditure from 1967 to 1973, and the occupation of Sinai.

Mounting economic and political crisis led Nasser in 1968 to begin a pattern of relaxing state control in the economy. The 30 March Programme conceded the need to give Egyptians greater freedom with overseas deposits of foreign currency. It was, however, Nasser's failure to promote democratic and participatory structures, alongside economic intervention and state management of the economy that ensured his fragile heritage. Despite the considerable improvement in rural and urban standards of living, the reform of tenure and attempts to reduce inequalities in holdings of land, Nasser was unable, or unwilling, to forge a strong organic link with workers and peasants. That link was crucial to prevent the 'bourgeois recapture of state power'.[12]

## Counter-revolution

Economic reform in the agricultural sector began in the mid-1980s but it had been preceded by Sadat's return of land to many large landowners in the 1970s. Sadat's economic opening or *infitah*, launched after the October 1973 war with Israel, aimed to combine Arab capital, Western technology and Egyptian resources.[13] The short-term boom at the start of *infitah* was driven by high oil prices and an accompanying neglect of agriculture. The economy benefited from high rents from the Suez canal, oil and labour remittances. Yet by 1981 Egypt's external debt had risen from $5 billion in 1970 to $30 billion. The regime became mired in corruption while inequality soared. Dissatisfaction with the regime came to a head in 1977 with unprecedented food riots protesting against price rises.

Agriculture was neglected in the 1970s and 1980s. By 1974 Egypt was the world's third largest importer of grain. Imports had quadrupled in the 1970s to fill the gap between wheat production—growing at less than 2% per annum and wheat consumption, which grew at close to 9%. This was paid by subsidised US loans, increased international borrowing and an enlarged external debt. In per capita terms imports of basic food grains and pulses increased almost eight times between 1970 and 1980. The trade balance for the agricultural sector, previously in surplus ($300 million in 1970) became a deficit of $800 million by 1977 and $2.5 billion by 1980–81. The annual net deficit in agricultural trade rose to $3 billion in the mid-1980s.[14] At the end of the 1980s Egypt imported more than half its food needs and food imports accounted for 25% of all imports.

Financial crisis drove Mubarak in 1991 to agree to an IMF and World Bank Economic Reform and Structural Adjustment Programme (ERSAP). Mubarak was mindful of the need for a cautious approach to reform. He had learnt the lesson of bread riots in Sadat's presidency. The IFIs also valued stability and the persistence of an authoritarian regime in the region. ERSAP was intended to liberalise markets and input provision and to promote production for export of high-value low nutritious foodstuffs (and cut flowers) for Europe.[15]

## Cropping patterns

The Egyptian government and IFIs blame the Nasser era for the under-performing agricultural sector. State intervention, the controls placed on farmers in relation to pricing, cropping and marketing, are seen to have restricted agricultural production and frustrated market efficiency. By 1987 the then Minister of Agriculture, Yusif Wali was promoting liberalisation with USAID advisors and funding.[16] The IFIs wanted a strategy to 'get the prices right' and a US farm-type model of extensive capital-intensive agriculture driven by market liberalisation, export-led growth and tenure reform. Although the government has not always complied, the key to the strategy was the removal of the state from production. USAID noted 'Due to state intervention, agricultural sector growth during the early to mid 80s was very poor with the value of production growing at less than 1 per cent per year'.[17]

The strategy freed prices to encourage 'farmers, buyers and processors of agricultural commodities to invest in productivity enhancing capital and technological improvements'. Crop production was encouraged to promote Egypt's comparative advantage.[18] USAID has invested more than $1.26 billion in Egypt's agricultural sector reform. US economic assistance since 1975 has totalled $26 billion.[19] Its programme budget declined from $573 953 million in 2004 to $455 000 in 2007—a fall of 21%.[20] Yet US military assistance remains huge, at $1.3 billion in 2006, and USAID continues to have enormous influence across government ministries and by strategising with the World Bank and IMF to add leverage for policy reform.[21] Nevertheless, despite all the investment (or perhaps because of it?), the reforms have been unsuccessful.

The first phase of the counter-revolution from the mid-1980s to mid-1990s emphasised market liberalisation, state removal from production and credit supply and attempts to alter cropping patterns. Reform advocates emphasised improvements in real value of crop production for 23 leading crops between 1980 and 1990; increases in farm incomes; and a doubling of wheat production from 1986 to 1992. These, along with declines in food subsidies and increases in size of cultivated area, were hailed as a vindication of the reform process.[22]

Critics of the early phases of reform highlighted the disjuncture between policy and actual outcome.[23] IFIs have repeatedly focused on early increases in performance but there is little evidence that, where there may have been productivity improvements, they were the result of changes in farm gate pricing.[24] It is more likely that there was an under-reporting of earlier yields and cropping patterns. Figures for increased wheat production after 1987 cannot be explained by price incentives to producers. Evidence for improved wheat production resulted instead, for Mitchell, because before 1987, when government tried to control cropping patterns, the *fellahin* did not disclose all that they grew. Small farmers also increased production for self-provisioning and protection from the market, not for the market[25].

Egypt does not seem to have made the conversion to an export-led agricultural economy. Although there have been improvements in the quantity of exports between 2002 and 2005 for potatoes, fresh tomatoes and fresh onions,[26] income generated and sustained levels of productivity and exports remain poor, patchy and problematic. Government figures show that between 1995 and 2003 there were falls in the area cultivated for seed cotton, wheat, alfalfa, clover, summer maize, dry beans and dry fenugreek.[27] Increases in potato, fresh tomato and fresh onion exports will do little to raise incomes or opportunities for rural poor.

The IFIs and the government use the rhetoric of the market, and of trade liberalisation, to promote agricultural growth subordinated to external economic interests. Where there have been improvements in some vegetable production there has also been a decline in berseem.[28] In the 1990s it was argued that one aspect of Egypt's agricultural crisis was the way in which farmer priorities had shifted in the 1970s from the production of cotton and other 'traditional' crops to focus on meat, poultry and dairy production, and on the cultivation of berseem as animal fodder.[29] This was promoted by a change in domestic elite consumption patterns away from traditional foodstuffs towards meat and it had been promoted by subsidised US loans and grain imports, as noted earlier. In contemporary Egypt it seems possible that small farmers shun the production of cotton favouring berseem, but not for the reasons of the 1970s and 1980s. The labour input for cotton is intense and liberalisation has undermined previous state input and marketing provision without any effective replacement. *Fellahin* will not jeopardise the well-being of their limited holdings of livestock, from which they get supplies of milk and cheese. They have refused to switch to market-driven crops since 2004. Many focus instead on self-provisioning and decisions shaped by the household.[30]

## Tenure reform

The second major dimension of market reform was the issuing of a new tenancy law. President Mubarak's Law 96 of 1992 reversed the tenancy guarantees of Nasser's Agrarian Reform Law of 1952. It stipulated a five-year transition period during which time rent was raised from seven to 22 times the land tax. The legislation was not intended to apply to Agrarian Reform and religious endowment (or *Awqaf*) land but Law 96 politicised land in an unprecedented way. After the transition period on 1 October 1997 landowners retook land from tenants and levied a market-based rent.

While there was a discrepancy between values and rents the strategy put in place by the government was an extraordinary culmination of the counter-revolution and the policy of de-nassirisation. Yet the government denied this, dressed the proposals as meeting everyone's needs and asserted agricultural productivity would improve as a result.[31] This was to be achieved, moreover, with the dismantling of the co-operative structures and end of access to credit for smallholders that had also been a hallmark of the Nasser legacy.

The speed of the way in which Nasser enacted the agrarian reform was now matched by Mubarak's haste to reward landowners. The 1991 ERSAP provided good cover for Law 96. Rents increased significantly during the transition period and many tenants who farmed up to 30% of Egypt's cultivable land simply either did not know about the reform or were confident the president would not sign the legislation to make it legally enforceable. There had been no census of tenants, little knowledge of how many there were or what their farming arrangements looked like. In 1997 there were probably about one million tenants. With family members they represented about 10% of Egypt's population. Parliamentary debate on tenants and rural dwellers in general was scathing. They were collectively accused of laziness, of spending too much time on entertainment and of enjoying the benefits of cheap rents while not increasing productivity.[32]

After 1997 rents jumped dramatically, sometimes by as much as 400%. Tenancies were annual but they were seldom formalised in a written contract and landowners could dispossess tenants summarily. Many women who had farmed land successfully were evicted—landlords favouring men from neighbouring villages who had a less strong and proximate attachment to the land. And many tenants lost crops in the ground as they were evicted without compensation. While not part of the IFI-driven reform programme both USAID and the Food and Agriculture Organisation (FAO) saw the reforms as an important element in constructing a land market and efficiency in the holding and utilising of agricultural land.[33] Rental values remained high compared with pre-1997 levels and were prohibitive for many tenants. In the village of Dandeet, for example, in the Governorate of Dakhalia in the eastern Delta annual rents in 2007 were LE4 800 per *feddan* compared with LE600 in 1997. And the price of agricultural land ranged from LE250 000 to LE300 00 per *feddan*, compared with LE50 000 in 1997—a fivefold increase over ten years.[34]

### Resistance

Violent opposition to Law 96 of 1992 was expected in some quarters but was little in evidence. That does not mean it did not exist. Much of it was covert and took the form of 'silent struggles'. Nevertheless 119 deaths, 846 injuries and 1409 arrests were recorded that were related to the law and the conflicts that emerged around its implementation.[35] There were also large demonstrations organised by the leftist Tagamu' party in Dakhalia and Cairo, and a petition with 350 000 names was rejected by the Minister of Agriculture, who said opposition to the act could not have been so strong. The government deplored any actions that resisted the Act, blaming opposition on radical Islamists. It recruited the support of the Fatwa committee of Al Azhar, headed by the Grand Sheikh, to demonstrate that the new law was consistent with Islam and the right of people to own private property.

Rural violence is systemic in Egypt and a persistent feature of the contemporary period of reform. It has been both open and obvious and it has been covert and subtle as tenants have been evicted from land and houses and it has been directed at the landless, tenants and legal smallholders. It has been caused by landowners raising rents and small holders contesting boundaries and water and other access rights.

Violence has persisted and may even have increased in 2007 between tenants and landlords and between smallholders. Farmers are now increasingly squeezed on limited and more expensive land where boundary and irrigation disputes assume an importance that may have previously been more easily and less violently resolved. Farmers now seem to use small disputes as opportunities to voice dissatisfaction over land. An incident in the village of Turk, Giza demonstrates this as violence flared during attempts to erect a mobile phone signal-strengthening tower, leading to the death of one farmer and the injury of 22 others.[36]

The politicisation of land has aggravated the level of violence. Landlords have used confusion regarding the exact terms of Law 96 to try and retake land reform land and also religiously endowed land from its rightful owners. In 2007 in the village of Mershak in the Governorate of Dahkalia heirs of a large landowning family who had lost land to Nasser's agrarian reform went to court to reclaim 100 *feddans* purchased legally by 50 families since the mid-1950s. The heirs argued that the wife of the original owner had not been legally divorced at the time of her death and the agrarian reform. She was therefore entitled to a separate dispensation of land at the time of her divorce. Yet the land has been farmed and legally owned by the beneficiaries of the agrarian reform law for the previous 40 years. They have legal titles and receipts for their payments and investigation has shown that, in fact, at the time of her death, the 'heir' was still married and was thus ineligible to separate land entitlement as part of a divorce settlement. The villagers, many of whom had been beaten and tortured by a combination of 'hired in' thugs and local police, had mobilised neighbouring villagers not to accept tenancies offered by the heirs of the original owners on the contested land.

The case of Mershak was symptomatic of the politicisation of land and the frailty of the idea of the security of the market: here legal land holders who had purchased agrarian reform land were being evicted by previous owners who had been dispossessed by Nasser—it may not be coincidental that neighbouring the village are drilling towers searching and discovering natural gas, dramatically raising the price of and struggle for land.[37] Smallholder owners in this village were angry that their legal rights were challenged by absentee owners who had no legal basis to contest ownership. There were many rumours that court officials and officials of the Agrarian Reform committee had been bribed to favour the heirs of the original owner—there certainly did not appear to be any legal reason why current owners should be dispossessed. Villagers had established a tent for a vigil on their land and they had become a focus for land struggles. The strategy of the heirs, however, was to combine violence and intimidation with legal challenge and to individualise court cases against the 50 owners. In these circumstances each holder would find it impossible, without considerable outside financial support, to meet costs of litigation.

Resistance to the transformation of tenure has also taken a less overt form. Tingay, for example, has noted how village norms and values were challenged by Law 96.[38] The introduction of market principles to defend landowner interests jeopardised reciprocal village rights and duties of good neighbourliness, care of the land and financial obligation that elders and the wealthy might be expected to use in their relations with the less poor. It is important to understand the contribution that social values can play in challenging the dominance of market principles. Tingay has shown how criticism of the wealthy did sometimes restrict their actions as they tried to raise rents without consideration of the social consequences and dispossessions that ensued. She also confirmed that widespread and organised violent opposition to the reform of tenancy was never a realistic option for smallholders. Extensive rural repression and the widespread deployment of security forces, as well as the use of torture and imprisonment, gave landowners the upper hand. The structure of landholdings may also have undermined concerted action against landlords. Tenants sometimes rent-in land from a number of owners and this can limit the possibility of political action against a single target. It is also not unusual for tenants themselves to rent out land and to sharecrop in what one author has called a 'tenancy web'.[39]

## Back to the future

According to the World Bank, 'The agricultural sector is now a fully private sector, operating in a market- and export-oriented economy.[40] Yet liberalisation has not delivered significant improvements in productivity, job creation or poverty reduction. Agricultural production reached 3% in the 1990s from 2.8% in the 1980s and there may have been a narrowing of the food gap.[41] But these growth rates have not met IFI expectations and they have been insufficient to boost agricultural growth.[42] Agriculture's contribution to Egypt's trade deficit increased from 21% in 1974 to 33% in 1998.[43] Total agricultural exports in 2005 were valued at LE6.2 billion compared with LE7.6 billion in 2004.[44]

The IFIs explain the persistent under-achievement of agriculture by (re)discovering two causes: the failure to generate trade in horticulture and cotton, and management inefficiencies. The World Bank laments that 'the main constraint is management inadequacy at all levels of production and post-harvest processing...the lack of skilled business management in agriculture is a serious limitation for more rapid expansion of horticultural exports'.[45]

The IFI response is to further encourage private entrepreneurs and to more fully integrate Egypt into the world capitalist system by reducing barriers to international trade. Egypt's macroeconomic achievements of the 1990s have 'not been sufficient to improve Egypt's agricultural export performance'.[46] The World Bank argues that there is much potential for increasing Egypt's horticultural exports and high-quality cotton products and yarn. Egypt is seen to have a comparative advantage in products like table grapes and strawberries, cut flowers, cherry tomatoes, melons and watermelons. But, although there has been an upward trend in production and the area planted to some cash crops, it is unclear just how much additional improvement is possible. Egypt's farmers responded in the 1990s to the call to raise strawberry production but most of what was produced seemed to end up on the streets of Cairo as rotting waste. The IFIs want to avoid a repeat of that kind of disaster by assisting with management reform, improving transport and giving incentives for private entrepreneurs to store and move Egypt's crops.

The IFIs are now calling for the further liberalisation of rice production, a reduction in tariffs on imported seed and improved dialogue between the government and entrepreneurs to boost investment. The IFIs want improved water management too; at the same time they are calling for increases in rice production—a water hungry crop—as well as poverty eradication. Here poverty reduction becomes a trope for market reform. But what is the role for the *fellahin*, who are being so unevenly incorporated into the newly reformed agricultural sector? Are they to become wage workers in new desert irrigated estates or lumpen and landless unemployed readied for occasional work in towns?

The EU has added to the IFI clamour for Egypt's incorporation into the global food system. The EU Ambassador to Egypt noted in 2006:

> We [the EU] need products from other countries to satisfy our consumers' needs. We also want to have quality standards for our consumers that will be compliant with our market requirements. Egypt has the weather and it is near. You can produce things which are in high demand in our market, like organic food. This is in our interest. And we have traders who are ready to invest in this area.[47]

The liberalisation of land rental markets is believed to have had the impact of encouraging the production of higher value crops and of stimulating productivity increases. Yet in 2005 total agricultural exports were only 3.9% of the value of Egypt's total exports.[48] There are two problems with the current strategy of agricultural modernisation. The first is the preoccupation with capital-intensive export agriculture. The second is the neglect of small farmers that follows from the contemporary drive to promote investment in the new lands rather than resolve issues of land and market access and rural development in the old lands. It is difficult to understand how Egypt's market share in horticulture or cotton exports can be dramatically improved with the current IFI-driven strategy. The USA continues to subsidise its cotton farmers, and East Asian technological innovation delivers high quality finished garments from lower grade raw materials, while the EU continues to subsidise and protect its agricultural sector.[49]

The idea that further liberalisation of Egypt's trade regime will enable the country to benefit from improved agricultural performance is a familiar call. In the 1990s, for instance, USAID advised a shift towards production of the same list of horticultural crops used by the World Bank at the start of the new millennium.[50] It believed Egypt could benefit from a boost of horticultural exports of $100 and $150 million a year.[51] That boost was particularly targeted for the newly reclaimed desert lands and in the 21st century to the new greening of the desert intended to reclaim 3.4 million *feddans* by 2017. The biggest of these schemes is Toshka in the New Valley Governorate west of Luxor, an area that represents close to 40% of Egypt's entire landmass. Other schemes include the East Oweinat project aimed at reclaiming 200 000 *feddans* and in North Sinai a scheme to reclaim a further 400 000 *feddans*. An estimated $3.7 billion is spent each year on these projects by the Egyptian government.[52]

The schemes are an important feature of contemporary Egyptian politics. They have helped sustain the centrality of the value of the Nile and Egypt's claims on its water, set by the 1959 Nile Water Treaty at 55 billion cubic metres a year. The importance of big projects has helped continue to frame the country's agricultural crisis in terms of limited land area, diminishing per capita water supply and population growth. This has provided fuel for strategies that have neglected farmers, boosted the importance of private investors and characterised Egypt somewhat romantically as a hydraulic society with the continued need for Mubarak to be an omnipotent pharaonic president. As one commentator noted at the start of the Toshka project 'moving to the desert is a must. There is no better way to inspire people than through a dramatic announcement. The President knows his people. Egyptians tend to join hands when they are inspired by an urgent national project.'[53]

Environmental determinism has been a strong current in the characterisation of Egypt's development problems, especially in relation to food security.[54] The irony is that project-led development similar to that in the newly reclaimed lands will not provide an opportunity for either the declared benefits of export-led growth or resettlement from the 'overcrowded' Nile valley. The Toshka project began in 1997 to enormous fanfare.[55] The plan was to pump water from behind the Aswan High Dam along a 74 km canal to irrigate 540 000 *feddans* of desert. The scheme was to produce fruit and vegetables for Europe and to provide a home for migrants from the 'overcrowded' cities of Alexandria and Cairo. Yet there is little basis upon which to assume that any of Egypt's big schemes will provide a panacea for agricultural growth. There is far more evidence that the schemes will promote environmental crisis, suck in available liquidity and provide opportunities for asset stripping by foreign and some Egyptian interests.

Toshka was implemented quickly. There was no full environmental impact assessment or understanding of the likelihood that settlers from the perceived overcrowded Nile Valley would move to a most inhospitable area hundreds of kilometres away from their homes. The government could not encourage the IFIs to fund the project, budgeted at $86.5 billion from 1997 to 2017.

Land was instead initially assigned to four investor groups that included Egypt's holding company for agricultural investment, a consortium of Egyptian private investors and public sector companies and the Abu Dhabi Development Fund. The most significant investor, however, and one that President Mubarak has relied on as others have withdrawn, is the Saudi Prince al-Walid bin Talal bin Abdulaziz. He is Chairman of The Kingdom Holding Company. The Kingdom Agricultural Development Company (KADCO) had been co-operating with the California agribusiness company Sun World, a producer of grapes and citrus, but in July 2002 the KADCO-Sunworld co-operation collapsed.[56] As Tim Mitchell noted:

> [Sun World] was to invest no money of its own in the Toshka project... In the excitement of the government's announcement that the project had found an American partner, the reason for this went unnoticed: Sun World had no money.[57]

Sun World's new holding company, Santa Monica based Cadiz Inc, has a bigger financial interest in selling patents and trademarks than in growing crops. The Egyptian government, moreover, has provided significant amounts of capital for the firm at Toskha and granted the US company a 20-year tax break.[58] The failure to generate long-term and sustainable investment seems to have left even the Saudi billionaire Prince Al-Walid less comfortable with remaining the project's biggest backer. On a visit to Cairo in 2007 he was forced to publicly defend the scheme, suggesting it still had a bright future and that he had no intention of withdrawing.[59]

For several years, during the building of the scheme and certainly since its operation, farmers in the Delta have complained about diminishing flows of water for irrigation as off-take to Toshka has increased. The scheme is likely to use up to 10% of Nile flows; this at a time when the World Bank is anxious to manage water use more efficiently and where the focus is increasingly on mechanisms for water use charging.[60] Yet these calls now run alongside recent unprecedented riots in the Delta in mid-2007, where villagers are struggling to access drinking water.[61] Water shortages also affect major urban centres in Cairo and its suburbs. But in rural Egypt the problem of accessing timely irrigation water is now increasingly being added to by the absence of any potable water.

Toskha has added to the debate about water access and usage and it has also provoked concern that it will not meet its projected level for job creation. One estimate is that it will provide no more than a maximum of 30 000 job opportunities and government subsidy to investors with water access, electricity and construction will exceed LE300 million per 100 000 *feddan*.[62] Access to the limited investment of a Saudi prince will not prevent the scheme sucking in liquidity that might have been spent instead on health and education and other poverty-ameliorating policies. There is certainly no longer even any pretence that the scheme will encourage large-scale migration from the Delta southwest to the desert for employment and housing.

Mubarak's attempt to bequeath a successful agricultural project has led to a pyramid in the desert. It highlights the fantasy of a flawed national agricultural strategy and subordination of policy to external financial control, asset stripping and state subsidy to local crony investors. In addition, neighbouring riparian states Sudan and Ethiopia are vexed that Egypt's schemes for land reclamation restrict upstream development opportunities.

## A subordinate agrarian capitalism?

The promotion of Egypt's comparative advantage as a producer of high-value horticulture and cotton marginalises smallholders. The strategy characterises them as incapable of being an engine for growth. Among other things we have seen that they have been blamed for a lack of management skills and effectively reduced to supernumeraries who may or may not be integrated into capital-intensive agriculture in the new lands.[63]

There is more inequality in landholdings in contemporary Egypt than there was at the time of Nasser's revolution. Before the 1952 agrarian reform law 0.1% of landowners owned 20% of the cultivated area. In 2000 0.05% of holders accounted for 11% of the total landholding area.[64] At the start of the new millennium there were fewer than four million land holders and a million landless *fellahin* plus family members. More than half of landholders (55%) farm five *feddan* or less. The dominance of smallholders hides significant inequalities in land holding—5% of landholders have 5–10 *feddan* but 2281 holders have land sizes in excess of 100 *feddan*, amounting almost a million *feddan* from the total of roughly nine million cultivable *feddans* in the old lands.[65]

Reliance on the world market and Egypt's increased integration with it will not deliver sustained growth and development for the majority of Egyptians. Difficulties in meeting policy aims and objectives are conveniently explained as government back-sliding or the intransigence of small farmers wedded to inefficient farming practices. The IFIs refuse to address the failures of market reform: increased poverty, greater social differentiation and rural decay. The IFIs are reluctant to also explore the likely impact of a further round of policy that encourages production of cash crops for European or Gulf markets. Egypt is persuaded to produce crops that are the object of fierce regional competition. There also remains confusion regarding the government role in facilitating or removing itself from production. There has been little discussion of the asset stripping that has taken place in the cotton sector since 1991 and which has led to enormous recent worker unrest. And there is little probing of links between government officials and owners and investors of big agricultural schemes, suggesting persistence and deepening of the spoils of politics.

It is likely that export strategies based on comparative advantage will reimpose the limitations of primary production. There has been a failure to explore the problems of how markets are organised beyond simple expressions of abstract principles, rationality and efficiency. Markets are determinations of power relations and they express relations of domination and subordination within the global order. IFI strategy focuses on the importance of market access to international capital characterised by a role for agribusiness in new land development and promotion of contract farming. This will be an integration that is subordinate to the more powerful forces and interests of US and EU capital. Contemporary strategy does not have at its core priorities of local food security, national development or poverty amelioration.

## Notes

Thanks to Abd-el Mawla Ismael and Adel William and colleagues at the Awlad al Ard human rights organisation, Cairo for research assistance.

1 J Beinen & H el-Hamalawy, 'Egyptian workers confront the new economic order', 2007, at www.merip.org/mero/mero032507.html; Beinen & el-Hamalawy, 'Strikes in Egypt spread from center of gravity', 2007, at www.merip.org/mero/mero050907.html.

2 World Bank, *Arab Republic of Egypt Toward Agricultural Competitiveness in the 21st Century: An Agricultural Export Oriented Strategy*, Report no 23405-EGT, Washington, DC: World Bank, 21 December 2001.

3 USAID, 'USAID/Egypt agriculture', 1998; USAID, *Agriculture: Vision for 2003*, MALR/USAID Agricultural Policy Reform Programme, RDI policy brief, no. 1, November, Cairo, 1999.

4 For the sake of simplicity I will refer to these lands as 'new'.

5 *Fellahin* (plural of *fellah*) means 'tillers of the soil'. The term is also used to describe a rural as opposed to an urban dweller.

6 KM Cuno, *The Pasha's Peasants: Land, Society and Economy in Lower Egypt, 1740–1858*, Cairo: American University in Cairo Press, 1992.

7 ME Yapp, *The Near East Since the First World War: A History to 1995*, London: Longman, 1996.

8 MS Sallam, 'Agrarian reform in Egypt', paper presented to the Land Reform Conference, Cascavel, Brazil, April, 1998, p 4.

9 MR El-Ghonemy, 'Food security and rural development in North Africa', *Middle Eastern Studies*, 29 (3), 1993, pp 445–466; and El-Ghonemy, 'Recent changes in agrarian reform and rural development strategies in the Near East', *Land Reform*, Vols 1& 2, 1999, pp 9–20.

10 S Radwan & E Lee, *Agrarian Change in Egypt: Anatomy of Rural Poverty*, London: Croom Helm, 1986.

11 R Hinnebusch, 'The formation of the contemporary Egyptian state from Nasser and Sadat to Mubarak', in IM Oweiss (ed), *The Political Economy of Egypt*, Washington, DC: Center for Contemporary Arab Studies, Georgetown University, 1990.

12 *Ibid*, p 190.

13 M Cooper, *The Transformation of Egypt*, London: Croom Helm, 1982.

14 USAID and Government of Egypt, 'Taking stock: eight years of Egyptian agricultural policy reforms', paper presented at the Agricultural Policy Conference, Cairo, 26–28 March 1995, p 4. See also R Bush, *Economic Crisis and the Politics of Reform in Egypt*, Boulder, CO: Westview Press, 1999.

15 USAID, 'USAID/Egypt agriculture'; USAID, USAID/Egypt economic growth overview', at http://www.info.usaid.gov/eg/econ-ovr.htm, 1998; and USAID, 'Egypt: Congressional presentation', at http://usaid.gov/pubs//cp2000/ane/egypt/html, 2000.

16 USAID, *Country Program Strategy FY 1992–1996: Egypt*, Cairo: USAID, 1992; World Bank, 'Arab Republic of Egypt: an agricultural strategy for the 1990s', Agricultural Operations Division, Country Department, II, Middle East and North African Region, Report no 11083-EAT, Washington, DC, 1992; and A Richards, 'Economic imperatives and political systems', *Middle East Journal*, 47 (2), Spring 1993, pp 217–227.

17 USAID, 'Egypt: Congressional presentation'.

18 USAID, *Country Programme Strategy*, p 15.

19 www.usaid.gov/locations/asia_near_east/countries/egypt/.

20 www.usaid.gov/policy/budget/cbj2007/ane/eg.html.

21 The Bush administration announced a further $13 billion pledge to Egypt for military assistance on 30 July 2007. Dan Glaister 'US accused of fuelling arms race with $20 bn Arab weapons sale', *Guardian*, 30 July 2007.

22 MA Faris & MH Khan (eds), *Sustainable Agriculture in Egypt*, Boulder, CO: Lynne Rienner; and LB Fletcher (ed), *Egypt's Agriculture in a Reform era*, Ames, IO: Iowa State University Press, 1996.

23 T Mitchell, 'The market's place' in N Hopkins & K Westergaard (eds), *Directions of Change in Rural Egypt*, Cairo: American University Press in Cairo, 1998; Bush, *Economic Crisis and the Politics of Reform in Egypt*; and Bush (ed), *Counter-Revolution in Egypt's Countryside: Land and Farmers in the Era of Economic Reform*, London: Zed Books, 2002.

24 Poor quality data collection also raises questions of the accuracy of the data used by the IFIs.

25 Mitchell, 'The market's place'.

26 Figures for 2005 taken from Ministry of Agriculture and Land Reclamation, *Bulletin of Foreign Trade*, Cairo: Government of Egypt, 2005 and for 2002 from Ministry of Agriculture and Land Reclamation, *Bulletin of Foreign Trade*, Cairo: Government of Egypt, 2003.

27 USAID and Government of Egypt, 'Taking stock'; Ministry of Agriculture and Land Reclamation, *Bulletin of Foreign Trade*, Cairo: Government of Egypt, 2003.

28 Ministry of Agriculture and Land Reclamation, *Crop Production Tables*, Cairo: Government of Egypt, 2006.

29 T Mitchell, 'The object of development: America's Egypt', in J Crush (ed), *Power of Development*, London: Routledge, 1995, p 135.

30 The counter-revolution has also dramatically increased rural poverty and unemployment. See N Fergany, 'Poverty and unemployment in rural Egypt', in Bush, *Counter Revolution in the Egyptian Countryside*.

31 R Saad, 'State, landlord, parliament and peasant: the story of the 1992 tenancy law in Egypt', in A Bowman & E Rogan (eds), *Agriculture in Egypt from Pharaonic to Modern Times*, Proceedings of the British Academy, Vol 96, Oxford: Oxford University Press, 1999; and Saad, 'Egyptian politics and the tenancy law', in Bush, *Counter Revolution in the Egyptian Countryside*.

32 Saad 'Egyptian politics and the tenancy law'.

33 See for instance, USAID and Government of Egypt, *A Study on Developing a Revised, Integrated Land and Water Plan*, USAID, Agricultural Policy Reform Programme, Reform Design and Implementation Unit, BB Attia *et al*, December 1997, p 1, Cairo.

34 Awlad al Ard, 'Violence in Egypt's countryside', mimeo, Cairo, 2007; and Awlad al Ard,' Report on Dandeet and survey of tenants and near landless', mimeo, Cairo, 2007.

35 Land Center for Human Rights (Markaz el Ard), 'Farmer struggles against Law 96 of 1992', in Bush, *Counter Revolution in Egypt's Countryside*, p 127.

36 Awlad al Ard, 'Violence in Egypt's countryside'.

37 Field visit and interviews with farmers, 23 April 2007.

38 C Tingay, 'Agrarian transformation in Egypt: conflict dynamics and the politics of power from a micro perspective', unpublished PhD thesis, Freie Universität, Berlin, 2004.

39 MH Abdel Aal, 'Agrarian reform and tenancy in Upper Egypt', in Bush, *Counter Revolution in Egypt's Countryside*.

40 World Bank, *Arab Republic of Egypt Toward Agricultural Competitiveness in the 21st Century*.

41 See also S El Saharty, G Richardson & S Chase, *Egypt and the Millennium Development Goals: Challenges and Opportunities*, HNP Discussion Paper, Washington, DC: World Bank, February 2005.

42 World Bank, *Arab Republic of Egypt Toward Agricultural Competitiveness in the 21st Century*, Annex A2.

43 GE El-Din, 'A future for fruits', *Al Ahram Weekly*, 13–19 January 2000.

44 Government of Egypt, *Bulletin of Foreign Trade*, Cairo: Ministry of Agriculture and Land Reclamation, 2005.

45 World Bank, *Arab Republic of Egypt Toward Agricultural Competitiveness in the 21st Century*, p 31.

46 *Ibid.*

47 N Wahish, 'Liberalise or bust', interview with Klaus Ebermann, Ambassador of the EU to Egypt, *Al Ahram Weekly*, 2006, at www.weekly.ahram.org.eg/print/2006/789/ec1.htm, accessed 15 May 2007.

48 Government of Egypt, *Bulletin of Foreign Trade*, 2005.

49 The USA spends at least $4.2 billion supporting its cotton farmers. Egypt's Minister for Foreign Trade and Industry noted in 2005 that US subsidies meant that American Pima cotton sold at $1.01/libra compared with $1.18/libra for Egyptian- produced Giza 70, $1.12/libra for Giza 88 and $1.09/libra for Giza 86. See Wahish (2006).

50 USAID, *Country Program Strategy*.

51 World Bank, 'Arab Republic of Egypt'.

52 Another estimate suggests that spending by 2017 for Upper Egypt development of the New Valley oases will be $90 billion. R Noeman, 'Egypt pours money into desert reclamation', at www.planetark.org/avantgo/dailynewsstory.cfm?newsid=9340, 2000, accessed 4 June 2007; and F Farag, 'Green desert—at what cost?', *Al Ahram Weekly*, 23–29 January 2003, at www.weekly. ahram.org.eg/2003/622/fel.htm, accessed 7 June 2007.

53 Beshai, quoted in 'Egypt survey', *Financial Times*, 13 May 1997.

54 R Kaplan, *The Ends of the Earth*, London: Papermac, 1996; K Ikram, *Egypt: Economic Management in a Period of Transition: The Report of a Mission Sent to the Arab Republic of Egypt by the World Bank*, Baltimore, MD: Johns Hopkins University Press, 1980; and J Waterbury, *Hydropolitics of the Nile Valley*, Syracuse, NY: Syracuse University Press, 1979. For a critique see Mitchell, 'The object of development'.

55 This was in fact the revival of a scheme suggested in the 1950s.

56 'California commodities', *Rural Migration News 2002*, at www.migration.ucdavis.edu/rmn/comments.php?id=607_0_5_0, accessed 4 June 2007.

57 T Mitchell, *Rule of Experts: Egypt, Techno-Politics, Modernity*, Berkeley, CA: University of California Press, 2002, p 274.

58 *Ibid*, p 274.

59 'Alwaleed backs Toshka', *Trade Arabia*, 12 March 2007, at www.tradearabia.com/news/newsprint.asp?Article=120294&Sn=AGRI, accessed 4 June 2007.

60 World Bank, *Arab Republic of Egypt Toward Agricultural Competitiveness in the 21st Century*; 2001a.

61 Dina Essat, 'Not a drop to drink', *Al Ahram Weekly*, at www.weekly.ahram.org.eg/print/2007/853/eg9.htm, accessed 26 July 2007.

62 R Said, *The Future of Egypt: Water, Energy and the Desert*, Cairo: Dar el Helal, 2004, p 145.

63 World Bank, *Arab Republic of Egypt Toward Agricultural Competitiveness in the 21st Century*, p viii.

64 Ministry of Agriculture, *Agricultural Census 2000*, Cairo: Ministry of Agriculture, 2000.

65 *Ibid*.

# Index

For Product Safety Concerns and Information please contact our EU
representative GPSR@taylorandfrancis.com
Taylor & Francis Verlag GmbH, Kaufingerstraße 24, 80331 München, Germany

www.ingramcontent.com/pod-product-compliance
Lightning Source LLC
Chambersburg PA
CBHW081434270326
41932CB00019B/3195